MARK TWAIN AND THE THREE R'S

BOOKS BY MAXWELL GEISMAR

THE NOVEL IN AMERICA

Writers in Crisis: The American Novel, 1925–1940
(*Studies of Ring Lardner, Ernest Hemingway, John Dos Passos,
William Faulkner, Thomas Wolfe, John Steinbeck*)
The Last of the Provincials: The American Novel, 1915–1925
(*Studies of H. L. Mencken, Sinclair Lewis, Willa Cather,
Sherwood Anderson, F. Scott Fitzgerald*)
Rebels and Ancestors: The American Novel, 1890–1915
(*Studies of Frank Norris, Stephen Crane, Jack London,
Ellen Glasgow, Theodore Dreiser*)
American Moderns: From Rebellion to Conformity
Henry James and the Jacobites
Mark Twain: An American Prophet

EDITOR

The Ring Lardner Reader
The Walt Whitman Reader
The Portable Thomas Wolfe
Sherwood Anderson: Short Stories
Jack London: Short Stories
Mark Twain and the Three R's

MARK TWAIN
and the
THREE R's

RACE, RELIGION, REVOLUTION
—AND RELATED MATTERS

edited and with an introduction by
Maxwell Geismar

THE BOBBS-MERRILL COMPANY, INC.
Indianapolis/New York

Thanks are due to Harper & Row, Publishers, Inc. for permission to quote from:

Letters From the Earth by Mark Twain, edited by Bernard DeVoto. Copyright ©
1938, 1944, 1946, 1959, 1962 by The Mark Twain Co. Reprinted by permission of
Harper & Row, Publishers, Inc.
Mark Twain in Eruption by Mark Twain, edited by Bernard DeVoto. Copyright ©
1922 by Harper & Row, Publishers, Inc.; renewed 1940 by The Mark Twain Co. Re-
printed by permission of Harper & Row, Publishers, Inc.
Mark Twain's Speeches by Mark Twain. Copyright © 1923 by The Mark Twain Co.;
renewed 1951 by The Mark Twain Co.
Mark Twain: a Biography by Albert Bigelow Paine. Copyright © 1912 by Harper &
Row, Publishers, Inc.; renewed 1940 by Dora F. Paine.
The Mysterious Stranger and Other Stories by Mark Twain. Copyright © 1916 by
Harper & Row, Publishers, Inc.; renewed 1944 by Clara Clemens Gabrilowitsch. Re-
printed by permission of Harper & Row, Publishers, Inc.
The Autobiography of Mark Twain, edited by Charles Neider. Copyright © 1959 by
The Mark Twain Company. Copyright 1952 by Clara Clemens Samossoud. Copyright
© 1959 by Charles Neider. Reprinted by permission of Harper & Row, Publishers, Inc.
Europe and Elsewhere by Mark Twain. Copyright © 1923, 1951 by The Mark Twain
Co. Reprinted by permission of Harper & Row, Publishers, Inc.
Mark Twain's Autobiography, Volume II, edited by Albert Bigelow Paine. Copyright
© 1924 by Clara Gabrilowitsch; renewed 1952 by Clara Clemens Samossoud. Re-
printed by permission of Harper & Row, Publishers, Inc.
Mark Twain's Letters, Volume II, edited by Albert Bigelow Paine. Copyright © 1917,
1945 by The Mark Twain Co. Reprinted by permission of Harper & Row, Publishers,
Inc.
A Pen Warmed-Up in Hell: Mark Twain in Protest, edited by Frederick Anderson.
Copyright © 1972 by The Mark Twain Co. Reprinted by permission of Harper & Row,
Publishers, Inc.
Mark Twain's Notebook, edited by Albert Bigelow Paine. Copyright © 1935, 1963 by
The Mark Twain Co. Reprinted by permission of Harper & Row, Publishers, Inc.
Thanks are due also to Farrar, Straus & Giroux, Inc., Hill & Wang Division, for per-
mission to quote from *Mark Twain on the Damned Human Race*, edited and with
an introduction by Janet Smith; preface by Maxwell Geismar. Copyright © 1962 by
Farrar, Straus & Giroux, Inc. Reprinted by permission of Farrar, Straus & Giroux, Inc.
Thanks are due also to International Publishers to quote from *Mark Twain: Social
Critic*, by Philip S. Foner. Copyright © 1958 by International Publishers. Reprinted
by permission of International Publishers.

The Bobbs-Merrill Company, Inc.
Publishers: Indianapolis/New York

Copyright © 1973 by Maxwell Geismar
All rights reserved
ISBN 0-672-51705-1
Library of Congress catalog card number 72-9882
Designed by A. Christopher Simon
Manufactured in the United States of America

TO ANNE—

The Christina of crisis, still and always

"EVIL BEARS DENIAL."

PEACE WITH HONOR

I pray you to pause and consider. Against our traditions we are now entering upon an unjust and trivial war, a war against a helpless people, and for a base object—robbery. At first our citizens spoke out against this thing by an impulse natural to their training. Today they have turned, and their voice is the other way. What caused this change? Merely a politician's trick—a high-sounding phrase, a blood-stirring phrase which turned their uncritical heads: *Our Country, right or wrong!* An empty phrase, a silly phrase. It was shouted by every newspaper, it was thundered from the pulpit, the Superintendent of Public Instruction placarded it in every schoolhouse in the land, the War Department inscribed it upon the flag. And every man who failed to shout it, or who was silent, was proclaimed a traitor—none but those others were patriots. To be a patriot, one had to say, and keep on saying, "Our Country, right or wrong," and urge on the little war. Have you not perceived that phrase is an insult to the nation. . . .

Only when a republic's *life* is in danger should a man uphold his government when it is in the wrong. There is no other time.

This Republic's life is not in peril. The nation has sold its honor for a phrase. It has swung itself loose from its safe anchorage and is drifting, its helm is in pirate hands. The stupid phrase needed help, and it got another one: "Even if the war be wrong we are in it and must fight it out: *we cannot retire from it without dishonor.*" Why, not even a burglar could have said it better. We cannot withdraw from this sordid raid because to grant peace to those little people upon their terms—independence —would dishonor us. You have flung away Adam's phrase—you should take it up and examine it again. He said, *"An inglorious peace is better than a dishonorable war."*

You have planted a seed, and it will grow.

> *—Mark Twain on the Philippine War,*
> *as widely used in the anti-Vietnam War*
> *protest in the sixties.*

I wish you could understand how unshaken you are, you old tower, in every way; your foundations are struck so deep that you will catch the sunshine of immortal years, and bask in the same light as Cervantes and Shakespeare.

—William Dean Howells to Mark Twain in a letter of January, 1898.

I love to think of the great and God-like Clemens. He is the biggest man you have on your side of the water by a damn sight, and don't you forget it. Cervantes was a relation of his.

—Rudyard Kipling in a
letter to the publisher Frank
Doubleday, October, 1903.

I am admonished in many ways that time is pushing me inexorably along. I am approaching the threshold of age: in 1977 I shall be 142.

—Mark Twain's letter of July 19, 1901.

TABLE OF CONTENTS

xi

INTRODUCTION

This is an anthology of Mark Twain's radical social commentary dealing with race, religion and revolution, but also covering a wider range of social and historical matters. The material ranges in time from 1869, the publication year of his first book, *The Innocents Abroad,* to 1970, when my own Mark Twain book appeared. I claim that, far from being the embittered old man of the scholarly legend, Twain was a revolutionary temperament from the very start of his literary career (or his life) to the end. Indeed, it is true that his best polemics and social satires were written after 1900, in the closing decade of his life.

Why, then, has there been such a cloud of ambiguity and more than a hint of censorship and suppression about this vein of Twain's work? In a larger sense, why has Twain's entire literary career been the source of critical dissension and disagreement from the very beginning until the present day?

During his own lifetime it was only a small group of discerning artists, including William Dean Howells in this country and, oddly enough, Rudyard Kipling in England, who traced Twain's affinity to Shakespeare and Cervantes. The majority of the professional and academic critics concurred in believing that Twain was common, vulgar, coarse; a popular "humorist" whose reputation would not survive him. The fact that his books were sold by subscription to mass audiences meant that they did not deserve the dignity of reviews in cultivated literary organs. We may remember how *Huck Finn* was greeted with a chorus of critical disapproval, and in some cases banned, for its immoral teachings and low manners. (We may suspect that part of this was due to the book's young heroes: Huck, the son of the village drunkard and the first drop-out in our literature; and Jim, the runaway slave and the first black hero in our letters.) And England itself, which has been usually faster in seeing the real dimensions of native American talent, and which had embraced Twain socially as well, was horrified at *A Connecticut Yankee in King Arthur's Court*. Mark Twain was always quick to bite the hand that fed him.

In the twenties, the great historian of our literature, Van Wyck Brooks, completely misunderstood Twain and made him an object lesson on the horrors of American civilization—those horrors which Twain was among the first to point out, just as he does in this book. After that critics were either pro-Brooks or pro-Twain until Bernard DeVoto pointed out Brooks' errors and vindicated Twain (again) as a major talent. But it was as an artist of the frontier that DeVoto saw Twain, as a vindication of the American spirit against those artists of the twenties and thirties who were highly critical of American society. And when, in the forties, DeVoto published some of Twain's later social satires and polemics in *Mark Twain in Eruption*, he was forced to fall back, alas, on almost the standard thesis of the sick, frustrated, bitter artist whose enigma could be resolved "only speculatively and only in analytical psychology."

By analytical psychology Mr. DeVoto presumably meant the same Freudian "speculations" he had attacked in Brooks' work on Twain, and which Justin Kaplan's *Mr. Clemens and Mark Twain*, in 1966, developed to an extraordinary density of surmise. This biography marked a peak of Freudian psychoanalysis in our literature and criticism during the cold war period, when social criticism was muted; and Charles Neider's new edition of Mark Twain's *Autobiography*, in the early sixties, completed the circle by reducing Twain to an "amusing" anecdotist. But it is hard to keep a good man down or a great artist silent, or, more subtly, to transmute his values; and in this case Twain was always too clear and too forthright in that luminous language of his which he alone could fashion.

Meanwhile, in one of those ironies which history delights to visit upon those who ignore her, both in the southern pilgrimage of the civil-rights advocates, in the early and mid-sixties, and in the anti-Vietnam War protest movement of the late sixties, the American student movement of our period had discovered that Twain was highly relevant today; that, in fact, speaking from the grave as he was, he was uttering words of fire and flame, of damning social indictment, of brilliant and hilarious social satire, of high-spirited polemics in a great tradition of polemical literature which had been vacated by contemporary American artists.

Such essays in the present collection as "The United States of Lyncherdom" could hardly be missed by a civil rights crusade (the term is appropriate; the southern pilgrimage had its historical effect) which was galvanized by the murder of two white northern boys along with a southern black youth. (Before that, of course, and no doubt after, young southern blacks had been disappearing steadily, their deaths never mentioned or recorded.) Similarly, in the Vietnam protest movement, both anti-war and anti-Vietnam War in particular, Twain's "War Prayer" had been reproduced and reprinted so steadily in the underground press and the New Left press of the sixties, that it achieved the dignity of a hardback edition, handsomely illustrated, as a collector's item.

Many of the essays collected in this volume were published originally as popular pamphlets—like the celebrated "King Leopold's Soliloquy" which described the massacre of ten million black souls in the Belgian Congo—in editions of a hundred thousand copies. In the nineteen sixties, right up to our own decade, and despite all the professional and literary disparagement of Twain and, in particular, of this vein of Twain's radical, political, and polemical writings, it appeared that he was being pamphletized all over again.

For the truth is that Twain was never the horrid old man, the embittered and failed artist, the drunken cynic that he was supposed to be. The myth is so consistent about him from his own time to ours that it almost seems he must represent some kind of literary *threat*, some barely concealed challenge, to our accepted literary and scholarly institutions—and that is just what he did—and does.

His beginning was so golden he could have called himself (and in fact he felt he was) Fortune's favorite child. At the onset of the seventies *The Innocents Abroad* had brought him fame overnight, riches beyond his dreams. The former Mississippi river pilot—the itinerant jour printer, silver miner, prospector, phony millionaire,

newspaper reporter, vagrant, and spree-drunkard—this authentic pro-
letarian bum and adventurer, whose early life, like his true inner spirit,
was not dissimilar to Charlie Chaplin's insouciant hobo, faced a
dazzling new literary career. Beyond that, he soon married a coal-
mining heiress from Elmira, New York, a cultivated and beautiful
heroine of fiction, it almost appeared, whom Sam Clemens was in love
with to his dying day. For a wedding present he was given part ownership of a Buffalo newspaper by his father-in-law, along with a sumptuous new home and a complete staff of domestics down to, or up to, a
coachman and carriage.

The early books (which some scholars consider his best books or his
only books, though this is not true) were a series of popular successes.
Among these, *Roughing It* (1872), *Life on the Mississippi* (1883), and
Huckleberry Finn (1885) are classics of our literature, at least in part,
since Twain was one of those nineteenth century "inspirational" writers whose work could vary from day to day or page to page. He must
be read this way, in fact, for the sake of the gems which we can
pick up in the most rough or arid-appearing territory; and contrariwise,
as with the end of *Huck*, the immortal pages of Huck's "confrontation"
about returning Jim to slavery are followed by a series of practical
jokes. As with Dickens, another Victorian giant who had been down-
graded for the same reasons, modern standards of "form" simply do
not apply to these natural geniuses; and when we try to apply formal-
istic standards at any cost, as with Whitman, we only succeed in block-
ing out invaluable areas of our cultural heritage.

But they will stand, those formless masters who in fact create their
own form which we must get to understand and to value; and our strict
formalists will disappear as they always do in the face of human nature
and history. In Twain's case again, *A Connecticut Yankee* (1889) was
a very badly wrought fictional tale which gained prominence and has
survived mainly because of its radical social commentary, some of
which, like the famous passage on the two French reigns of terror, is
included in this volume. But here we are on the edge of what was
indeed a dark *period* in Twain's career, from the mid-eighties to the
mid-nineties; but not at all a breaking point or a major split in his
literary career.

Popular, rich, pleasure-loving and living high, Sam and Livy had
built their Hartford mansion and expanded the scale of their domestic

and social life to the point where often they had to flee from their own home to get away from their friends. They were a closely-knit family group . . . with the three daughters whom Livy worked to educate, and Sam to entertain. The letters and diaries up to this point seem to describe a domestic idyll—perhaps the children were only jealous of the close, affectionate, and openly physical relationship of the parents. (I say this with all due regard to the ominously Freudian "analyses" of a famous literary couple.)

But Clemens had founded a publishing house which had a sensational beginning with General Grant's *Memoirs,* eventually paying the hero's widow about half a million dollars, and which ran steadily down hill after that. Moreover, he had, in the eighties, invested his own money and most of Livy's fortune in a fabulous typesetter which was supposed to beat out the Mergenthaler. It has been described as the most expensive machine of its type ever built, and the greatest mechanical failure. Twain's first biographer, Albert Bigelow Paine, estimated that he lost almost two hundred thousand dollars on the never-to-be-finished Paige typesetter and over one hundred thousand dollars in the Charles Webster publishing firm, sums of money which were fantastically large for that period and for a popular writer in any period. In the panic of 1893–94, Clemens, worn out by worries, exhausted, depressed, and black-hearted, went into the ordeal of bankruptcy, and from this crisis there ensued a series of dark and enigmatic parables from *Pudd'nhead Wilson* in 1894 to "The Man That Corrupted Hadleyburg" in 1900 and "The $30,000 Bequest" in 1906.

What is usually overlooked in·this period of Twain's work is that like every great writer he made his art his salvation. He rejoiced in rejecting business forever (though he would live to dally with the idea of further fortunes in other inventions). He vowed to go back to his trade and to swim in ink. And like all major writers he identified his own experience with his country's and his culture. He was deeply identified not merely with the moral evil and spiritual debasement of slavery but with the financial corruption of the old republic under the impact of the great fortunes which were being accumulated in this period, and which were indeed changing the nature, the domestic rituals, the world outlook of the American democracy.

The cash nexus, the huge and powerful corporations of finance capitalism, the pomp and power as the means and ends of human existence, the growing territorial ambitions, and the obvious imperialism of an emerging world power—Sam Clemens did not like any of this. Moreover, in "The $30,000 Bequest" he had reached a perspective on his own personal misfortunes which could make a comedy out of human avarice. He had been befriended by a Standard Oil tycoon named H. H. Rogers; his financial troubles were clearing up; his world-wide lecture tour in 1895 paid off his remaining creditors—when further tragedy even harder in personal terms again pursued him. From his world tour he had returned to London triumphantly only to learn that their most beloved daughter Susy had come down with meningitis. Susy did indeed die a horrible death before Livy and Clara could get back to America, and the Clemens family was enshrouded by a darkness from which it never recovered. Perhaps Susy had been too much of a prodigy, perhaps the parents lavished too much love and devotion on her, perhaps they mourned too deeply and too long. At any rate their domestic idyll, so fortunate, so blessed, so charming, was over. Livy's own spiritual and physical decline can be dated from this point; and Clara also had a kind of nervous breakdown after her mother's death. At York Harbor, Maine, in August, 1902, Livy had collapsed; and after almost two more years of suffering and torment as a bed-ridden invalid who was isolated from the family she loved so much, she died in Italy in May, 1904. As Sam Clemens wrote in his notebook, "At a quarter past 9 this evening she that was the life of my life passed to the relief & the peace of death after 22 months of unjust and unearned suffering. I first saw her 37 years ago & now I have looked upon her face for the last time. Oh, so unexpected! . . . I was full of remorse for things done & said in these 34 years of married life that hurt Livy's heart."

And indeed he was, and how the tributes to Livy poured forth from his affectionate and grieving heart in both the personal and the literary utterances of those years. But the point of Twain's final period, and the true background of the polemical and satirical social commentary collected in this volume, is that he lived to survive even the worst of these personal blows—to survive quite triumphantly, and to climax his literary career.

Though he was alone and lonely during these years, he established a comfortable residence at 21 Fifth Avenue in a city where he had always loved social festivities, even during the worst of his financial troubles, and parties and drinking and dancing late into the night. At one point he had been called the Belle of New York. For there existed in Sam Clemens, along with his radicalism and revolutionary side—as the "double" driving force of his temperament which was really two sides of the same coin—a deep sense of pleasure and comfort and joy in life (or what was life for?) which most of us have experienced in childhood, but which in him was the secret of his maturity. Yes, and a sense of material pomp. On his seventieth birthday there was a great banquet for him at Delmonico's on December 5, 1905, with a forty-piece orchestra from the Metropolitan Opera House, an epicurean dinner, five hours of toasts and talks, and then one of Twain's most hilarious and brilliant speeches about the "secret" of his success in life—a talk that undercut the whole fantastic pageant.

Later on he even built another mansion for himself at Redding, Connecticut; and there with his daughter Jeanne as secretary and companion, he had once more the sense of family happiness. He had a final flowering. During all this time he had been working on *The Mysterious Stranger*,* one of the great short stories (or novelettes) of world literature, and on the epical book of his old age, the *Autobiography*, which has also been called one of the great "daylight books" of American literature.

If *The Mysterious Stranger* is almost a compendium of life's fatalities, ironies, hoaxes, and cruelties, the point is that Satan, the book's hero, the true creator of human existence, according to Twain, and the glamorous "teacher" of the group of innocent young boys in the narrative (who is not even the true Satan but a distant nephew), is a remarkably entertaining literary creation. Almost alone among the great despairing fables of man's deluded and painful existence, the *Stranger* proclaims—and illustrates—the efficacy of laughter as a saving grace. In the end, Twain's Satan-Creator is even a joyous and gay creature as he displays and dispels a wide variety of human delusions, evasions,

---

* Despite the academic controversy about "the *Mysterious Stranger* manuscripts," there is only one version of the story, the final one which Twain evolved, that makes any sense—but that one makes great sense indeed. And while it is true that A. B. Paine inserted the ending from one of the other drafts, the ending is not relevant to the story's real import. Twain never had good endings.

and fabrications. The desperate nihilism of the tale turns out to be very comical. That famous "black despair" of Twain's final period has undergone the purgation of his own irrepressible humor. Evil is not quite evil when it becomes parody, or a comedy of evil; and this remarkable story also has its undertone of the pagan-plenary world of comic make-believe in *Tom Sawyer* and *Huck Finn*. The beautiful and devastating irony of *The Mysterious Stranger*—an irony which contains all of Twain's final wisdom about life—is permeated by a sense of human absurdity and hilarity. The Twainian man has entered the black pit of mortal disaster—and has survived to laugh. Though Mark Twain, like every great artist, never attempted to deny the basic tragedy of life, he succeeded in diminishing our large stock of vile and sordid and vicious accomplishments, including those social crimes which he attacks so brilliantly in the present volume. He makes life worth living again; at his best he makes life heroic, when it is now generally conceived as hopeless and degrading. He reminds us of what great literature should do, because he is great literature.

Though the categories of this anthology rise directly from Twain's work, the placement of the selections is often arbitrary or by a kind of association which the essays themselves lead to. Thus many of the items under "Race" are related to such religious themes as Twain's early and constant hatred of missionaries, particularly in China. And many of the items under "Religion" are devoted to themes of race and imperialism. Similarly, while Twain's direct comments on "Revolution" are less extended than one might expect (he remained a radical democrat all his life and never succumbed to his friend William Dean Howells' utopian socialism), Twain's whole temperament was revolutionary. Everything he touched seemed to change in his hands, becoming its polar and dialectical opposite.

That is why in a sense I am fondest of the final section in this book, "Related Matters," where we can see the range of his curiosity and insight upon a wide variety of things, big and small. But the myth of Twain's final despair and frustration being the *cause* of his radical social commentary (which we have seen to be false) is also dispelled by the fact that his rebellious satire opens with his career, remains constant throughout it, and was simply enhanced in his maturity by what had become of his *country* in this period. Very early on, Sam Clemens had escaped from the "civilization" of the western mining towns to the paradisiacal air of the Sandwich Islands; and one of his earliest satires was the proposal, included in this volume, to annex those blessed isles and give them all the benefits of the corrupt political, moral, and commercial life in the United States. (He was prophetic; we did it.)

Was there one book of his *without* passages of social satire, in the beginning, in the middle, or at the end of his career? If *The Gilded Age* (1873) was a hodge-podge collaboration with Charles Dudley Warner, what redeems it is the description of the whole new age of get-rich-quick vulgarity and corruption. The picture of Washington finance-politics is searing; the book's title became a byword. If *A Connecticut Yankee* was another rough and implausible fictional narrative, it was again marked by brilliant passages of social and historical reflections on the feudal ages, the French Revolution—and our own society.

No—though tempered by life's losses, illusions, and sufferings, Sam Clemens was inherently himself from start to end. Very few artists have remained so true to their own temperaments as he was through such extremes of riches and poverty, obscurity and renown; poverty and obscurity again—and then again fame, wealth, and prestige in his final flowering. This was not the celebrated split personality which we have heard so much about. He just embodied the polar opposites of any major writer, artist, or of life itself. The polarity of his own career seemed to touch him relatively little indeed; perhaps that was another distinguishing mark of his talent, and a key to his work.

What changed in the later phase of his career, however—and what some of Twain's biographers and critics have seemed singularly neglectful about, or deliberately obtuse to—was our own American society in the closing decade of the nineteenth century. We had gone to hell in 1896, Twain once declared flatly, and he was not far from the truth. The early nineties saw one of the worst American depressions, and by 1895, in New England for example, it was still around. But the late nineties saw the United States as the dominant power in both North and South America, having replaced both the English empire and the declining Spanish empire. (We had openly announced our plans to take over Canada in case of any conflict in South America.)

Having completed the conquest of our own frontier, while destroying a native Indian culture, carving out a large piece of land from Mexico for the southern slave owners, surviving an agonizing Civil War over slavery only to become the most potent new financial and industrial power in the world, the United States naturally began to look outward, first to South America, our natural colony under the Monroe Doctrine, and then to Europe, Asia, and Africa. We annexed Hawaii in the face of the English, and we faced England down in the Venezuela border crisis. We threw Spain out of Cuba under the pretext of "liberation" and took over the Philippines by crushing their own liberation movement. Puerto Rico was another item on the agenda, since we needed bases for the new American navy which was being established, not coincidentally, at the same time.

This was no secret at the time, though it has remained semi-secret in many history books today. "Failure of the home market provided the stimulus for the full development of imperial policies in the United States. . . . The growth of American industry made the conquest of foreign markets not only an inviting possibility, but a hard-felt necessity."* Such famous political figures as Teddy Roosevelt, who felt the Spanish war would be good for the American spirit, and Henry Cabot Lodge, aided by the leading industrialists, financiers, and politicians of the country, all agreed on the new Manifest Destiny of America's taking its part, or its lead, among those other great powers, like England and Germany, who were carving up the "backward areas" of the world. It was now or never, do or die. And both ambitious or reluctant American presidents or presidential candidates—Harrison, Blaine, Cleveland, McKinley, and Roosevelt—yielded to the historical impetus of the period.

This was a watershed—or a chasm—in our history. The old republic of Mark Twain's day became the new American empire right before his face. He was there, he saw it, he wrote about it on the spot—if he did not always publish it. (Some of the essays in this volume are almost a secret history of American low-life in very high places.) And Twain was primarily the philosopher-poet of the old American republic whose aspirations he, along with Whitman and Melville, had voiced most

* Daniel B. Schirmer, *Republic or Empire*. Preface by Howard Zinn. Schenkman Publishing Co., 1972. I am indebted to this book for one of the most closely detailed studies of American imperialism in the nineties which I have yet seen.

fully, profoundly, eloquently. No wonder these essays are filled with anger, despair, desperation, biting satire, and furious polemics! Only a professor of English might not understand this. The wonder is that they are not more so, that Twain somehow kept his balance in this area too. The marvel of these writings is how often they make you laugh in the midst of the most desperate fury—this is always the stamp of Mark Twain's writings, and what makes them so special in the annals of literature, and indeed so reminiscent of Cervantes.

Seeing this spread out before his eyes in Europe and America, Twain was not slow to identify the American oligarchy (whose pet he had been) for what it was, along with the American political figures who served their masters so well, when they were not themselves of the oligarchy. He was ripe with comparisons of the American and the Roman empires. He was haunted by visions of the coming American monarchy and the rise of a shoemaker-dictator in the southern states. Because he was still primarily an "innocent"—a pagan spirit trapped by the cage of civilization, just as Melville's psyche indicated the same dilemma—Twain could not even believe his own deepest premonitions. When describing the collapse of his beloved American republic, he was forced to seek remote religious imagery, upon occasions, and to designate himself as the "mad prophet." But we know what such madness means.

A word about "method," as the New Critics used to say when they were still around, or on the composition of this anthology. In the four main categories of this Twainian collection, it has not been difficult to support the more famous and well-known essays with corresponding or complementary essays and passages from less well-known and usually earlier books of Twain. The problem was not lack of material but only of space and a choice of relevance. I might personally have preferred a volume larger than this one, which documented Twain's radical utterances from start to end and in various other ways, but my editors have prevailed on me to be more pertinent. Even so, behind Twain's commentary on the Anglo-Saxon race, on the scandalous behavior of American missionaries (and all the missionaries) in China, on imperialism and the darker races, on our brutal and disgraceful conquest of the Philippines (a model for Vietnam and My Lai), on King

Leopold of Belgium and the Russian Czar—behind these essays I have included less well-known passages and sections from *Following the Equator* (1897) on the slave trade in Australia, guerrilla warfare in South Africa, and again, and always, the cruel subjugation of the native blacks. It even turns out that the Christian heaven of Captain Stormfield's visit is populated by a motley collection of darker skinned peoples—a white man hasn't got a chance there.

And while Twain was intensely interested in the hypocrisy of conventional Christianity—or that of a besmirched "Christendom" at the close of the nineteenth century—it is also true that some of his best social and historical indictments were couched under the formal guise of religious commentary. Or even more profoundly, perhaps, he was absorbed all his life in the imagery of the Garden, Adam and Eve, the Serpent of knowledge, the Fall. Here again the natural innocence of man was always contrasted in Twain's mind with the harsh repressions of "formal" (or social, or civilizing) Christianity. This lifelong advocate of Satan, this rebellious angel himself, was also fascinated by the moral turpitude of the Old Testament to the point that his reflections on God's sins would have constituted a new Twainian Bible.

In Part Two there is the essay on Bible Teaching and Twain's talk on Plymouth Rock and the Pilgrims as early as 1881 (and what a natural wit was there, the wit of genius). There are the discussions of patriotism and Christianity, and of the manifold blessings of Christian civilization. . . .

But the book is here, and in the book I have tried to keep editorial comment to a minimum. As usual Mark Twain speaks for himself better than anybody can speak for him, and that is what he is doing in these pages.

MAXWELL GEISMAR
July 4th, 1972

PART ONE

Race

THE ANGLO-SAXON RACE*

For good or for evil we continue to educate Europe. We have held the post of instructor for more than a century and a quarter now. We were not elected to it, we merely took it. We are of the Anglo-Saxon race. At the banquet last winter of that organization which calls itself the Ends of the Earth Club, the chairman, a retired regular army officer of high grade, proclaimed in a loud voice, and with fervency, "We are of the Anglo-Saxon race, and when the Anglo-Saxon wants a thing *he just takes it.*"

That utterance was applauded to the echo. There were perhaps seventy-five civilians present and twenty-five military and naval men. It took those people nearly two minutes to work off their stormy admiration of that great sentiment; and meanwhile the inspired prophet who had discharged it—from his liver, or his intestines, or his esophagus, or wherever he had bred it—stood there glowing and beaming and smiling and issuing rays of happiness from every pore, rays that were so intense that they were visible and made him look like the old-time picture in the Almanac of the man who stands discharging signs of the zodiac in every direction, and so absorbed in happiness, so steeped in happiness, that he smiles and smiles and has plainly forgotten that he is painfully and dangerously ruptured and exposed amidships and needs sewing up right away.

The soldier man's great utterance, interpreted by the expression which he put into it, meant in plain English, "The English and the Americans are thieves, highwaymen, pirates, and we are proud to be of the combination."

* Bernard DeVoto, editor, *Mark Twain in Eruption*, 1940. (Written in 1906.)

3

Out of all the English and Americans present, there was not one with the grace to get up and say he was ashamed of being an Anglo-Saxon, and also ashamed of being a member of the human race since the race must abide under the presence upon it of the Anglo-Saxon taint. I could not perform this office. I could not afford to lose my temper and make a self-righteous exhibition of myself and my superior morals that I might teach this infant class in decency the rudiments of that cult, for they would not be able to grasp it; they would not be able to understand it.

It was an amazing thing to see, that boyishly frank and honest and delighted outburst of enthusiasm over the soldier prophet's mephitic remark. It looked suspiciously like a revelation, a secret feeling of the national heart surprised into expression and exposure by untoward accident, for it was a representative assemblage. All the chief mechanisms that constitute the machine which drives and vitalizes the national civilization were present—lawyers, bankers, merchants, manufacturers, journalists, politicians, soldiers, sailors—they were all there. Apparently it was the United States in banquet assembled, and qualified to speak with authority for the nation and reveal its private morals to the public view.

The initial welcome of that strange sentiment was not an unwary betrayal, to be repented of upon reflection; and this was shown by the fact that whenever during the rest of the evening a speaker found that he was becoming uninteresting and wearisome, he only needed to inject that great Anglo-Saxon moral into the midst of his platitudes to start up that glad storm again. After all, it was only the human race on exhibition. It has always been a peculiarity of the human race that it keeps two sets of morals in stock—the private and real, and the public and artificial.

Our public motto is "In God we trust," and when we see those gracious words on the trade-dollar (worth sixty cents) they always seem to tremble and whimper with pious emotion. That is our public motto. It transpires that our private one is, "When the Anglo-Saxon wants a thing *he just takes it.*" Our public morals are touchingly set forth in that stately and yet gentle and kindly motto which indicates that we are a nation of gracious and affectionate multitudinous brothers compacted into one—"*e pluribus unum.*" Our private morals find the light in the sacred phrase, "Come, *step* lively!"

We imported our imperialism from monarchical Europe, also our curious notions of patriotism—that is, if we have any principle of patriotism which any person can definitely and intelligibly define. It is but fair then, no doubt, that we should instruct Europe in return for these and the other kinds of instruction which we have received from that source.

Something more than a century ago we gave Europe the first notions of liberty it had ever had, and thereby largely and happily helped to bring on the French Revolution and claim a share in its beneficent results. We have taught Europe many lessons since. But for us, Europe might never have known the interviewer; but for us certain of the European states might never have experienced the blessing of extravagant imposts; but for us the European Food Trust might never have acquired the art of poisoning the world for cash; but for us her Insurance Trusts might never have found out the best way to work the widow and orphan for profit; but for us the long delayed resumption of Yellow Journalism in Europe might have been postponed for generations to come. Steadily, continuously, persistently, we are Americanizing Europe, and all in good time we shall get the job perfected.*

TO THE PERSON SITTING IN DARKNESS†

The following news from China appeared in the *Sun,* of New York, on Christmas Eve. The italics are mine:

The Rev. Mr. Ament, of the American Board of Foreign Missions, has returned from a trip which he made for the purpose of collecting indemnities for damages done by Boxers. *Everywhere he went he compelled the Chinese to pay.* He says that all his native Christians are now provided for. He had 700 of them under his charge, and 300 were killed. He has collected *300 taels for each* of these murders, and

---

* And compare this blunt statement with Henry James' quaint notion, during the same years, that the Old World was educating the New in civilizational graces. *Ed.*

† *North American Review,* 1901. Reprinted in *Europe and Elsewhere* (1923).

has *compelled full payment for all the property belonging to Christians* that was destroyed. He also assessed *fines* amounting to THIRTEEN TIMES the amount of the indemnity. *This money will be used for the propagation of the Gospel.*

Mr. Ament declares that the compensation he has collected is *moderate* when compared with the amount secured by the Catholics, who demand, in addition to money, *head for head.* They collect 500 taels for each murder of a Catholic. In the Wenchiu country, 680 Catholics were killed, and for this the European Catholics here demand 750,000 strings of cash and 680 *heads.*

In the course of a conversation, Mr. Ament referred to the attitude of the missionaries toward the Chinese. He said:

"I deny emphatically that the missionaries are *vindictive,* that they *generally* looted, or that they have done anything *since* the siege that *the circumstances did not demand.* I criticize the Americans. *The soft hand of the Americans is not as good as the mailed fist of the Germans.* If you deal with the Chinese with a soft hand they will take advantage of it.

"The statement that the French government will return the loot taken by the French soldiers is the source of the greatest amusement here. The French soldiers were more systematic looters than the Germans, and it is a fact that to-day *Catholic Christians,* carrying French flags and armed with modern guns, *are looting villages* in the Province of Chili."

By happy luck, we get all these glad tidings on Christmas Eve—just in time enable us to celebrate the day with proper gayety and enthusiasm. Our spirits soar, and we find we can even make jokes: Taels, I win, Heads you lose.

Our Reverend Ament is the right man in the right place. What we want of our missionaries out there is, not that they shall merely represent in their acts and persons the grace and gentleness and charity and loving-kindness of our religion, but that they shall also represent the American spirit. The oldest Americans are the Pawnees. Macallum's History says:

When a white Boxer kills a Pawnee and destroys his property, the other Pawnees do not trouble to seek *him* out, they kill any white person that comes along; also, they make some white village pay deceased's heirs the full cash value of deceased, together with full cash value of the property destroyed; they also make the village pay, in addition, *thirteen times* the value of that property into a fund for the dissemination of the Pawnee religion, which they regard as the best of all religions for the softening and humanizing of the heart of man. It is their idea that it is only fair and right that the innocent should be made to suffer for the guilty, and that it is better that ninety and nine innocent should suffer than that one guilty person should escape.

Our Reverend Ament is justifiably jealous of those enterprising Catholics, who not only get big money for each lost convert, but get "head for head" besides. But he should soothe himself with the reflections that the entirety of their exactions are for their own pockets, whereas he, less selfishly, devotes only 300 taels per head to that service, and gives the whole vast thirteen repetitions of the property-indemnity to the service of propagating the Gospel. His magnanimity has won him the approval of his nation, and will get him a monument. Let him be content with these rewards. We all hold him dear for manfully defending his fellow missionaries from exaggerated charges which were beginning to distress us, but which his testimony has so considerably modified that we can now contemplate them without noticeable pain. For now we know that, even before the siege, the missionaries were not "generally" out looting, and that, "since the siege," they have acted quite handsomely, except when "circumstances" crowded them. I am arranging for the monument. Subscriptions for it can be sent to the American Board; designs for it can be sent to me. Designs must allegorically set forth the Thirteen Reduplications of the Indemnity, and the Object for which they were exacted; as Ornaments, the designs must exhibit 680 Heads, so disposed as to give a pleasing and pretty effect; for the Catholics have done nicely, and are entitled to notice in the monument. Mottoes may be suggested, if any shall be discovered that will satisfactorily cover the ground.

Mr. Ament's financial feat of squeezing a thirteen-fold indemnity out of the pauper peasants to square other people's offenses, thus condemning them and their women and innocent little children to inevitable starvation and lingering death, in order that the blood money so acquired might be *"used for the propagation of the Gospel,"* does not flutter my serenity; although the act and the words, taken together, concrete a blasphemy so hideous and so colossal that, without doubt, its mate is not findable in the history of this or of any other age. Yet, if a layman had done that thing and justified it with those words, I should have shuddered, I know. Or, if I had done the thing and said the words myself—However, the thought is unthinkable, irreverent as some imperfectly informed people think me. Sometimes an ordained minister sets out to be blasphemous. When this happens, the layman is out of the running; he stands no chance.

We have Mr. Ament's impassioned assurance that the missionaries are not "vindicative." Let us hope and pray that they will never become so, but will remain in the almost morbidly fair and just and gentle temper which is affording so much satisfaction to their brother and champion to-day.

The following is from the New York *Tribune* of Christmas Eve. It comes from that journal's Tokyo correspondent. It has a strange and impudent sound, but the Japanese are but partially civilized as yet. When they become wholly civilized they will not talk so:

> The missionary question, of course, occupies a foremost place in the discussion. It is now felt as essential that the Western Powers take cognizance of the sentiment here, that religious invasions of Oriental countries by powerful Western organizations are tantamount to filibustering expeditions, and should not only be discountenanced, but that stern measures should be adopted for their suppression. The feeling here is that the missionary organizations constitute a constant menace to peaceful international relations.

Shall we? That is, shall we go on conferring our Civilization upon the peoples that sit in darkness, or shall we give those poor things a rest? Shall we bang right ahead in our old-time, loud, pious way, and commit the new century to the game; or shall we sober up and sit down and think it over first? Would it not be prudent to get our Civilization tools together, and see how much stock is left on hand in the way of Glass Beads and Theology, and Maxim Guns and Hymn Books, and Trade Gin and Torches of Progress and Enlightenment (patent adjustable ones, good to fire villages with, upon occasion), and balance the books, and arrive at the profit and loss, so that we may intelligently decide whether to continue the business or sell out the property and start a new Civilization Scheme on the proceeds?

Extending the Blessings of Civilization to our Brother who Sits in Darkness has been a good trade and has paid well, on the whole; and there is money in it yet, if carefully worked—but not enough, in my judgment, to make any considerable risk advisable. The People that Sit in Darkness are getting to be too scarce—too scarce and too shy. And such darkness as is now left is really of but an indifferent quality, and not dark enough for the game. The most of those People that Sit in Darkness have been furnished with more light than was good for them or profitable for us. We have been injudicious.

The Blessings-of-Civilization Trust, wisely and cautiously administered, is a Daisy. There is more money in it, more territory, more sovereignty, and other kinds of emolument, than there is in any other game that is played. But Christendom has been playing it badly of late years, and must certainly suffer by it, in my opinion. She has been so eager to get every stake that appeared on the green cloth, that the People who Sit in Darkness have noticed it—they have noticed it, and have begun to show alarm. They have become suspicious of the Blessings of Civilization. More—they have begun to examine them. This is not well. The Blessings of Civilization are all right, and a good commercial property; there could not be a better, in a dim light. In the right kind of a light, and at a proper distance, with the goods a little out of focus, they furnish this desirable exhibit to the Gentlemen who Sit in Darkness:

LOVE,	LAW AND ORDER,
JUSTICE,	LIBERTY,
GENTLENESS,	EQUALITY,
CHRISTIANITY,	HONORABLE DEALING,
PROTECTION TO THE WEAK,	MERCY,
TEMPERANCE,	EDUCATION,

—and so on.

There. Is it good? Sir, it is pie. It will bring into camp any idiot that sits in darkness anywhere. But not if we adulterate it. It is proper to be emphatic upon that point. This brand is strictly for Export—apparently. *Apparently.* Privately and confidentially, it is nothing of the kind. Privately and confidentially, it is merely an outside cover, gay and pretty and attractive, displaying the special patterns of our Civilization which we reserve for Home Consumption, while *inside* the bale is the Actual Thing that the Customer Sitting in Darkness buys with his blood and tears and land and liberty. That Actual Thing is, indeed, Civilization, but it is only for Export. Is there a difference between the two brands? In some of the details, yes.

We all know that the Business is being ruined. The reason is not far to seek. It is because our Mr. McKinley, and Mr. Chamberlain, and the Kaiser, and the Tsar and the French have been exporting the Actual Thing *with the outside cover left off*. This is bad for the Game. It shows that these new players of it are not sufficiently acquainted with it.

It is a distress to look on and note the mismoves, they are so strange and so awkward. Mr. Chamberlain manufactures a war out of materials so inadequate and so fanciful that they make the boxes grieve and the gallery laugh, and he tries hard to persuade himself that it isn't purely a private raid for cash, but has a sort of dim, vague respectability about it somewhere, if he could only find the spot; and that, by and by, he can scour the flag clean again after he has finished dragging it through the mud, and make it shine and flash in the vault of heaven once more as it has shown and flashed there a thousand years in the world's respect until he laid his unfaithful hand upon it. It is bad play—bad. For it exposes the Actual Thing to Them that Sit in Darkness, and they say: "What! Christian against Christian? And only for money? Is *this* a case of magnanimity, forbearance, love, gentleness, mercy, protection of the weak—this strange and overshowy onslaught of an elephant upon a nest of field mice, on the pretext that the mice had squeaked an insolence at him—conduct which "no self-respecting government could allow to pass unavenged"? as Mr. Chamberlain said. Was that a good pretext in a small case, when it had not been a good pretext in a large one—for only recently Russia had affronted the elephant three times and survived alive and unsmitten. Is this Civilization and Progress? Is it something better than we already possess? These harryings and burnings and desert-makings in the Transvaal—is this an improvement on our darkness? Is it, perhaps, possible that there are two kinds of Civilization—one for home consumption and one for the heathen market?"

Then They that Sit in Darkness are troubled, and shake their heads; and they read this extract from a letter of a British private, recounting his exploits in one of Methuen's victories, some days before the affair of Magersfontein, and they are troubled again:

> We tore up the hill and into the intrenchments, and the Boers saw we had them; so they dropped their guns and went down on their knees and put up their hands clasped, and begged for mercy. And we gave it them—*with the long spoon.*

The long spoon is the bayonet. See *Lloyd's Weekly,* London, of those days. The same number—and the same column—contained some quite unconscious satire in the form of shocked and bitter upbraidings of the Boers for their brutalities and inhumanities!

Next, to our heavy damage, the Kaiser went to playing the game without first mastering it. He lost a couple of missionaries in a riot in Shantung, and in his account he made an overcharge for them. China had to pay a hundred thousand dollars apiece for them, in money; twelve miles of territory, containing several millions of inhabitants and worth twenty million dollars; and to build a monument, and also a Christian church; whereas the people of China could have been depended upon to remember the missionaries without the help of these expensive memorials. This was all bad play. Bad, because it would not, and could not, and will not now or ever, deceive the Person Sitting in Darkness. He knows that it was an overcharge. He knows that a missionary is like any other man: he is worth merely what you can supply his place for, and no more. He is useful, but so is a doctor, so is a sheriff, so is an editor; but a just Emperor does not charge war prices for such. A diligent, intelligent, but obscure missionary, and a diligent, intelligent country editor are worth much, and we know it; but they are not worth the earth. We esteem such an editor, and we are sorry to see him go; but, when he goes, we should consider twelve miles of territory, and a church, and a fortune, overcompensation for his loss. I mean, if he was a Chinese editor, and we had to settle for him. It is no proper figure for an editor or a missionary; one can get shop-worn kings for less. It was bad play on the Kaiser's part. It got this property, true; but it *produced the Chinese revolt,* the indignant uprising of China's traduced patriots, the Boxers. The results have been expensive to Germany, and to the other Disseminators of Progress and the Blessings of Civilization.

The Kaiser's claim was paid, yet it was bad play, for it could not fail to have an evil effect upon Persons Sitting in Darkness in China. They would muse upon the event, and be likely to say: "Civilization is gracious and beautiful, for such is its reputation; but can we afford it? There are rich Chinamen, perhaps they can afford it; but this tax is not laid upon them, it is laid upon the peasants of Shantung; it is they that must pay this mighty sum, and their wages are but four cents a day. Is this a better civilization than ours, and holier and higher and nobler? Is not this rapacity? Is not this extortion? Would Germany charge America two hundred thousand dollars for two missionaries, and shake the mailed fist in her face, and send warships, and send soldiers, and say: 'Seize twelve miles of territory, worth twenty millions of dollars, as additional pay for the missionaries; and make those peasants build a monument to the missionaries, and a costly Christian church to remember them by?' And later would Germany say to her soldiers: 'March through America and slay, *giving no quarter;* make the German face there, as has been our Hun-face here, a terror for a thousand years; march through the Great Republic and slay, slay, slay, carving a road for our offended religion through its heart and bowels?' Would Germany do like this to America, to England, to France, to Russia? Or only to China, the helpless—imitating the elephant's assault upon the field mice? Had we better invest in this Civilization—this Civilization which called Napoleon a buccaneer for carrying off Venice's bronze horses, but which steals our ancient astronomical instruments from our walls, and goes looting like common bandits—that is, all the alien soldiers except America's; and (Americans again excepted) storms frightened villages and cables the result to glad journals at home every day: 'Chinese losses, 450 killed; ours, *one officer and two men wounded.* Shall proceed against neighboring village to-morrow, where a *massacre* is reported.' Can we afford Civilization?"

And next Russia must go and play the game injudiciously. She affronts England once or twice—with the Person Sitting in Darkness observing and noting; by moral assistance of France and Germany, she robs Japan of her hard-earned spoil, all swimming in Chinese blood— Port Arthur—with the Person again observing and noting; then she seizes Manchuria, raids its villages, and chokes its great river with the swollen corpses of countless massacred peasants—that astonished Person still observing and noting. And perhaps he is saying to himself: "It is yet *another* Civilized Power, with its banner of the Prince of Peace in one hand and its loot basket and its butcher knife in the other. Is there no salvation for us but to adopt Civilization and lift ourselves down to its level?"

And by and by comes America, and our Master of the Game plays it badly—plays it as Mr. Chamberlain was playing it in South Africa. It was a mistake to do that; also, it was one which was quite unlooked for in a Master who was playing it so well in Cuba. In Cuba, he was playing the usual and regular *American* game, and it was winning, for there is no way to beat it. The Master, contemplating Cuba, said: "Here is an oppressed and friendless little nation which is willing to fight to be free; we go partners, and put up the strength of seventy million sympathizers and the resources of the United States: play!" Nothing but Europe combined could call that hand: and Europe cannot combine on anything. There, in Cuba, he was following our great traditions in a way which made us very proud of him, and proud of the deep dissatisfaction'which his play was provoking in continental Europe. Moved by a high inspiration, he threw out those stirring words which proclaimed that forcible annexation would be "criminal aggression"; and in that utterance fired another "shot heard round the world." The memory of that fine saying will be outlived by the remembrance of no act of his but one—that he forgot it within the twelvemonth, and its honorable gospel along with it.

For, presently, came the Philippine temptation. It was strong; it was too strong, and he made that bad mistake: he played the European game, the Chamberlain game. It was a pity; it was a great pity, that error; that one grievous error, that irrevocable error. For it was the very place and time to play the American game again. And at no cost. Rich winnings to be gathered in, too; rich and permanent; indestructible; a fortune transmissible forever to the children of the flag. Not land, not money, not dominion—no, something worth many times more than that dross: our share, the spectacle of a nation of long harassed and persecuted slaves set free through our influence; our posterity's share, the golden memory of that fair deed. The game was in our hands. If it had been played according to the American rules, Dewey would have sailed away from Manila as soon as he had destroyed the Spanish fleet—after putting up a sign on shore guaranteeing foreign property and life against damage by the Filipinos, and warning the Powers that interference with the emancipated patriots would be regarded as an act unfriendly to the United States. The Powers cannot combine, in even a bad cause, and the sign would not have been molested.

Dewey could have gone about his affairs elsewhere, and left the competent Filipino army to starve out the little Spanish garrison and send it home, and the Filipino citizens to set up the form of government they might prefer, and deal with the friars and their doubtful acquisitions according to Filipino ideas of fairness and justice—ideas which have since been tested and found to be of as high an order as any that prevail in Europe or America.

But we played the Chamberlain game, and lost the chance to add another Cuba and another honorable deed to our good record.

The more we examine the mistake, the more clearly we perceive that it is going to be bad for the Business. The Person Sitting in Darkness is almost sure to say: "There is something curious about this—curious and unaccountable. There must be two Americas: one that sets the captive free, and one that takes a once-captive's new freedom away from him, and picks a quarrel with him with nothing to found it on; then kills him to get his land."

The truth is, the Person Sitting in Darkness *is* saying things like that; and for the sake of the Business we must persuade him to look at the Philippine matter in another and healthier way. We must arrange his opinions for him. I believe it can be done; for Mr. Chamberlain has arranged England's opinion of the South African matter, and done it most cleverly and successfully. He presented the facts—some of the facts—and showed those confiding people what the facts meant. He did it statistically, which is a good way. He used the formula: "Twice 2 are 14, and 2 from 9 leaves 35." Figures are effective; figures will convince the elect.

Now, my plan is a still bolder one than Mr. Chamberlain's, though apparently a copy of it. Let us be franker than Mr. Chamberlain; let us audaciously present the whole of the facts, shirking none, then explain them according to Mr. Chamberlain's formula. This daring truthfulness will astonish and dazzle the Person Sitting in Darkness, and he will take the Explanation down before his mental vision has had time to get back into focus. Let us say to him:

"Our case is simple. On the 1st of May, Dewey destroyed the Spanish fleet. This left the Archipelago in the hands of its proper and rightful owners, the Filipino nation. Their army numbered 30,000 men, and they were competent to whip out or starve out the little Spanish garrison; then the people could set up a government of their own devising. Our traditions required that Dewey should now set up his warning sign, and go away. But Master of the Game happened to think of another plan—the European plan. He acted upon it. This was, to send out an army—ostensibly to help the native patriots put the finishing touch upon their long and plucky struggle for independence, but really to take their land away from them and keep it. That is, in the interest of Progress and Civilization. The plan developed, stage by stage, and quite satisfactorily. We entered into a military alliance with the trusting Filipinos, and they hemmed in Manila on the land side, and by their valuable help the place, with its garrison of 8,000 or 10,000 Spaniards, was captured—a thing which we could not have accomplished unaided at that time. We got their help by—by ingenuity. We knew they were fighting for their independence, and that they had been at it for two years. We knew they supposed that we also were fighting in their worthy cause—just as we had helped the Cubans fight for Cuban independence—and we allowed them to go on thinking so. *Until Manila was ours and we could get along without them.* Then we showed our hand. Of course, they were surprised—that was natural; surprised and disappointed; disappointed and grieved. To them it looked un-American; uncharacteristic; foreign to our established traditions. And this was natural, too; for we were only playing the American Game in public—in private it was the European. It was neatly done, very neatly, and it bewildered them. They could not understand it; for we had been so friendly—so affectionate, even—with those simple-minded patriots! We, our own selves, had brought back out of exile their leader, their hero, their hope, their Washington—Aguinaldo; brought him in a warship, in high honor, under the sacred shelter and hospitality of the flag; brought him back and restored him to his people, and got their moving and eloquent gratitude for it. Yes, we had been so friendly to them, and had heartened them up in so many ways! We had lent them guns and ammunition; advised with them; exchanged pleasant courtesies with them; placed our sick and wounded in their kindly care; intrusted our Spanish prisoners to their humane and honest hands; fought shoulder to shoulder with them against "the common enemy" (our own phrase); praised their courage, praised their gallantry, praised their mercifulness, praised their fine and honorable conduct; borrowed their trenches, borrowed strong positions which they had previously captured from the Spaniards; petted them, lied to them—officially proclaiming that our land and naval forces came to give them their freedom and displace the bad Spanish Government—fooled them, used them until we needed them no longer; then derided the sucked orange and threw it away. We kept the positions which we had beguiled them of; by and by, we moved a force forward and overlapped patriot ground—a clever thought, for we needed trouble, and this would produce it. A Filipino soldier, crossing the ground, where no one had a right to forbid him, was shot by our sentry. The badgered patriots resented this with arms, without waiting to know whether Aguinaldo, who was absent, would approve or not. Aguinaldo did not approve; but that availed nothing. What we wanted, in the interest of Progress and Civilization, was the Archipelago, unencumbered by patriots struggling for independence; and War was what we needed. We clinched our opportunity. It is Mr. Chamberlain's case over again—at least in its motive and intention; and we played the game as adroitly as he played it himself."

At this point in our frank statement of fact to the Person Sitting in Darkness, we should throw in a little trade taffy about the Blessings of Civilization—for a change, and for the refreshment of his spirit—then go on with our tale:

"We and the patriots having captured Manila, Spain's ownership of the Archipelago and her sovereignty over it were at an end—obliterated—annihilated—not a rag or shred of either remaining behind. It was then that we conceived the divinely humorous idea of *buying* both of these specters from Spain! [It is quite safe to confess this to the Person Sitting in Darkness, since neither he nor any other sane person will believe it.] In buying those ghosts for twenty millions, we also contracted to take care of the friars and their accumulations. I think we also agreed to propagate leprosy and smallpox, but as to this there is doubt. But it is not important; persons afflicted with the friars do not mind other diseases.

With our Treaty ratified, Manila subdued, and our Ghosts secured, we had no further use for Aguinaldo and the owners of the Archipelago. We forced a war, and we have been hunting America's guest and ally through the woods and swamps ever since.

At this point in the tale, it will be well to boast a little of our war work and our heroisms in the field, so as to make our performance look as fine as England's in South Africa; but I believe it will not be best to emphasize this too much. We must be cautious. Of course, we must read the war telegrams to the Person, in order to keep up our frankness; but we can throw an air of humorousness over them, and that will modify their grim eloquence a little, and their rather indiscreet exhibitions of gory exultation. Before reading to him the following display heads of the dispatches of November 18, 1900, it will be well to practice on them in private first, so as to get the right tang of lightness and gayety into them:

ADMINISTRATION WEARY OF
PROTRACTED HOSTILITIES!

REAL WAR AHEAD FOR FILIPINO
REBELS!*

WILL SHOW NO MERCY!
KITCHENER'S PLAN ADOPTED!

Kitchener knows how to handle disagreeable people who are fighting for their homes and their liberties, and we must let on that we are merely imitating Kitchener, and have no national interest in the matter, further than to get ourselves admired by the Great Family of Nations, in which august company our Master of the Game has bought a place for us in the back row.

Of course, we must not venture to ignore our General MacArthur's reports—oh, why do they keep on printing those embarrassing things?—we must drop them trippingly from the tongue and take the chances:

* "Rebels!" Mumble that funny word—don't let the Person catch it distinctly.

During the last ten months our losses have been 268 killed and 750 wounded; Filipino loss, *three thousand two hundred and twenty-seven killed*, and 694 wounded.

We must stand ready to grab the Person Sitting in Darkness, for he will swoon away at this confession, saying: "Good God! those 'niggers' spare their wounded, and the Americans massacre theirs!"

We must bring him to, and coax him and coddle him, and assure him that the ways of Providence are best, and that it would not become us to find fault with them; and then, to show him that we are only imitators, not originators, we must read the following passage from the letter of an American soldier lad in the Philippines to his mother, published in *Public Opinion*, of Decorah, Iowa, describing the finish of a victorious battle:

"WE NEVER LEFT ONE ALIVE. IF ONE WAS WOUNDED, WE WOULD RUN OUR BAYONETS THROUGH HIM."

Having now laid all the historical facts before the Person Sitting in Darkness, we should bring him to again, and explain them to him. We should say to him:

"They look doubtful, but in reality they are not. There have been lies; yes, but they were told in a good cause. We have been treacherous; but that was only in order that real good might come out of apparent evil. True, we have crushed a deceived and confiding people; we have turned against the weak and the friendless who trusted us; we have stamped out a just and intelligent and well-ordered republic; we have stabbed an ally in the back and slapped the face of a guest; we have bought a Shadow from an enemy that hadn't it to sell; we have robbed a trusting friend of his land and his liberty; we have invited our clean young men to shoulder a discredited musket and do bandits' work under a flag which bandits have been accustomed to fear, not to follow; we have debauched America's honor and blackened her face before the world; but each detail was for the best. We know this. The Head of every State and Sovereignty in Christendom and 90 per cent of every legislative body in Christendom, including our Congress and our fifty state legislatures, are members not only of the church, but also of the Blessings-of-Civilization Trust. This world-girdling accumulation of trained morals, high principles. and justice cannot do an unright thing, an unfair thing, an ungenerous thing, an unclean thing. It knows what it is about. Give yourself no uneasiness; it is all right."

Now then, that will convince the Person. You will see. It will restore the Business. Also, it will elect the Master of the Game to the vacant place in the Trinity of our national gods; and there on their high thrones the Three will sit, age after age, in the people's sight, each bearing the Emblem of his service: Washington, the Sword of the Liberator; Lincoln, the Slave's Broken Chains; the Master,* the Chains Repaired.

It will give the Business a splendid new start. You will see.

Everything is prosperous, now; everything is just as we should wish it. We have got the Archipelago, and we shall never give it up. Also, we have every reason to hope that we shall have an opportunity before very long to slip out of our congressional contract with Cuba and give her something better in the place of it. It is a rich country, and many of us are already beginning to see that the contract was a sentimental mistake. But now—right now—is the best time to do some profitable rehabilitating work—work that will set us up and make us comfortable, and discourage gossip. We cannot conceal from ourselves that, privately, we are a little troubled about our uniform. It is one of our prides; it is acquainted with honor; it is familiar with great deeds and noble; we love it, we revere it; and so this errand it is on makes us uneasy. And our flag—another pride of ours, our chiefest! We have worshiped it so; and when we have seen it in far lands—glimpsing it unexpectedly in that strange sky, waving its welcome and benediction to us—we have caught our breaths, and uncovered our heads, and couldn't speak, for a moment, for the thought of what it was to us and the great ideals it stood for. Indeed, we *must* do something about these things; it is easily managed. We can have a special one—our states do it: we can have just our usual flag, with the white stripes painted black and the stars replaced by the skull and crossbones.

And we do not need that Civil Commission out there. Having no powers, it has to invent them, and that kind of work cannot be effectively done by just anybody; an expert is required. Mr. Croker can be spared. We do not want the United States represented there, but only the Game.

* In turn Presidents William McKinley and Theodore Roosevelt. *Ed.*

By help of these suggested amendments, Progress and Civilization in that country can have a boom, and it will take in the Persons who are Sitting in Darkness and we can resume Business at the old stand.

THE CONQUEST OF THE PHILIPPINES:

The Moros*

There was nothing left for us to do but to take them all and civilize and Christianize them, and by God's grace do the very best by them as our fellow-men for whom Christ also died.

—PRESIDENT MCKINLEY
to a delegation of Methodists
in 1899

. . . This incident burst upon the world last Friday in an official cablegram from the commander of our forces in the Philippines to our government at Washington. The substance of it was as follows:

A tribe of Moros, dark-skinned savages, had fortified themselves in the bowl of an extinct crater not many miles from Jolo; and as they were hostiles, and bitter against us because we have been trying for eight years to take their liberties away from them, their presence in that position was a menace. Our commander, Gen. Leonard Wood, ordered a reconnoissance. It was found that the Moros numbered six hundred, counting women and children; that their crater bowl was in the summit of a peak or mountain twenty-two hundred feet above sea level, and very difficult of access for Christian troops and artillery. Then General Wood ordered a surprise, and went along himself to see the order carried out. Our troops climbed the heights by devious and difficult trails, and even took some artillery with them. The kind of artillery is not specified, but in one place it was hoisted up a sharp acclivity by tackle a distance of some three hundred feet. Arrived at the rim of the crater, the battle began. Our soldiers numbered five hundred

* *Autobiography*, A. B. Paine edition (Harper and Brothers: New York and London, 1924). Not included in the Charles Neider edition in 1959.

and forty. They were assisted by auxiliaries consisting of a detachment of native constabulary in our pay—their numbers not given—and by a naval detachment, whose numbers are not stated. But apparently the contending parties were about equal as to number—six hundred men on our side, on the edge of the bowl; six hundred men, women, and children in the bottom of the bowl. Depth of the bowl, 50 feet.

General Wood's order was, "Kill or capture the six hundred."

The battle began—it is officially called by that name—our forces firing down into the crater with their artillery and their deadly small arms of precision; the savages furiously returning the fire, probably with brickbats—though this is merely a surmise of mine, as the weapons used by the savages are not nominated in the cablegram. Heretofore the Moros have used knives and clubs mainly; also ineffectual trade-muskets when they had any.

The official report stated that the battle was fought with prodigious energy on both sides during a day and a half, and that it ended with a complete victory for the American arms. The completeness of the victory is established by this fact: that of the six hundred Moros not one was left alive. The brilliancy of the victory is established by this other fact, to wit: that of our six hundred heroes only fifteen lost their lives.

General Wood was present and looking on. His order had been, "Kill *or* capture those savages." Apparently our little army considered that the "or" left them authorized to kill *or* capture according to taste, and that their taste had remained what it has been for eight years, in our army out there—the taste of Christian butchers.

The official report quite properly extolled and magnified the "heroism" and "gallantry" of our troops, lamented the loss of the fifteen who perished, and elaborated the wounds of thirty-two of our men who suffered injury, and even minutely and faithfully described the nature of the wounds, in the interest of future historians of the United States. It mentioned that a private had one of his elbows scraped by a missile, and the private's name was mentioned. Another private had the end of his nose scraped by a missile. His name was also mentioned—by cable, at one dollar and fifty cents a word.

Next day's news confirmed the previous day's report and named our fifteen killed and thirty-two wounded *again*, and once more described the wounds and gilded them with the right adjectives.

Let us now consider two or three details of our military history. In one of the great battles of the Civil War 10 per cent of the forces engaged on the two sides were killed and wounded. At Waterloo, where four hundred thousand men were present on the two sides, fifty thousand fell, killed and wounded, in five hours, leaving three hundred and fifty thousand sound and all right for further adventures. Eight years ago, when the pathetic comedy called the Cuban War was played, we summoned two hundred and fifty thousand men. We fought a number of showy battles, and when the war was over we had lost two hundred and sixty-eight men out of our two hundred and fifty thousand, in killed and wounded in the field, and just *fourteen times as many* by the gallantry of the army doctors in the hospitals and camps. We did not exterminate the Spaniards—far from it. In each engagement we left an average of *2 per cent* of the enemy killed or crippled on the field.

Contrast these things with the great statistics which have arrived from that Moro crater! There, with six hundred engaged on each side, we lost fifteen men killed outright, and we had thirty-two wounded— counting that nose and that elbow. The enemy numbered six hundred—including women and children—and we abolished them utterly, leaving not even a baby alive to cry for its dead mother. *This is incomparably the greatest victory that was ever achieved by the Christian soldiers of the United States.*

Now then, how has it been received? The splendid news appeared with splendid display heads in every newspaper in this city of four million and thirteen thousand inhabitants, on Friday morning. But there was not a single reference to it in the editorial columns of any one of those newspapers. The news appeared again in all the evening papers of Friday, and again those papers were editorially silent upon our vast achievement. Next day's additional statistics and particulars appeared in all the morning papers, and still without a line of editorial rejoicing or a mention of the matter in any way. These additions appeared in the evening papers of that same day (Saturday) and again without a word of comment. In the columns devoted to correspondence, in the morning and evening papers of Friday and Saturday, nobody said a word about the "battle." Ordinarily those columns are teeming with the passions of the citizen; he lets no incident go by, whether it be large or small, without pouring out his praise or blame, his joy or his indignation, about the matter in the correspondence column. But, as I have said, during those two days he was as silent as the editors themselves. So far as I can find out, there was only one person among our eighty millions who allowed himself the privilege of a public remark on this great occasion—that was the President of the United States. All day Friday he was as studiously silent as the rest. But on Saturday he recognized that his duty required him to say something, and he took his pen and performed that duty. If I know President Roosevelt—and I am sure I do—this utterance cost him more pain and shame than any other that ever issued from his pen or his mouth. I am far from blaming him. If I had been in his place my official duty would have compelled me to say what he said. It was a convention, an old tradition, and he had to be loyal to it. There was no help for it. This is what he said:

WASHINGTON, *March 10, 1906.*

WOOD, MANILA:

I congratulate you and the officers and men of your command upon the brilliant feat of arms wherein you and they so well upheld the honor of the American flag.

(Signed) THEODORE ROOSEVELT.

His whole utterance is merely a convention. Not a word of what he said came out of his heart. He knew perfectly well that to pen six hundred helpless and weaponless savages in a hole like rats in a trap and massacre them in detail during a stretch of day and a half, from a safe position on the heights above, was no brilliant feat of arms—and would not have been a brilliant feat of arms even if Christian America, represented by its salaried soldiers, had shot them down with bibles and the Golden Rule instead of bullets. He knew perfectly well that our uniformed assassins had *not* upheld the honor of the American flag, but had done as they have been doing continuously for eight years in the Philippines—that is to say, they had dishonored it.

The next day, Sunday—which was yesterday—the cable brought us additional news—still more splendid news—still more honor for the flag. The first display head shouts this information at us in stentorian capitals: "WOMEN SLAIN IN MORO SLAUGHTER."

"Slaughter" is a good word. Certainly there is not a better one in the Unabridged Dictionary for this occasion.

The next display line says:

"With Children They Mixed in Mob in Crater, and All Died To-gether."

They were mere naked savages, and yet there is a sort of pathos about it when that word *children* falls under your eye, for it always brings before us our perfectest symbol of innocence and helplessness; and by help of its deathless eloquence color, creed, and nationality vanish away and we see only that they are children—merely children. And if they are frightened and crying and in trouble, our pity goes out to them by natural impulse. We see a picture. We see the small forms. We see the terrified faces. We see the tears. We see the small hands clinging in supplication to the mother; but we do not see those children that we are speaking about. We see in their places the little creatures whom we know and love.

The next heading blazes with American and Christian glory like to the sun in the zenith:

"Death List is Now 900."

I was never so enthusiastically proud of the flag till now!

The next heading explains how safely our daring soldiers were located. It says:

"Impossible to Tell Sexes Apart in Fierce Battle on Top of Mount Dajo."

The naked savages were so far away, down in the bottom of that trap, that our soldiers could not tell the breasts of a woman from the rudimentary paps of a man—so far away that they couldn't tell a toddling little child from a black six-footer. *This was by all odds the least dangerous battle that Christian soldiers of any nationality were ever engaged in.*

The next heading says:

"Fighting for Four Days."

So our men were at it four days instead of a day and a half. It was a long and happy picnic with nothing to do but sit in comfort and fire the Golden Rule into those people down there and imagine letters to write home to the admiring families, and pile glory upon glory. Those savages fighting for their liberties had the four days, too, but it must have been a sorrowful time for them. Every day they saw two hundred and twenty-five of their number slain, and this provided them grief and mourning for the night—and doubtless without even the relief and consolation of knowing that in the meantime they had slain four of their enemies and wounded some more on the elbow and the nose.

The closing heading says:

"Lieutenant Johnson Blown from Parapet by Exploding Artillery Gallantly Leading Charge."

Lieutenant Johnson had pervaded the cablegrams from the first. He and his wound have sparkled around through them like the serpentine thread of fire that goes excursioning through the black crisp fabric of a fragment of burnt paper. It reminds one of Gillette's comedy farce of a few years ago, "Too Much Johnson." Apparently Johnson was the only wounded man on our side whose wound was worth anything as an advertisement. It has made a great deal more noise in the world than has any similar event since "Humpty Dumpty" fell off the wall and got injured. The official dispatches do not know which to admire most, Johnson's adorable wound or the nine hundred murders. The ecstasies flowing from army headquarters on the other side of the globe to the White House, at one dollar and a half a word, have set fire to similar ecstasies in the President's breast. It appears that the immortally wounded was a Rough Rider under Lieutenant-Colonel Theodore Roosevelt at San Juan Hill—that twin of Waterloo—when the colonel of the regiment, the present Major-General Dr. Leonard Wood, went to the rear to bring up the pills and missed the fight. The President has a warm place in his heart for anybody who was present at that bloody collision of military solar systems, and so he lost no time in cabling to the wounded hero, "How are you?" And got a cable answer, "Fine, thanks." This is historical. This will go down to posterity.

Johnson was wounded in the shoulder with a slug. The slug was in a shell—for the account says the damage was caused by an exploding shell which blew Johnson off the rim. The people down in the hole had no artillery; therefore it was our artillery that blew Johnson off the rim. And so it is now a matter of historical record that the only officer of ours who acquired a wound of advertising dimensions got it at our hands, and not the enemies'. It seems more than probable that if we had placed our soldiers out of the way of our own weapons, we should have come out of the most extraordinary battle in all history without a scratch. . . .

The ominous paralysis continues. There has been a slight sprinkle— an exceedingly slight sprinkle—in the correspondence columns, of angry rebukes of the President for calling this cowardly massacre a "brilliant feat of arms" and for praising our butchers for "holding up the honor of the flag" in that singular way; but there is hardly a ghost of a whisper about the feat of arms in the editorial columns of the papers.

I hope that this silence will continue. It is about as eloquent and as damaging and effective as the most indignant words could be, I think. When a man is sleeping in a noise, his sleep goes placidly on; but if the noise stops, the stillness wakes him. This silence has continued five days now. Surely it must be waking the drowsy nation. Surely the nation must be wondering what it means. A five-day silence following a world-astonishing event has not happened on this planet since the daily newspaper was invented.

At a luncheon party of men convened yesterday to God-speed George Harvey, who is leaving to-day for a vacation in Europe, all the talk was about the brilliant feat of arms; and no one had anything to say about it that either the President or Major-General Dr. Wood or the damaged Johnson would regard as complimentary, or as proper comment to put into our histories. Harvey said he believed that the shock and shame of this episode would eat down deeper and deeper into the hearts of the nation and fester there and produce results. He believed it would destroy the Republican party and President Roosevelt. I cannot believe that the prediction will come true, for the reason that prophecies which promise valuable things, desirable things, good things, worthy things, never come true. Prophecies of this kind are like wars fought in a good cause—they are so rare that they don't count.

Day before yesterday the cable note from the happy General Doctor Wood was still all glorious. There was still proud mention and elaboration of what was called the "desperate hand-to-hand fight," Doctor Wood not seeming to suspect that he was giving himself away, as the phrase goes—since if there was any very desperate hand-to-hand fighters, if really desperate, would surely be able to kill more than fifteen of our men before their last man and woman and child perished.

Very well, there was a new note in the dispatches yesterday afternoon—just a faint suggestion that Doctor Wood was getting ready to lower his tone and begin to apologize and explain. He announces that he assumes full responsibility for the fight. It indicates that he is aware that there is a lurking disposition here amid all this silence to blame somebody. He says there was "no wanton destruction of women and children in the fight, though many of them were killed by force of necessity because the Moros used them as shields in the hand-to-hand fighting."

This explanation is better than none; indeed, it is considerably better than none. Yet if there was so much hand-to-hand fighting there must have arrived a time, toward the end of the four days' butchery, when only one native was left alive. We had six hundred men present; we had lost only fifteen; why did the six hundred kill that remaining man—or woman, or child?

Doctor Wood will find that explaining things is not in his line. He will find that where a man has the proper spirit in him and the proper force at his command, it is easier to massacre nine hundred unarmed animals than it is to explain why he made it so remorselessly complete. Next he furnishes us this sudden burst of unconscious humor, which shows that he ought to edit his reports before he cables them:

"Many of the Moros feigned death and butchered the American hospital men who were relieving the wounded."

We have the curious spectacle of hospital men going around trying to relieve the wounded savages—for what reason? The savages were all massacred. The plain intention was to massacre them all and leave none alive. Then where was the use in furnishing mere temporary relief to a person who was presently to be exterminated? The dispatches call this battle a "battle." In what way was it a battle? It has no resemblance to a battle. In a battle there are always as many as five wounded men to one killed outright. When this so-called battle was over, there were certainly not fewer than two hundred wounded savages lying on the field. What became of them? Since not one savage was left alive!

The inference seems plain. We cleaned up our four days' work and made it complete by butchering those helpless people.

The President's joy over this achievement brings to mind an earlier presidential ecstasy. When the news came, in 1901, that Colonel Funston had penetrated to the refuge of the patriot, Aguinaldo, in the mountains, and had captured him by the use of these arts, to wit: by forgery, by lies, by disguising his military marauders in the uniform of the enemy, by pretending to be friends of Aguinaldo's and by disarming suspicion by cordially shaking hands with Aguinaldo's officers and in that moment shooting them down—when the cablegram announcing this "brilliant feat of arms" reached the White House, the newspapers said that that meekest and mildest and gentlest of men, President Mc-Kinley, could not control his joy and gratitude, but was obliged to express it in motions resembling a dance.

THE CONQUEST OF THE PHILIPPINES:

The Destruction of the Filipino Patriot and President, Aguinaldo, by US General Funston*

. . . I have been absent several weeks in the West Indies; I will now resume this Defence.

It seems to me that General Funston's appreciation of the capture needs editing. It seems to me that, in his after-dinner speeches, he spreads out the heroisms of it—I say it with deference, and subject to correction—with an almost too generous hand. He is a brave man; his dearest enemy will cordially grant him that credit. For his sake it is a pity that somewhat of that quality was not needed in the episode under consideration; that he would have furnished it, no one doubts. But, by his own showing, he ran but one danger—that of starving. He and his party were well disguised, in dishonored uniforms, American and Insurgent; they greatly outnumbered Aguinaldo's guard;† by his forgeries and falsehoods he had lulled suspicion to sleep; his coming was expected, his way was prepared; his course was through a solitude, unfriendly interruption was unlikely; his party were well armed; they would catch their prey with welcoming smiles in their faces, and with hospitable hands extended for the friendly shake—nothing would be

---

* "A Defense of General Funston" (*North American Review*, 1902), reprinted in Janet Smith, *Mark Twain on the Damned Human Race* (Hill and Wang: New York, 1962). Frederick Funston, Brigadier General of Volunteers in the American army, returned from the Philippines in 1901 with a "heroic" account of how, by deception, treachery, and guile—and through Aguinaldo's gift of food to the starving Americans —they succeeded in penetrating the Filipino's camp and massacred his bodyguard. Twain was afraid that Funston's treachery and boastfulness would set an example for future military commanders in places, let us say, like Vietnam. *Ed.*

† Eighty-nine to forty-eight.—*Funston's Lotus Club Confession.* (M.T.)

necessary but to shoot these people down. That is what they did. It was hospitality repaid in a brand-new, up-to-date, modern civilization fashion, and would be admired by many.

The spokesman so completely hoodwinked Aguinaldo that he did not suspect the ruse. In the meantime, the Macabebes maneuvered around into advantageous positions, directed by the Spaniard, until all were in readiness; then he shouted, "Macabebes, now is your turn!" whereupon they emptied their rifles into Aguinaldo's body-guard.

The utter completeness of the surprise, the total absence of suspicion which had been secured by the forgeries and falsehoods, is best brought out in Funston's humorous account of the episode in one of his rollicking speeches . . . :

The Macabebes fired on those men and two fell dead; the others retreated, firing as they ran, and I might say here that they retreated with such great alacrity and enthusiasm that they dropped eighteen rifles and a thousand rounds of ammunition.

Sigismondo rushed back into the house, pulled his revolver, and told the insurgent officers to surrender. They all threw up their hands except Villia, Aguinaldo's chief of staff; he had on one of those new-fangled Mauser revolvers and he wanted to try it. But before he had the Mauser out of its scabbard he was shot twice; Sigismondo was a pretty fair marksman himself.

Alambra was shot in the face. He jumped out of the window; the house, by the way, stood on the bank of the river. He went out of the window and went clear down into the river, the water being twenty-five feet below the bank. He escaped, swam across the river and got away, and surrendered five months afterwards.

Villia, shot in the shoulder, followed him out of the window and into the river, but the Macabebes saw him and ran down to the river bank, and they waded in and fished him out, and kicked him all the way up the bank, and asked him how he liked it. (Laughter.)

While it is true that the daredevils were not in danger upon this occasion, they *were* in awful peril at one time; in peril of a death so awful that swift extinction by bullet, by the axe, by the sword, by the rope, by drowning, by fire, is a kindly mercy contrasted with it; a death so awful that it holds its place unchallenged as the supremest of human agonies—death by starvation. Aguinaldo saved them from that.

These being the facts, we come now to the question, Is Funston to blame? I think not. And for that reason I think too much is being made of this matter. He did not make his own disposition, It was born with him. It chose his ideals for him, he did not choose them. It chose the kind of society It liked, the kind of comrades It preferred, . . . It admired everything that Washington did not admire, and hospitably received and coddled everything that Washington would have turned out of doors—but It, and It only, was to blame, not Funston . . . It had a native predilection for unsavory conduct, but it would be in the last degree unfair to hold Funston to blame for the outcome of his infirmity; as clearly unfair as it would be to blame him because his conscience leaked out through one of his pores when he was little—a thing which he could not help, and he couldn't have raised it, anyway; It was able to say to an enemy, "Have pity on me, I am starving; I am too weak to move, give me food; I am your friend, I am your fellow patriot, your fellow Filipino, and am fighting for our dear country's liberties, like you—have pity, give me food, save my life, there is no other help!" and It was able to refresh and restore Its marionette with the food, and then shoot down the giver of it while his hand was stretched out in welcome . . . It has the noble gift of humor, and can make a banquet almost die with laughter when It has a funny incident to tell about; this one will bear reading again—and over and over again, in fact . . .

But it is only It that is speaking, not Funston. With youthful glee It can see sink down in death the simple creatures who had answered Its fainting prayer for food, and without remorse It can note the reproachful look in their dimming eyes; but in fairness we must remember that this is only It, not Funston; . . . And It—not Funston —comes home now, to teach us children what patriotism is! Surely It ought to know.

It is plain to me, and I think it ought to be plain to all, that Funston is not in any way to blame for the things he has done, does, thinks, and says.

Now, then, we have Funston; he has happened, and is on our hands.

The question is, What are we going to do about it? How are we going
to meet the emergency? We have seen what happened in Washington's
case: he became a colossal example, an example to the whole world,
and for all time—because his name and deeds went everywhere, and
inspired, as they still inspire, and will always inspire, admiration, and
compel emulation. Then the thing for the world to do in the present
case is to turn the gilt front of Funston's evil notoriety to the rear, and
expose the back aspect of it, the right and black aspect of it, to the
youth of the land; otherwise *he* will become an example and a boy-
admiration, and will most sorrowfully and grotesquely bring his breed
of patriotism into competition with Washington's. This competition
has already begun, in fact. Some may not believe it, but it is nevertheless true, that there are now public-school teachers and superintendents
who are holding up Funston as a model hero and patriot in the schools.

If this Funstonian boom continues, Funstonism will presently affect
the army. In fact, this has already happened. There are weak-headed
and weak-principled officers in all armies, and these are always ready
to imitate successful notoriety-breeding methods, let them be good or
bad. . . . Funston's example has bred many imitators, and many
ghastly additions to our history: the torturing of Filipinos by the awful
"water cure," for instance, to make them confess—what? Truth? Or
lies? How can one know which it is they are telling? For under unendurable pain a man confesses anything that is required of him, true
or false, and his evidence is worthless. Yet upon such evidence American officers have actually—but you know about those atrocities which
the War Office has been hiding a year or two; and about General
Smith's now world-celebrated order of *massacre*—thus summarized by
the press from Major Waller's testimony:

> *Kill and burn—this is no time to take prisoners—the more you kill*
> *and burn, the better—Kill all above the age of ten—make Samar a*
> *howling wilderness!*

You see what Funston's example has produced, just in this little
while—even before he produced the example. It has advanced our
civilization ever so far—fully as far as Europe advanced it in China.
Also, no doubt, it was Funston's example that made us (and England)
copy Weyler's *reconcentrado* horror after the pair of us, with our
Sunday-school smirk on, and our goody-goody noses upturned toward

heaven, had been calling him a "fiend." And the fearful earthquake out there in Krakatoa, that destroyed the island and killed two million people— No, that could not have been Funston's example; I remember now, he was not born then.

However, for all these things I blame only his It, not him. In conclusion, I have defended him as well as I could, and indeed I have found it quite easy, and have removed prejudice from him and rehabilitated him in the public esteem and regard, I think. I was not able to do anything for his It, It being out of my jurisdiction, and out of Funston's and everybody's. As I have shown, Funston is not to blame for his fearful deed; and, if I tried, I might also show that he is not to blame for our still holding in bondage the man he captured by unlawful means, and who is not any more rightfully our prisoner and spoil than he would be if he were stolen money. He is entitled to his freedom. If he were a king of a great power, or an ex-president of our republic, instead of an ex-president of a destroyed and abolished little republic, Civilization (with a large C) would criticize and complain until he got it.

SUMMARY OF THE PHILIPPINE "INCIDENT"*

We may now take an account of stock and find out how much we have made by the speculation—or lost. The Government went into the speculation on certain definite grounds which it believed from the viewpoint of statesmanship, to be good & sufficient. To wit: 1, for the sake of the money supposed to be in it; 2, in order to become a World Power and get a back seat in the Family of Nations.

We have scored on number 2. We have secured a back seat in the Family of Nations. We have scored it & [are] trying to enjoy the tacks that are in it. We are a World Power, no one can deny it, a brass-gilt one, a tuppence, ha'penny one, but a World Power just the same.† We

* Philip S. Foner, *Mark Twain: Social Critic* (International Publishers: New York, 1958).

† Twain was wrong here in asserting that America was only a halfpenny World Power with a back seat in the Family of Nations, but elsewhere he rectified this error. *Ed.*

have bought some islands from a party that did not own them; with real smartness & a good counterfeit of disinterested friendliness, we coaxed a weak nation into a trap, & closed it upon them; we went back on our honored guest of the stars & stripes when we had no further use for him, & chased him into the mountains; we are as indisputably in possession of a wide-spreading archipelago as if it were our property; we have pacified some thousands of the islanders & buried them; destroyed their fields; burned their villages & turned their widows & orphans out of doors; furnished heart-breaking exile to dozens of disagreeable patriots & subjugated the remaining millions by Benevolent Assimilation which is the pious new name of the musket; we have acquired property in the three hundred concubines & other slaves of our business-partner, the Sultan of Sulu, & hoisted our protecting swag over that flag.

And so, by these providences of God—the phrase is the Government's, not mine—we are a World Power; & are glad & proud, & have a Back Seat in the Family. With tacks in it. At least we are letting on to be glad & proud; & it is the best way. Indeed, it is the only way. We must maintain our dignity for people are looking. . . .

THE UNITED STATES OF LYNCHERDOM*

And so Missouri has fallen, that great state! Certain of her children have joined the lynchers, and the smirch is upon the rest of us. That handful of her children have given us a character and labeled us with a name, and to the dwellers in the four quarters of the earth we are "lynchers," now, and ever shall be. For the world will not stop and think—it never does, it is not its way; its way is to generalize from a single sample. It will not say, "Those Missourians have been busy eighty years in building an honorable good name for themselves; these hundred lynchers down in the corner of the state are not real Mis-

---

* *Europe and Elsewhere.* (Written in 1901.) According to Philip Foner's *Mark Twain: Social Critic*, Twain wrote this famous essay as the introduction for a proposed book on the history of lynching in the United States; for the writing of which, he declared, he needed only a scissors and the daily newspapers. *Ed.*

sourians, they are renegades." No, that truth will not enter its mind; it
will generalize from the one or two misleading samples and say, "The
Missourians are lynchers." It has no reflection, no logic, no sense of
proportion. With it, figures go for nothing; to it, figures reveal nothing,
it cannot reason upon them rationally; it would say, for instance, that
China is being swiftly and surely Christianized, since nine Chinese
Christians are being made every day; and it would fail, with him, to
notice that the fact that 33,000 pagans are *born* there every day,
damages the argument. It would say, "There are a hundred lynchers
there, therefore the Missourians are lynchers"; the considerable fact
that there are two and a half million Missourians who are *not* lynchers
would not affect their verdict.

   Oh, Missouri!
   The tragedy occurred near Pierce City, down in the southwestern
corner of the state. On a Sunday afternoon a young white woman who
had started alone from church was found murdered. For there are
churches there; in my time religion was more general, more pervasive,
in the South than it was in the North, and more virile and earnest, too,
I think; I have some reason to believe that this is still the case. The
young woman was found murdered. Although it was a region of
churches and schools the people rose, lynched three negroes—two of
them very aged ones—burned out five negro households, and drove
thirty negro families into the woods.
   I do not dwell upon the provocation which moved the people to these
crimes, for that has nothing to do with the matter; the only question is,
does the assassin *take the law into his own hands?* It is very simple,
and very just. If the assassin be proved to have usurped the law's
prerogative in righting his wrongs, that ends the matter; a thousand
provocations are no defense. The Pierce City people had bitter provocation—indeed, as revealed by certain of the particulars, the bitterest
of all provocations—but no matter, they took the law into their own
hands, when by the terms of their statutes their victim would certainly
hang if the law had been allowed to take its course, for there are but
few negroes in that region and they are without authority and without
influence in overawing juries.

Why has lynching, with various barbaric accompaniments, become a favorite regulator in cases of "the usual crime" in several parts of the country? Is it because men think a lurid and terrible punishment a more forcible object lesson and a more effective deterrent than a sober and colorless hanging done privately in a jail would be? Surely sane men do not think that. Even the average child should know better. It should know that any strange and much-talked-of event is always followed by imitations, the world being so well supplied with excitable people who only need a little stirring up to make them lose what is left of their heads and do mad things which they would not have thought of ordinarily. It should know that if a man jump off Brooklyn Bridge another will imitate him; that if a person venture down Niagara Whirlpool in a barrel another will imitate him; that if a Jack the Ripper make notoriety by slaughtering women in dark alleys he will be imitated; that if a man attempt a king's life and the newspapers carry the noise of it around the globe, regicides will crop up all around. The child should know that one much-talked-of outrage and murder committed by a negro will upset the disturbed intellects of several other negroes and produce a series of the very tragedies the community would so strenuously wish to prevent; that each of these crimes will produce another series, and year by year steadily increase the tale of these disasters instead of diminishing it; that, in a word, the lynchers are themselves the worst enemies of their women. The child should also know that by a law of our make, communities, as well as individuals, are imitators; and that a much-talked-of lynching will infallibly produce other lynchings here and there and yonder, and that in time these will breed a mania, a fashion; a fashion which will spread wide and wider, year by year, covering state after state, as with an advancing disease. Lynching has reached Colorado, it has reached California, it has reached Indiana—and now Missouri! I may live to see a negro burned in Union Square, New York, with fifty thousand people present, and not a sheriff visible, not a governor, not a constable, not a colonel, not a clergyman, not a law-and-order representative of any sort.

Increase in Lynching.—In 1900 there were eight more cases than in 1899, and probably this year will be more than there were last year. The year is little more than half gone, and yet there are eighty-eight cases as compared with one hundred and fifteen for all of last year. The four Southern states, Alabama, Georgia, Louisiana, and Mississippi are the worst offenders. Last year there were eight cases in Alabama, sixteen in Georgia, twenty in Louisiana, and twenty in Mississippi—over one-half the total. This year to date there have been nine in Alabama, twelve in Georgia, eleven in Louisiana, and thirteen in Mississippi—again more than one-half the total number in the whole United States.—Chicago *Tribune*.

It must be that the increase comes of the inborn human instinct to imitate—that and man's commonest weakness, his aversion to being unpleasantly conspicuous, pointed at, shunned, as being on the unpopular side. Its other name is Moral Cowardice, and is the commanding feature of the make-up of 9,999 men in the 10,000. I am not offering this as a discovery; privately the dullest of us knows it to be true. History will not allow us to forget or ignore this supreme trait of our character. It persistently and sardonically reminds us that from the beginning of the world no revolt against a public infamy or oppression has ever been begun but by the one daring man in the 10,000, the rest timidly waiting, and slowly and reluctantly joining, under the influence of that man and his fellows from the other ten thousands. The abolitionists remember. Privately the public feeling was with them early, but each man was afraid to speak out until he got some hint that his neighbor was privately feeling as he privately felt himself. Then the boom followed. It always does. It will occur in New York, some day; and even in Pennsylvania.

It has been supposed—and said—that the people at a lynching enjoy the spectacle and are glad of a chance to see it. It cannot be true; all experience is against it. The people in the South are made like the people in the North—the vast majority of whom are right-hearted and compassionate, and would be cruelly pained by such a spectacle—and *would attend it,* and let on to be pleased with it, if the public approval seemed to require it. We are made like that, and we cannot help it. The other animals are not so, but we cannot help that, either. They lack the Moral Sense; we have no way of trading ours off, for a nickel or some other thing above its value. The Moral Sense teaches us what is right, and how to avoid it—when unpopular.

It is thought, as I have said, that a lynching crowd enjoys a lynching. It certainly is not true; it is impossible of belief. It is freely
asserted—you have seen it in print many times of late—that the lynching impulse has been misinterpreted; that it is *not* the outcome of a
spirit of revenge, but of a "mere atrocious hunger *to look upon human
suffering.*" If that were so, the crowds that saw the Windsor Hotel burn
down would have enjoyed the horrors that fell under their eyes. Did
they? No one will think that of them, no one will make that charge.
Many risked their lives to save the men and women who were in peril.
Why did they do that? Because *none would disapprove.* There was no
restraint; they could follow their natural impulse. Why does a crowd of
the same kind of people in Texas, Colorado, Indiana, stand by, smitten
to the heart and miserable, and by ostentatious outward signs pretend
to enjoy a lynching? Why does it lift no hand or voice in protest? Only
because it would be unpopular to do it, I think; each man is afraid of
his neighbor's disapproval—a thing which, to the general run of the
race, is more dreaded than wounds and death. When there is to be a
lynching the people hitch up and comes miles to see it, bringing their
wives and children. Really to see it? No—they come only because they
are afraid to stay at home, lest it be noticed and offensively commented
upon. We may believe this, for we all know how *we* feel about such
spectacles—also, how we would act under the like pressure. We are not
any better nor any braver than anybody else, and we must not try to
creep out of it.

A Savonarola can quell and scatter a mob of lynchers with a mere
glance of his eye: so can a Merrill* or a Beloat.† For no mob has any
sand in the presence of a man known to be splendidly brave. Besides, a
lynching mob would *like* to be scattered, for of a certainty there are
never ten men in it who would not prefer to be somewhere else—and
would be, if they but had the courage to go. When I was a boy I saw a
brave gentleman deride and insult a mob and drive it away; and
afterward, in Nevada, I saw a noted desperado make two hundred men
sit still, with the house burning under them, until he gave them permis-

---

* Sheriff of Carroll County, Georgia. (M.T.)

† Sheriff, Princeton, Indiana. By that formidable power which lies in an established
reputation for cold pluck they faced lynching mobs and securely held the field against
them. (M.T.)

sion to retire. A plucky man can rob a whole passenger train by himself; and the half of a brave man can hold up a stagecoach and strip its occupants.

Then perhaps the remedy for lynchings comes to this: station a brave man in each affected community to encourage, support, and bring to light the deep disapproval of lynching hidden in the secret places of its heart—for it is there, beyond question. Then those communities will find something better to imitate—of course, being human, they must imitate something. Where shall these brave men be found? That is indeed a difficulty; there are not three hundred of them in the earth. If merely *physically* brave men would do, then it were easy; they could be furnished by the cargo. When Hobson called for seven volunteers to go with him to what promised to be certain death, four thousand men responded—the whole fleet, in fact. Because *all the world would approve.* They knew that; but if Hobson's project had been charged with the scoffs and jeers of the friends and associates, whose good opinion and approval the sailors valued, he could not have got his seven.

No, upon reflection, the scheme will not work. There are not enough morally brave men in stock. We are out of moral-courage material; we are in a condition of profound poverty. We have those two sheriffs down South who—but never mind, it is not enough to go around; they have to stay and take care of their own communities.

But if we only *could* have three or four more sheriffs of that great breed! Would it help? I think so. For we are all imitators: other brave sheriffs would follow; to be a dauntless sheriff would come to be recognized as the correct and only thing, and the dreaded disapproval would fall to the share of the other kind; courage in this office would become custom, the absence of it a dishonor, just as courage presently replaces the timidity of the new soldier; then the mobs and the lynchings would disappear, and—

However. It can never be done without some starters, and where are we to get the starters? Advertise? Very well, then, let us advertise.

In the meantime, there is another plan. Let us import American missionaries from China, and send them into the lynching field. With 1,511 of them out there converting two Chinamen apiece per annum

against an uphill birth rate of 33,000 pagans per day,* it will take
upward of a million years to make the conversions balance the output
and bring the Christianizing of the country in sight to the naked eye;
therefore, if we can offer our missionaries as rich a field at home at
lighter expense and quite satisfactory in the matter of danger, why
shouldn't they find it fair and right to come back and give us a trial?
The Chinese are universally conceded to be excellent people, honest,
honorable, industrious, trustworthy, kind-hearted, and all that—leave
them alone, they are plenty good enough just as they are; and besides,
almost every convert runs a risk of catching our civilization. We ought
to be careful. We ought to think twice before we encourage a risk like
that; for, *once civilized, China can never be uncivilized again.* We have
not been thinking of that. Very well, we ought to think of it now. Our
missionaries will find that we have a field for them—and not only for
the 1,511, but for 15,011. Let them look at the following telegram and
see if they have anything in China that is more appetizing. It is from
Texas:

> The negro was taken to a tree and swung in the air. Wood and
> fodder were piled beneath his body and a hot fire was made. *Then it
> was suggested that the man ought not to die too quickly, and he was
> let down to the ground while a party went to Dexter, about two miles
> distant, to procure coal oil.* This was thrown on the flames and the
> work completed.

We implore them to come back and help us in our need. Patriotism
imposes this duty on them. Our country is worse off than China; they
are our countrymen, their motherland supplicates their aid in this her
hour of deep distress. They are competent; our people are not. They
are used to scoffs, sneers, revilings, danger; our people are not. They
have the martyr spirit; nothing but the martyr spirit can brave a lynching mob, and cow it and scatter it. They can save their country, we
beseech them to come home and do it. We ask them to read that

---

* These figures are not fanciful; all of them are genuine and authentic. They are
from official missionary records in China. See Doctor Morrison's book on his pedestrian
journey across China; he quotes them and gives his authorities. For several years he
has been the London *Times's* representative in Peking, and was there through the
siege. (M.T.)

telegram again, and yet again, and picture the scene in their minds, and soberly ponder it; then multipy it by 115, add 88; place the 203 in a row, allowing 600 feet of space for each human torch, so that there may be viewing room around it for 5,000 Christian American men, women, and children, youths and maidens; make it night, for grim effect; have the show in a gradually rising plain, and let the course of the stakes be uphill; the eye can then take in the whole line of twenty-four miles of blood-and-flesh bonfires unbroken, whereas if it occupied level ground the ends of the line would bend down and be hidden from view by the curvature of the earth. All being ready, now, and the darkness opaque, the stillness impressive—for there should be no sound but the soft moaning of the night wind and the muffled sobbing of the sacrifices—let all the far stretch of kerosened pyres be touched off simultaneously and the glare and the shrieks and the agonies burst heavenward to the Throne.

There are more than a million persons present; the light from the fires flushes into vague outline against the night the spires of five thousand churches. O kind missionary, O compassionate missionary, leave China! come home and convert these Christians!

"A THANKSGIVING SENTIMENT" ON THE CONGO*

We have much to be thankful for. Our free Republic being the official godfather of the Congo Graveyard; first of the Powers to recognize its pirate flag & become responsible through silence for the prodigious depredations & multitudinous murders committed under it upon the helpless natives by King Leopold of Belgium in the past twenty years: now therefore let us be humbly thankful that this last twelvemonth has seen the King's usual annual myriad of murders reduced by nearly one & one half per cent; let us be humbly grateful that the good King, our pet & protégé, due in hell these sixty-five years, is still spared to us to continue his work & ours among the friendless & the forsaken; & finally let us live in the blessed hope that when in the Last

* Unpublished, Thanksgiving Day, 1904. From *Mark Twain: Social Critic*, by Philip S. Foner.

Great Day he is confronted with his unoffending millions upon millions of robbed, mutilated and massacred men, women & children, & required to explain, he will be as politely silent about us as we have been about him.

KING LEOPOLD'S SOLILOQUY
ON THE BELGIAN CONGO*

[*Throws down pamphlets which he has been reading. Excitedly combs his flowing spread of whiskers with his fingers; pounds the table with his fists; lets off brisk volleys of unsanctified language at brief intervals, repentantly drooping his head, between volleys, and kissing the Louis XI crucifix hanging from his neck, accompanying the kisses with mumbled apologies; presently rises, flushed and perspiring, and walks the floor, gesticulating*]

—— !! —— !! If I had them by the throat!! [*Hastily kisses the crucifix, and mumbles*] In these twenty years I have spent millions to keep the press of the two hemispheres quiet, and still these leaks keep on occurring. I have spent other millions on religion and art, and what do I get for it? Nothing. Not a compliment. These generosities are studiedly ignored, in print. In print I get nothing but slanders—and slanders again—and still slanders, and slanders on top of slanders! Grant them true, what of it? They are slanders all the same, when uttered against a king.

Miscreants—they are telling *everything!* Oh, everything: how I went pilgriming among the Powers in tears, with my mouth full of Bible and my pelt oozing piety at every pore, and implored them to place the vast and rich and populous Congo Free State in trust in my hands as their agent, so that I might root out slavery and stop the slave raids, and lift up those twenty-five millions of gentle and harmless blacks out of dark-

* Pamphlet, 1905, published by American Anti-Imperialist League, with many subsequent printings.

ness into light, the light of our blessed Redeemer, the light that streams from his holy Word, the light that makes glorious our noble civilization—lift them up and dry their tears and fill their bruised hearts with joy and gratitude—lift them up and make them comprehend that they were no longer outcasts and forsaken, but our very brothers in Christ; how America and thirteen great European states wept in sympathy with me, and were persuaded; how their representatives met in convention in Berlin and made me Head Foreman and Superintendent of the Congo State, and drafted out my powers and limitations, carefully guarding the persons and liberties and properties of the natives against hurt and harm; forbidding whiskey traffic and gun traffic; providing courts of justice; making commerce free and fetterless to the merchants and traders of all nations, and welcoming and safeguarding all missionaries of all creeds and denominations. They have told how I planned and prepared my establishment and selected my horde of officials—"pals" and "pimps" of mine, "unspeakable Belgians" every one—and hoisted my flag, and "took in" a President of the United States, and got him to be the first to recognize it and salute it. Oh, well, let them blackguard me if they like; it is a deep satisfaction to me to remember that I was a shade too smart for that nation that thinks itself so smart. Yes, I certainly did bunco a Yankee—as those people phrase it. Pirate flag? Let them call it so—perhaps it is. All the same, *they were the first to salute it.*

These meddlesome American missionaries! these frank British consuls! these blabbing Belgian-born traitor officials!—those tiresome parrots are always talking, always telling. They have told how for twenty years I have ruled the Congo State not as a trustee of the Powers, an agent, a subordinate, a foreman, but as a sovereign—sovereign over a fruitful domain four times as large as the German Empire—sovereign absolute, irresponsible, above all law; trampling the Berlin-made Congo charter under foot; barring out all foreign traders but myself; restricting commerce to myself, through concessionaires who are my creatures and confederates; seizing and holding the State as my personal property, the whole of its vast revenues as my private "swag"—mine, solely mine—claiming and holding its millions of people as my private property, my serfs, my slaves; their labor mine, with or without wage; the food they raise not their property but mine; the rubber, the ivory and all the other riches of the land mine—mine solely—and gathered for me by the men, the women and the little children under compulsion of lash and bullet, fire, starvation, multilation and the halter.

These pests!—it is as I say, they have kept back nothing! They have revealed these and yet other details which shame should have kept them silent about, since they were exposures of a king, a sacred personage and immune from reproach, by right of his selection and appointment to his great office by God himself; a king whose acts cannot be criticized without blasphemy, since God has observed them from the beginning and has manifested no dissatisfaction with them, nor shown disapproval of them, nor hampered nor interrupted them in any way. By this sign I recognize his approval of what I have done; his cordial and glad approval, I am sure I may say.

Blest, crowned, beatified with this great reward, this golden reward, this unspeakably precious reward, why should I care for men's cursings and revilings of me? [*With a sudden outburst of feeling*] May they roast a million aeons in—

[*Catches his breath and effusively kisses the crucifix; sorrowfully murmurs, "I shall get myself damned yet, with these indiscretions of speech."*]

Yes, they go on telling everything, these chatterers! They tell how I levy incredibly burdensome taxes upon the natives—taxes which are a pure theft; taxes which they must satisfy by gathering rubber under hard and constantly harder conditions, and by raising and furnishing food supplies gratis—and it all comes out that, when they fall short of their tasks through hunger, sickness, despair, and ceaseless and exhausting labor without rest, and forsake their homes and flee to the woods to escape punishment, my black soldiers, drawn from unfriendly tribes, and instigated and directed by my Belgians, hunt them down and butcher them and burn their villages—reserving some of the girls. They tell it all: how I am wiping a nation of friendless creatures out of existence by every form of murder, for my private pocket's sake, and how every shilling I get costs a rape, a mutilation or a life. But they never say, although they know it, that I have labored in the cause of religion at the same time and all the time, and have sent missionaries there (of a "convenient stripe," as they phrase it), to teach them the error of their ways and bring them to Him who is all mercy and love, and who is the sleepless guardian and friend of all who suffer. They tell only what is against me, they will not tell what is in my favor.

They tell how England required of me a Commission of Inquiry into Congo atrocities, and how, to quiet that meddling country, with its disagreeable Congo Reform Association, made up of earls and bishops and John Morleys and university grandees and other dudes, more interested in other people's business than in their own, I appointed it. Did it stop their mouths? No, they merely pointed out that it was a commission composed wholly of my "Congo butchers," "the very men whose acts were to be inquired into." They said it was equivalent to appointing a commission of wolves to inquire into depredations committed upon a sheepfold. *Nothing* can satisfy a cursed Englishman!*

And were the fault-finders frank with my private character? They could not be more so if I were a plebeian, a peasant, a mechanic. They remind the world that from the earliest days my house has been chapel and brothel combined, and both industries working full time; that I practised cruelties upon my queen and my daughters, and supplemented them with daily shame and humiliations; that, when my queen lay in the happy refuge of her coffin, and a daughter implored me on her knees to let her look for the last time upon her mother's face, I refused; and that, three years ago, not being satisfied with the stolen spoils of a whole alien nation, I robbed my own child of her property and appeared by proxy in court, a spectacle to the civilized world, to defend the act and complete the crime. It is as I have said: they are unfair, unjust; they will resurrect and give new currency to such things as those, or to any other things that count against me, but they will not mention any act of mine that is in my favor. I have spent more money on art than any other monarch of my time, and they know it. Do they

---

* This visit had a more fortunate result than was anticipated. One member of the Commission was a leading Congo official, another an official of the government in Belgium, the third a Swiss jurist. It was feared that the work of the Commission would not be more genuine than that of innumerable so-called "investigations" by local officials. But it appears that the Commission was met by a very avalanche of awful testimony. One who was present at a public hearing writes: "Men of stone would be moved by the stories that are being unfolded as the Commission probes into the awful history of rubber collection." It is evident the commissioners were moved. Certain reforms were ordered by the Commission of Inquiry in the one section visited, but the latest word is that after its departure conditions were soon worse than before its coming. (M.T.)

speak of it, do they tell about it? No, they do not. They prefer to work up what they call "ghastly statistics" into offensive kindergarten object lessons, whose purpose is to make sentimental people shudder, and prejudice them against me. They remark that "if the innocent blood shed in the Congo State by King Leopold were put in buckets and the buckets placed side by side, the line would stretch 2,000 miles; if the skeletons of his ten millions of starved and butchered dead could rise up and march in single file, it would take them seven months and four days to pass a given point; if compacted together in a body, they would occupy more ground than St. Louis covers, World's Fair and all; if they should all clap their bony hands at once, the grisly crash would be heard at a distance of—" Damnation, it makes me tired! And they do similar miracles with the money I have distilled from that blood and put into my pocket. They pile it into Egyptian pyramids; they carpet Saharas with it; they spread it across the sky, and the shadow it casts makes twilight in the earth. And the tears I have caused, the hearts I have broken—oh, nothing can persuade them to let *them* alone!

[*Meditative pause*] Well . . . no matter, I *did* beat the Yankees, anyway! there's comfort in that.

[*Reads with mocking smile, the President's Order of Recognition of April 22, 1884*]

> . . . the government of the United States announces its sympathy with and approval of the humane and benevolent purposes of (my Congo scheme), and will order the officers of the United States, both on land and sea, to recognize its flag as the flag of a friendly government.

Possibly the Yankees would like to take that back, now, but they will find that my agents are not over there in America for nothing. But there is no danger; neither nations nor governments can afford to confess a blunder.

[*With a contented smile, begins to read from "Report by Rev. W. M. Morrison, American missionary in the Congo Free State"*]

> I furnish herewith some of the many atrocious incidents which have come under my own personal observation; they reveal the *organized*

system of plunder and outrage which has been perpetrated and is now being carried on in that unfortunate country by King Leopold of Belgium. I say King Leopold, because he and he *alone* is now responsible, since he is the *absolute sovereign. He styles himself such.* When our government in 1884 laid the foundation of the Congo Free State, by recognizing its flag, little did it know that this concern, parading under the guise of philanthropy—was really King Leopold of Belgium, one of the shrewdest, most heartless and most conscienceless rulers that ever sat on a throne. This is apart from his known corrupt morals, which have made his name and his family a byword in two continents. Our government would most certainly not have recognized that flag had it known that it was really King Leopold individually who was asking for recognition; had it known that it was setting up in the heart of Africa an *absolute monarchy;* had it known that, having put down African slavery in our own country at great cost of blood and money, it was *establishing a worse form of slavery right in Africa.*

[*With evil joy*] Yes, I certainly was a shade too clever for the Yankees. It hurts; it gravels them. They can't get over it! Puts a shame upon them in another way, too, and a graver way; for they never can rid their records of the reproachful fact that their vain Republic, self-appointed Champion and Promoter of the Liberties of the World, is the only democracy in history that has lent its power and influence to the establishing of an *absolute monarchy!*

[*Contemplating, with an unfriendly eye, a stately pile of pamphlets*] Blister the meddlesome missionaries! They write tons of these things. They seem to be always around, always spying, always eyewitnessing the happenings; and everything they see they commit to paper. They are always prowling from place to place; the natives consider them their only friends; they go to them with their sorrows; they show them their scars and their wounds, inflicted by my soldier police; they hold up the stumps of their arms and lament because their hands have been chopped off, as punishment for not bringing in enough rubber, and as proof to be laid before my officers that the required punishment was well and truly carried out. One of these missionaries saw eighty-one of these hands drying over a fire for transmission to my officials—and of course he must go and set it down and print it. They travel and travel, they spy and spy! And nothing is too trivial for them to print.

[*Takes up a pamphlet. Reads a passage from Report of a "Journey made in July, August and September, 1903, by Rev. A. E. Scrivener, a British missionary"*]

. . . . Soon we began talking, and without any encouragement on my part the natives began the tales I had become so accustomed to. They were living in peace and quietness when the white men came in from the lake with all sorts of requests to do this and that, and they thought it meant slavery. So they attempted to keep the white men out of their country but without avail. The rifles were too much for them. So they submitted and made up their minds to do the best they could under the altered circumstances. First came the command to build houses for the soldiers, and this was done without a murmur. Then they had to feed the soldiers and all the men and women—hangers on—who accompanied them. Then they were told to bring in rubber. This was quite a new thing for them to do. There was rubber in the forest several days away from their home, but that it was worth anything was news to them. A small reward was offered and a rush was made for the rubber. "What strange white men, to give us cloth and beads for the sap of a wild vine." They rejoiced in what they thought their good fortune. But soon the reward was reduced until at last they were told to bring in the rubber for nothing. To this they tried to demur; but to their great surprise several were shot by the soldiers, and the rest were told, with many curses and blows, to go at once or more would be killed. Terrified, they began to prepare their food for the fortnight's absence from the village which the collection of rubber entailed. The soldiers discovered them sitting about. "What, not gone yet?" Bang! bang! bang! and down fell one and another, dead, in the midst of wives and companions. There is a terrible wail and an attempt made to prepare the dead for burial, but this is not allowed. All must go at once to the forest. Without food? Yes, without food. And off the poor wretches had to go without even their tinder boxes to make fires. Many died in the forests of hunger and exposure, and still more from the rifles of the ferocious soldiers in charge of the post. In spite of all their efforts the amount fell off and more and more were killed. I was shown around the place, and the sites of former big chiefs' settlements were pointed out. A careful estimate made the population of, say, seven years ago, to be 2,000 people in and about the post, within a radius of, say, a quarter of a mile. All told, they would not muster 200 now, and there is so much sadness and gloom about them that they are fast decreasing.

We stayed there all day on Monday and had many talks with the people. On the Sunday some of the boys had told me of some bones which they had seen, so on the Monday I asked to be shown these bones. Lying about on the grass, within a few yards of the house I was oc-cupying, were numbers of human skulls, bones, in some cases complete skeletons. I counted thirty-six skulls, and saw many sets of bones from which the skulls were missing. I called one of the men and asked the meaning of it. "When the rubber palaver began," said he, "the soldiers shot so many we grew tired of burying, and very often we were not allowed to bury; and so just dragged the bodies out into the grass and left them. There are hundreds all around if you would like to see them." But I had seen more than enough, and was sickened by the stories that came from men and women alike of the awful time they had passed through. The Bulgarian atrocities might be considered as mildness itself when compared with what was done here. How the people submitted I don't know, and even now I wonder as I think of their patience. That some of them managed to run away is some cause for thankfulness. I stayed there two days and the one thing that impressed itself upon me was the collection of rubber. I saw long files of men come in, as at Bongo, with their little baskets under their arms; saw them paid their milk tin full of salt, and the two yards of calico flung to the headmen; saw their trembling timidity, and in fact a great deal that all went to prove the state of terrorism that exists and the virtual slavery in which the people are held.

That is their way; they spy and spy, and run into print with every foolish trifle. And that British consul, Mr. Casement, is just like them. He gets hold of a *diary which had been kept by one of my government officers,* and, although it is a private diary and intended for no eye but its owner's, Mr. Casement is so lacking in delicacy and refinement as to print passages from it.

[Reads a passage from the diary]

Each time the corporal goes out to get rubber, cartridges are given him. He must bring back all not used, and for every one used he must bring back a right hand. M. P. told me that sometimes they shot a cartridge at an animal in hunting; they then cut off a hand from a living man. As to the extent to which this is carried on, he informed me that in six months the State on the Mambogo River had used

6,000 cartridges, which means that 6,000 people are killed or mutilated. It means more than 6,000 . . . for the people have told me repeatedly that the soldiers kill the children with the butt of their guns.

When the subtle consul thinks silence will be more effective than words, he employs it. Here he leaves it to be recognized that a thousand killings and mutilations a month is a large output for so small a region as the Mambogo River concession, silently indicating the dimensions of it by accompanying his report with a map of the prodigious Congo State, in which there is not room for so small an object as that river. That silence is intended to say, "If it is a thousand a month in this little corner, imagine the output of the whole vast State!" A gentleman would not descend to these furtivenesses.

Now as to the mutilations. You can't head off a Congo critic and make him stay headed-off; he dodges, and straightway comes back at you from another direction. They are full of slippery arts. When the mutilations (severing hands, unsexing men, etc.) began to stir Europe, we hit upon the idea of excusing them with a retort which we judged would knock them dizzy on that subject for good and all, and leave them nothing more to say; to wit, we boldly laid the custom on the natives, and said we did not invent it, but only followed it. Did it knock them dizzy? did it shut their mouths? Not for an hour. They dodged, and came straight back at us with the remark that "if a Christian king can perceive a saving moral difference between inventing bloody barbarities, and *imitating them from savages,* for charity's sake let him get what comfort he can out of his confession!"

It is most amazing, the way that that consul acts—that spy, that busybody.

[*Takes up pamphlet "Treatment of Women and Children in the Congo State; what Mr. Casement Saw in 1903"*]

Hardly two years ago! Intruding that date upon the public was a piece of cold malice. It is intended to weaken the force of my press syndicate's assurances to the public that my severities in the Congo *ceased,* and ceased utterly, *years and years ago.* This man is fond of trifles—revels in them, gloats over them, pets them, fondles them, sets them all down. One doesn't need to drowse through his monotonous report to see that; the mere sub-headings of its chapters prove it. [*Reads*]

> Two hundred and forty persons, *men, women and children*, compelled to supply government with *one ton* of carefully prepared foodstuffs *per week*, receiving in remuneration, all told, the princely sum of 15s 10d.!

Very well, it was liberal. It was not much short of a penny a week for each nigger. It suits this consul to belittle it, yet he knows very well that I could have had both the food and the labor for nothing. I can prove it by a thousand instances. [*Reads*]

> Expedition against a village behindhand in its (compulsory) supplies; result, slaughter of sixteen persons; among them three women and a boy of five years. Ten carried off, to be prisoners till ransomed; among them a child, who died during the march.

But he is careful not to explain that we are *obliged* to resort to ransom to collect debts, where the people have nothing to pay with. Families that escape to the woods sell some of their members into slavery and thus provide the ransom. He knows that I would stop this if I could find a less objectionable way to collect their debts. . . . Mm— here is some more of the consul's delicacy! He reports a conversation he had with some natives:

> Q.   How do you know it was the *white* men themselves who ordered these cruel things to be done to you? These things must have been done without the white man's knowledge by the black soldiers.
> A.   These white men told their soldiers: "You only kill *women;* you cannot kill men. You must prove that you kill men." So then the soldiers when they killed us (here he stopped and hesitated and then pointing to . . . he said:) then they . . . and took them to the white men, who said: "It is true, you have killed *men.*"
> Q.   You say this is true? Were many of you so treated after being shot?
> All [*shouting out*]: Nkoto! Nkoto! (Very many! Very many!)
> There was no doubt that these people were not inventing. Their vehemence, their flashing eyes, their excitement, were not simulated.

Of course the critic had to divulge that; he has no self-respect. All his kind reproach me, although they know quite well that I took no pleasure in punishing the men in that particular way, but only did it as a warning to other delinquents. Ordinary punishments are no good with ignorant savages; they make no impression.

[*Reads more sub-heads*]

Devastated region; population reduced from 40,000 to 8,000.

He does not take the trouble to say how it happened. He is fertile in concealments. He hopes his readers and his Congo reformers, of the Lord-Aberdeen-Norbury-John-Morley-Sir-Gilbert-Parker stripe, will think they were all killed. They were not. The great majority of them escaped. They fled to the bush with their families because of the rubber raids, and it was there they died of hunger. Could we help that?

One of my sorrowing critics observes: "Other Christian rulers tax their people, but furnish schools, courts of law, roads, light, water and protection to life and limb in return; King Leopold taxes his stolen nation, but provides *nothing in return but hunger, terror, grief, shame, captivity, mutilation and massacre.*" That is their style! I furnish "nothing"! I send the gospel to the survivors; these censure-mongers know it, but they would rather have their tongues cut out than mention it. I have several times required my raiders to give the dying an opportunity to kiss the sacred emblem; and if they obeyed me I have without doubt been the humble means of saving many souls. None of my traducers have had the fairness to mention this; but let it pass; there is One who has not overlooked it, and that is my solace, that is my consolation.

[*Puts down the Report, takes up a pamphlet, glances along the middle of it.*]

This is where the "death-trap" comes in. Meddlesome missionary spying around—Rev. W. H. Sheppard. Talks with a black raider of mine after a raid; cozens him into giving away some particulars. The raider remarks:

"I demanded 30 slaves from this side of the stream and 30 from the other side; 2 points of ivory, 2,500 balls of rubber, 13 goats, 10 fowls and 6 dogs, some corn chumy, etc."

"How did the fight come up?" I asked.

"I sent for all their chiefs, sub-chiefs, men and women, to come on a certain day, saying that I was going to finish all the palaver. When they entered these small gates (the walls being made of fences brought from other villages, the high native ones) I demanded all my pay or I would kill them; so they refused to pay me, and I ordered the fence to be closed so they couldn't run away; then we killed them here inside the fence. The panels of the fence fell down and some escaped."

"How many did you kill?" I asked.

"We killed plenty, will you see some of them?"

That was just what I wanted.

He said: "I think we have killed between eighty and ninety, and those in the other villages I don't know, I did not go out but sent my people."

He and I walked out on the plain just near the camp. There were three dead bodies with the flesh carved off from the waist down.

"Why are they carved so, only leaving the bones?" I asked.

"My people ate them," he answered promptly. He then explained, "The men who have young children do not eat people, but all the rest ate them."

On the left was a big man, shot in the back and without a head. (All corpses were nude.)

"Where is the man's head?" I asked.

"Oh, they made a bowl of the forehead to rub up tobacco and diamba in."

We continued to walk and examine until late in the afternoon, and counted forty-one bodies. The rest had been eaten up by the people.

On returning to the camp, we crossed a young woman, shot in the back of the head, one hand was cut away. I asked why, and Mulunba N'Cusa explained that they always cut off the right hand to give to the State on their return.

"Can you not show me some of the hands?" I asked.

So he conducted us to a framework of sticks, under which was burning a slow fire, and there they were, the right hands—I counted eighty-one in all.

There were not less than sixty women (Bena Pianga) prisoners. I saw them.

We say that we have as fully as possible investigated the whole outrage, and find it was a plan previously made to get all the stuff possible and to catch and kill the poor people in the death-trap.

Another detail, as we see!—cannibalism. They report cases of it with a most offensive frequency. My traducers do not forget to remark that, inasmuch as I am absolute and with a word can prevent in the Congo anything I choose to prevent, then whatsoever is done there by my permission is my act, my *personal* act; that *I* do it; that the hand of my agent is as truly *my* hand as if it were attached to my own arm; and so they picture me in my robes of state, with my crown on my head, munching human flesh, saying grace, mumbling thanks to Him from whom all good things come. Dear, dear, when the soft-hearts get hold of a thing like that missionary's contribution they completely lose their tranquillity over it. They speak profanely and reproach Heaven for allowing such a fiend to live. Meaning me. They think it irregular. They go shuddering around, brooding over the reduction of that Congo population from 25,000,000 to 15,000,000 in the twenty years of my administration; then they burst out and call me "the King with Ten Million Murders on his Soul." They call me a "record." The most of them do not stop with charging merely the 10,000,000 against me. No, they reflect that but for me the population, by natural increase, would now be 30,000,000, so they charge another 5,000,000 against me and make my total death-harvest 15,000,000. They remark that the man who killed the goose that laid the golden egg was responsible for the eggs she would subsequently have laid if she had been let alone. Oh, yes, they call me a "record." They remark that twice in a generation, in India, the Great Famine destroys 2,000,000 out of a population of 320,000,000, and the whole world holds up its hands in pity and horror; then they fall to wondering where the world would find room for its emotions if I had a chance to trade places with the Great Famine for twenty years! The idea fires their fancy, and they go on and imagine the Famine coming in state at the end of the twenty years and prostrating itself before me, saying: "Teach me, Lord, I perceive that I am but an apprentice." And next they imagine Death coming, with his scythe and hour-glass, and begging me to marry his daughter and reorganize his plant and run the business. For the whole world, you see! By this time their diseased minds are under full steam, and they get down their books and expand their labors, with me for text. They hunt through all biography for my match, working Attila, Torquemada, Ghengis Khan, Ivan the Terrible, and the rest of that crowd for all they are worth, and evilly exulting when they cannot find it. Then they examine the historical earthquakes and cyclones and blizzards and cataclysms and volcanic eruptions: verdict, none of them "in it" with me. At last they do really hit it (as they think), and they close their labors with conceding—reluctantly—that I have *one* match in history, but only one—the *Flood*. This is intemperate.

But they are always that, when they think of me. They can no more keep quiet when my name is mentioned than can a glass of water control its feelings with a seidlitz powder in its bowels. The bizarre things they can imagine, with me for an inspiration! One Englishman offers to give me the odds of three to one and bet me anything I like, up to 20,000 guineas, that for 2,000,000 years I am going to be the most conspicuous foreigner in hell. The man is so beside himself with anger that he does not perceive that the idea is foolish. Foolish and unbusinesslike: you see, there could be no winner; both of us would be losers, on account of the loss of interest on the stakes; at four or five per cent. compounded, this would amount to—I do not know how much, exactly, but, by the time the term was up and the bet payable, a person could buy hell itself with the accumulation.

Another madman wants to construct a memorial for the perpetuation of my name, out of my 15,000,000 skulls and skeletons, and is full of vindictive enthusiasm over his strange project. He has it all ciphered out and drawn to scale. Out of the skulls he will build a combined monument and mausoleum to me which shall exactly duplicate the Great Pyramid of Cheops, whose base covers thirteen acres, and whose apex is 451 feet above ground. He desires to stuff me and stand me up in the sky on that apex, robed and crowned, with my "pirate flag" in one hand and a butcher-knife and pendant handcuffs in the other. He will build the pyramid in the center of a depopulated tract, a brooding solitude covered with weeds and the mouldering ruins of burned villages, where the spirits of the starved and murdered dead will voice their laments forever in the whispers of the wandering winds. Radiating from the pyramid, like the spokes of a wheel, there are to be forty grand avenues of approach, each thirty-five miles long, and each fenced on both sides by skulless skeletons standing a yard and a half apart and festooned together in line by short chains stretching from wrist to wrist and attached to tried and true old handcuffs stamped with my private trade-mark, a crucifix and butcher-knife crossed, with motto, "By this sign we prosper"; each osseous fence to consist of 200,000 skeletons on a side, which is 400,000 to each avenue. It is remarked with satisfaction that it aggregates three or four thousand miles (single-ranked) of skeletons—15,000,000 all told—and would stretch across America from New York to San Francisco. It is remarked further, in the hopeful tone of a railroad company forecasting showy extensions of its mileage, that my output is 500,000 corpses a year when my plant is running full time, and that therefore if I am spared ten years longer there will be fresh skulls enough to add 175 feet to the pyramid, making it by a long way the loftiest architectural construction on the earth, and fresh skeletons enough to continue the transcontinental file (on piles) a thousand miles into the Pacific. The cost of gathering the materials from my "widely scattered and innumerable private graveyards," and transporting them, and building the monument and the radiating grand avenues, is duly ciphered out, running into an aggregate of millions of guineas, and then—why then, (— —!!— — !!) this idiot asks me to *furnish the money!* [*Sudden and effusive application of the crucifix*] He reminds me that my yearly income from the Congo is millions of guineas, and that *only* 5,000,000 would be required for his enterprise. Every day wild attempts are made upon my purse; they do not affect me, they cost me not a thought. But *this one*—this one troubles me, makes me nervous; for there is no telling what an unhinged creature like this may think of next. . . . *If he should think of Carnegie*—but I must banish that thought out of my mind! it worries my days; it troubles my sleep. That way lies madness. [*After a pause*] There is no other way—I have got to buy Carnegie.

[*Harassed and muttering, walks the floor a while, then takes to the Consul's chapter-headings again. Reads*]

Government starved a woman's children to death and killed her sons.

Butchery of women and children.

The native has been converted into a being without ambition because without hope.

Women chained by the neck by rubber sentries.

Women refuse to bear children because, with a baby to carry, they cannot well run away and hide from the soldiers.

Statement of a child: "I, my mother, my grandmother and my sister, we ran away into the bush. A great number of our people were killed by the soldiers. . . . After that they saw a little bit of my mother's head, and the soldiers ran quickly to where we were and caught my grandmother, my mother, my sister and another little one younger than us. Each wanted my mother for a wife, and argued about it, so they finally decided to kill her. They shot her through the stomach with a gun and she fell, and when I saw that I cried very much, because they killed my grandmother and mother and I was left alone. I saw it all done!"

It has a sort of pitiful sound, although they are only blacks. It carries me back and back into the past, to when my children were little, and would fly—to the bush, so to speak—when they saw me coming. . . .

[*Resumes the reading of chapter-headings of the Consul's report*]

They put a knife through a child's stomach.

They cut off the hands and brought them to C. D. (white officer) and spread them out in a row for him to see. They left them lying there, because the white man had seen them, so they did not need to take them to P.

Captured children left in the bush to die, by the soldiers.

Friends came to ransom a captured girl; but sentry refused, saying the white man wanted her because she was young.

Extract from a native girl's testimony:
"On our way the soldiers saw a little child, and when they went to kill it the child laughed, so the soldier took the butt of his gun and struck the child with it and then cut off its head. One day they

killed my half-sister and cut off her head, hands and feet, because she had bangles on. Then they caught another sister, and sold her to the W. W. people and now she is a slave there."

The little child laughed! [*A long pause. Musing*] That innocent creature. Somehow—I wish it had not laughed.

[*Reads*]

Mutilated children.

Government encouragement of inter-tribal slave-traffic. The monstrous fines levied upon villages tardy in their supplies of foodstuffs compel the natives to sell their fellows—and children—to other tribes in order to meet the fine.

A father and mother forced to sell their boy.

Widow forced to sell her little girl.

[*Irritated*] Hang the monotonous grumbler, what would he have me do! Let a widow off merely because she is a widow? He knows quite well that there is nothing much left, now, *but* widows. I have nothing against widows, as a class, but business is business, and I've got to live haven't I, even if it does cause inconvenience to somebody here and there?

[*Reads*]

Men intimidated by the torture of their wives and daughters. (To make the men furnish rubber and supplies and so get their captured women released from chains and detention.) The sentry explained to me that he caught the women and brought them in (chained together neck to neck) by direction of his employer.

An agent explained that he was forced to catch women in preference to men, as then the men brought in supplies quicker; but he did not explain how the children deprived of their parents obtained their own food supplies.

A file of 15 (captured) women.

Allowing women and children to die of starvation in prison.

[*Musing*] Death from *hunger*. A lingering, long misery that must be. Day and days, and still days and days, the forces of the body failing, dribbling away, little by little—yes, it must be the hardest death of all. And to see food carried by, every day, and you can have none of it! Of course the little children cry for it, and that wrings the mother's heart. . . .

[*A sigh*] Ah, well, it cannot be helped; circumstances make this discipline necessary.

[*Reads*]

The crucifying of sixty women!

How stupid, how tactless! Christendom's goose flesh will rise with horror at the news. "Profanation of the sacred emblem!" That is what Christendom will shout. Yes, Christendom will buzz. It can hear me charged with half a million murders a year for twenty years and keep its composure, but to profane the Symbol is quite another matter. It will regard this as serious. It will wake up and want to look into my record. Buzz? Indeed it will; I seem to hear the distant hum already. . . . It was wrong to crucify the women, clearly wrong, manifestly wrong, I can see it now, myself, and am sorry it happened, sincerely sorry. I believe it would have answered just as well to skin them. . . . [*With a sigh*] But none of us thought of that; one cannot think of everything; and after all it is but human to err.

It will make a stir, no doubt, these crucifixions. . . .

[*Rests himself with some more chapter-headings. Reads*]

More mutilation of children. (Hands cut off.)

Testimony of American Missionaries.

Evidence of British Missionaries.

It is all the same old thing—tedious repetitions and duplications of shop-worn episodes; mutilations, murders, massacres, and so on, and so on, till one gets drowsy over it. Mr. Morel intrudes at this point, and contributes a comment which he could just as well have kept to himself—and throws in some italics, of course; these people can never get along without italics:

It is one heartrending story of human misery from beginning to end, and *it is all recent.*

Meaning 1904 and 1905. I do not see how a person can act so. This Morel is a king's subject, and reverence for monarchy should have restrained him from reflecting upon me with that exposure. This Morel is a reformer; a Congo reformer. That sizes *him* up. He publishes a sheet in Liverpool called *The West African Mail,* which is supported by the voluntary contributions of the sap-headed and the soft-hearted; and every week it steams and reeks and festers with up-to-date "Congo atrocities" of the sort detailed in this pile of pamphlets here. I will suppress it. I suppressed a Congo atrocity book there, after it was actually in print; it should not be difficult for me to suppress a newspaper.

[*Studies some photographs of mutilated Negroes, throws them down. Sighs*]

The kodak has been a sore calamity to us. The most powerful enemy indeed. In the early years we had no touble in getting the press to "expose" the tales of the mutilations as slanders, lies, inventions of busy-body American missionaries and exasperated foreigners who found the "open door" of the Berlin-Congo charter closed against them when they innocently went out there to trade; and by the press's help we got the Christian nations everywhere to turn an irritated and un-believing ear to those tales and say hard things about the tellers of them. Yes, all things went harmoniously and pleasantly in those good days, and I was looked up to as the benefactor of a down-trodden and friendless people. Then all of a sudden came the crash! That is to say, the incorruptible *kodak*—and all the harmony went to hell! The only witness I have encountered in my long experience that I couldn't bribe. Every Yankee missionary and every interrupted trader sent home and got one; and now—oh, well, the pictures get sneaked around every-where, in spite of all we can do to ferret them out and suppress them. Ten thousand pulpits and ten thousand presses are saying the good word for me all the time and placidly and convincingly denying the mutilations. Then that trivial little kodak, that a child can carry in its pocket, gets up, uttering never a word, and knocks them dumb!

. . . . What is this fragment?

[*Reads*]

But enough of trying to tally off his crimes! His list is interminable, we should never get to the end of it. His awful shadow lies across his Congo Free State, and under it an unoffending nation of 15,000,000 is withering away and swiftly succumbing of their miseries. It is a land of graves; it is *The* Land of Graves; it is the Congo Free Graveyard. It is a majestic thought: that is, this ghastliest episode in all human history is the work of *one man alone;* one solitary man; just a single idividual—Leopold, King of the Belgians. He is personally and solely responsible for all the myriad crimes that have blackened the history of the Congo State. He is *sole* master there; he is absolute. He could have prevented the crimes by his mere command; he could stop them today with a word. He withholds the word. For his pocket's sake.

It seems strange to see a king destroying a nation and laying waste a country for mere sordid money's sake, and solely and only for that. Lust of conquest is royal; kings have always exercised that stately vice; we are used to it, by old habit we condone it, perceiving a certain dignity in it; but *lust of money—lust of shillings—lust of nickels—lust of dirty coin,* not for the nation's enrichment but for *the king's alone*—this is new. It distinctly revolts us, we cannot seem to reconcile ourselves to it, we resent it, we despise it, we say it is shabby, unkingly, out of character. Being democrats we ought to jeer and jest, we ought to rejoice to see the purple dragged in the dirt, but —well, account for it as we may, we don't. We see this awful king, this pitiless and blood-drenched king, this money-crazy king towering toward the sky in a world-solitude of sordid crime, unfellowed and apart from the human race, sole butcher for personal gain findable in all his caste, ancient or modern, pagan or Christian, proper and legitimate target for the scorn of the lowest and the highest, and the execrations of all who hold in cold esteem the oppressor and the coward; and—well, it is a mystery, but *we do not wish to look;* for he is a king, and it hurts us, it troubles us, by ancient and inherited instinct it shames us to see a king degraded to this aspect, and we shrink from hearing the particulars of how it happened. *We shudder* and *turn away* when we come upon them in print.

Why, certainly—THAT IS MY PROTECTION. And you will continue to do it. I know the human race.

THE MISSIONARIES IN CHINA

Letter to Rev. J. H. Twitchell in Hartford, July 28, 1901,
on being asked to assist a movement to help the
starving Chinese.*

AMPERSAND, N.Y., *July 28, '01.*

DEAR JOE,—As you say, it is impracticable—in my case, certainly. For me to assist in an appeal to that Congress of land-thieves and liars would be to bring derision upon it; and for me to assist in an appeal for cash to pass through the hands of those missionaries out there, of any denomination, Catholic or Protestant, wouldn't do at all. They wouldn't handle money which I had soiled, and I wouldn't trust them with it, anyway. They would devote it to the relief of suffering—I know that—but the sufferers selected would be converts. The missionary-utterances exhibit no humane feeling toward the others, but in place of it a spirit of hate and hostility. And it is natural; the Bible forbids their presence there, their trade is unlawful, why shouldn't their characters be of necessity in harmony with—but never mind, let it go, it irritates me.

Later. I have been reading Yung Wing's letter again. It may be that he is over-wrought by his sympathies, but it may not be so. There may be other reasons why the missionaries are silent about the Shensi-2-year famine and cannibalism. It may be that there are so few Protestant converts there that the missionaries are able to take care of them. That they are not likely to largely concern themselves about Catholic converts and the others, is quite natural, I think.

That crude way of appealing to this Government for help in a cause which has no money in it, and no politics, rises before me again in all

* *Mark Twain's Letters*, arranged with comment by A. B. Paine (Harper and Brothers: New York and London, 1917).

its admirable innocence! Doesn't Yung Wing know us yet? However, he has been absent since '96 or '97. We have gone to hell since then. Kossuth couldn't raise 30 cents in Congress, now, if he were back with his moving Magyar-Tale.

In 1895 Mark Twain made a worldwide lecture tour in order to pay off his creditors in bankruptcy. He was sixty years old, in poor health, and spiritually depressed. He visited such varied countries as the Sandwich Islands (Hawaii today), Australia, India, and South Africa just before the Boer War. The tour was an immense success financially, and he spoke to crowded houses everywhere. It enabled him to pay off his creditors completely, and he discovered that he was a world figure as well as an American folk hero. But during this tour he discovered something else of far greater spiritual import and of much greater importance to his career. He witnessed the actual conditions, habits and rituals, the primary ideas and fundamental facts of imperialism as it was being practised on the "inferior"—that is to say, weaker—nations and darker peoples of the world. (It was typical of Twain that the material success of this trip never affected his unflinching view of the world around him.) The book that recorded these findings was perhaps Twain's poorest work for other, personal and tragic reasons. But it contained Twain's descriptions and observations of imperialism at work. The following selections move from Australia to India and South Africa, as they appear in the book, and as Twain's interest moved from the white man's arsenic to Indian clothes and skin color and to the Boers' extinction of the blacks. But the unifying theme—the hatred and condemnation of imperialism—is obvious; and it is on-the-spot reporting that speaks to us today. Ed.

THE COLONIZING OF AUSTRALIA*

Captain Cook found Australia in 1770, and eighteen years later the British government began to transport convicts to it. Altogether, New

* *Following the Equator* (Harper and Brothers: New York, 1897).

South Wales received eighty-three thousand in fifty-three years. The convicts wore heavy chains; they were ill-fed and badly treated by the officers set over them; they were heavily punished for even slight infractions of the rules; "the cruelest discipline ever known" is one historian's description of their life.

English law was hard-hearted in those days. For trifling offenses which in our day would be punished by a small fine or a few days' confinement, men, women, and boys were sent to this other end of the earth to serve terms of seven and fourteen years; and for serious crimes they were transported for life. Children were sent to the penal colonies for seven years for stealing a rabbit!

When I was in London twenty-three years ago there was a new penalty in force for diminishing garroting and wife-beating—twenty-five lashes on the bare back with the cat-o'-nine-tails. It was said that this terrible punishment was able to bring the stubbornest ruffians to terms; and that no man had been found with grit enough to keep his emotions to himself beyond the ninth blow; as a rule the man shrieked earlier. That penalty had a great and wholesome effect upon the garroters and wife-beaters; but humane modern London could not endure it; it got its law rescinded. Many a bruised and battered English wife has since had occasion to deplore that cruel achievement of sentimental "humanity."

Twenty-five lashes! In Australia and Tasmania they gave a convict fifty for almost any little offense; and sometimes a brutal officer would add fifty, and then another fifty, and so on, as long as the sufferer could endure the torture and live. In Tasmania I read the entry, in an old manuscript official record, of a case where a convict was given *three hundred* lashes—for stealing some silver spoons. And men got more than that, sometimes. Who handled the cat? Often it was another convict; sometimes it was the culprit's dearest comrade; and he had to lay on with all his might; otherwise he would get a flogging himself for his mercy—for he was under watch—and yet not do his friend any good: the friend would be attended to by another hand and suffer no lack in the matter of full punishment.

The convict life in Tasmania was so unendurable, and suicide so difficult to accomplish, that once or twice despairing men got together and drew straws to determine which of them should kill another of the group—this murder to secure death to the perpetrator and to the witnesses of it by the hand of the hangman!

The incidents quoted above are mere hints, mere suggestions of what convict life was like—they are but a couple of details tossed into view out of a shoreless sea of such; or, to change the figure, they are but a pair of flaming steeples photographed from a point which hides from sight the burning city which stretches away from their bases on every hand.

Some of the convicts—indeed, a good many of them—were very bad people, even for that day; but the most of them were probably not noticeably worse than the average of the people they left behind them at home. We must believe this; we cannot avoid it. We are obliged to believe that a nation that could look on, unmoved, and see starving or freezing women hanged for stealing twenty-six cents' worth of bacon or rags, and boys snatched from their mothers, and men from their families, and sent to the other side of the world for long terms of years for similar trifling offenses, was a nation to whom the term "civilized" could not in any large way be applied. And we must also believe that a nation that knew, during more than forty years, what was happening to those exiles and was still content with it, was not advancing in any showy way toward a higher grade of civilization.

If we look into the characters and conduct of the officers and gentlemen who had charge of the convicts and attended to their backs and stomachs, we must grant again that as between the convict and his masters, and between both and the nation at home, there was a quite noticeable monotony of sameness.

Four years had gone by, and many convicts had come. Respectable settlers were beginning to arrive. These two classes of colonists had to be protected, in case of trouble among themselves or with the natives. It is proper to mention the natives, though they could hardly count, they were so scarce. At a time when they had not as yet begun to be much disturbed—not as yet being in the way—it was estimated that in New South Wales there was but one native to forty-five thousand acres of territory.

People had to be protected. Officers of the regular army did not want this service—away off there where neither honor nor distinction was to be gained. So England recruited and officered a kind of militia force of one thousand uniformed civilians called the "New South Wales Corps" and shipped it.

This was the worst blow of all. The colony fairly staggered under it. The Corps was an object-lesson of the moral condition of England outside of the jails. The colonists trembled. It was feared that next there would be an importation of the nobility.

In those early days the colony was non-supporting. All the necessaries of life—food, clothing, and all—were sent out from England, and kept in great government storehouses, and given to the convicts and sold to the settlers—sold at a trifling advance upon cost. The Corps saw its opportunity. Its officers went into commerce, and in a most lawless way. They went to importing rum, and also to manufacturing it in private stills, in defiance of the government's commands and protests. They leagued themselves together and ruled the market; they boycotted the government and the other dealers; they established a close monopoly and kept it strictly in their own hands. When a vessel arrived with spirits, they allowed nobody to buy but themselves, and they forced the owner to sell to them at a price named by themselves—and it was always low enough. They bought rum at an average of two dollars a gallon and sold it at an average of ten. They *made rum the currency of the country*—for there was little or no money—and they maintained their devastating hold and kept the colony under their heel for eighteen or twenty years before they were finally conquered and routed by the government.

Meantime, they had spread intemperance everywhere. And they had squeezed farm after farm out of the settlers' hands for rum, and thus had bountifully enriched themselves. When a farmer was caught in the last agonies of thirst they took advantage of him and sweated him for a drink.

In one instance they sold a man a gallon of rum worth two dollars for a piece of property which was sold some years later for one hundred thousand dollars.

When the colony was about eighteen or twenty years old it was discovered that the land was specially fitted for the wool culture. Prosperity followed, commerce with the world began, by and by rich mines of the noble metals were opened, immigrants flowed in, capital likewise. The result is the great and wealthy and enlightened common-wealth of New South Wales.

CIVILIZATION COMES TO AUSTRALIA:

or Arsenic Pudding for Savages.*

Before I saw Australia I had never heard of the "weet-weet" at all. I met but few men who had seen it thrown—at least I met but few who mentioned having seen it thrown. Roughly described, it is a fat wooden cigar with its butt-end fastened to a flexible twig. The whole thing is only a couple of feet long, and weighs less than two ounces. This feather—so to call it—is not thrown through the air, but is flung with an underhanded throw and made to strike the ground a little way in front of the thrower; then it glances and makes a long skip; glances again, skips again, and again and again, like the flat stone which a boy sends skating over the water. The water is smooth, and the stone has a good chance; so a strong man may make it travel fifty or seventy-five yards; but the weet-weet has no such good chance, for it strikes sand, grass, and earth in its course. Yet an expert aboriginal has sent it a measured distance of *two hundred and twenty yards*. It would have gone even further, but it encountered rank ferns and underwood on its passage and they damaged its speed. Two hundred and twenty yards; and so weightless a toy—a mouse on the end of a bit of wire, in effect; and not sailing through the accommodating air, but encountering grass and sand and stuff at every jump. It looks wholly impossible; but Mr. Brough Smyth saw the feat and did the measuring, and set down the facts in his book about aboriginal life, which he wrote by command of the Victorian Government.

What is the secret of the feat? No one explains. It cannot be physical strength, for that could not drive such a feather-weight any distance. It must be art. But no one explains what the art of it is; nor how it gets around that law of nature which says you shall not throw any two-

* *Following the Equator.*

ounce thing two hundred and twenty yards, either through the air or bumping along the ground. Rev. J. G. Wood says:

> The distance to which the weet-weet or kangaroo-rat can be thrown is truly astonishing. I have seen an Australian stand at one side of Kennington Oval and throw the kangaroo-rat completely across it. [Width of Kennington Oval not stated.] It darts through the air with the sharp and menacing hiss of a rifle-ball, its greatest height from the ground being some seven or eight feet. . . . When properly thrown it looks just like a living animal leaping along. . . . Its movements have a wonderful resemblance to the long leaps of a kangaroo-rat fleeing in alarm, with its long tail trailing behind it.

The Old Settler said that he had seen distances made by the weet-weet, in the early days, which almost convinced him that it was as extraordinary an instrument as the boomerang.

There must have been a large distribution of acuteness among those naked, skinny aboriginals, or they couldn't have been such unapproachable trackers and boomerangers and weet-weeters. It must have been race-aversion that put upon them a good deal of the low-rate intellectual reputation which they bear and have borne this long time in the world's estimate of them.

They were lazy—always lazy. Perhaps that was their trouble. It is a killing defect. Surely they could have invented and built a competent house, but they didn't. And they could have invented and developed the agricultural arts, but they didn't. They went naked and houseless, and lived on fish and grubs and worms and wild fruits, and were just plain savages, for all their smartness.

With a country as big as the United States to live and multiply in, and with no epidemic diseases among them till the white man came with those and his other appliances of civilization, it is quite probable that there was never a day in his history when he could muster one hundred thousand of his race in all Australia. He diligently and deliberately kept population down by infanticide—largely; but mainly by certain other methods. He did not need to practise these artificialities any more after the white man came. The white man knew ways of keeping down population which were worth several of his. The white man knew ways of reducing a native population eighty per cent in twenty years. The native had never seen anything as fine as that before.

For example, there is the case of the country now called Victoria—a country eighty times as large as Rhode Island, as I have already said. By the best official guess there were forty-five hundred aboriginals in it when the whites came along in the middle of the thirties. Of these one thousand lived in Gippsland, a patch of territory the size of fifteen or sixteen Rhode Islands: they did not diminish as fast as some of the other communities; indeed, at the end of forty years there were still two hundred of them left. The Geelong tribe diminished more satisfactorily: from one hundred and seventy-three persons it faded to thirty-four in twenty years; at the end of another twenty the tribe numbered one person altogether. The two Melbourne tribes could muster almost three hundred when the white man came; they could muster but twenty thirty-seven years later, in 1875. In that year there were still odds and ends of tribes scattered about the colony of Victoria, but I was told that natives of full blood are very scarce now. It is said that the aboriginals continue in some force in the huge territory called Queensland.

The early whites were not used to savages. They could not understand the primary law of savage life: that if a man do you a wrong, his whole tribe is responsible—each individual of it—and you may take your change out of any individual of it, without bothering to seek out the guilty one. When a white killed an aboriginal, the tribe applied the ancient law, and killed the first white they came across. To the whites this was a monstrous thing. Extermination seemed to be the proper medicine for such creatures as this. They did not kill all the blacks, but they promptly killed enough of them to make their own persons safe. From the dawn of civilization down to this day the white man has always used that very precaution. Mrs. Campbell Praed lived in Queensland, as a child, in the early days, and in her *Sketches of Australian Life* we get informing pictures of the early struggles of the white and the black to reform each other.

Speaking of pioneer days in the mighty wilderness of Queensland, Mrs. Praed says:

> At first the natives retreated before the whites; and, except that they every now and then speared a beast in one of the herds, gave little cause for uneasiness. But, as the number of squatters increased, each one taking up miles of country and bringing two or three men in his train, so that shepherds' huts and stockmen's camps lay far apart, and

defenseless in the midst of hostile tribes, the Blacks' depredations became more frequent and murder was no unusual event.

The loneliness of the Australian bush can hardly be painted in
words. Here extends mile after mile of primeval forest where perhaps
foot of white man has never trod—interminable vistas where the
eucalyptus trees rear their lofty trunks and spread forth their lanky
limbs, from which the red gum oozes and hangs in fantastic pendants
like crimson stalactites; ravines along the sides of which the long-
bladed grass grows rankly; level untimbered plains alternating with
undulating tracts of pasture, here and there broken by a stony ridge,
steep gully, or dried-up creek. All wild, vast, and desolate; all the same
monotonous gray coloring, except where the wattle, when in blossom,
shows patches of feathery gold, or a belt of scrub lies green, glossy,
and impenetrable as Indian jungle.

The solitude seems intensified by the strange sounds of reptiles,
birds, and insects, and by the absence of larger creatures; of which
in the daytime the only audible signs are the stampede of a herd of
kangaroo, or the rustle of a wallabi, or a dingo stirring the grass as it
creeps to its lair. But there are the whirring of locusts, the demoniac
chuckle of the laughing jackass, the screeching of cockatoos and parrots, the hissing of the frilled lizard, and the buzzing of innumerable
insects hidden under the dense undergrowth. And then at night, the
melancholy wailing of the curlews, the dismal howling of dingoes,
the discordant croaking of tree-frogs, might well shake the nerves of
the solitary watcher.

That is the theater for the drama. When you comprehend one or two
other details, you will perceive how well suited for trouble it was, and
how loudly it invited it. The cattlemen's stations were scattered over
that profound wilderness miles and miles apart—at each station half a
dozen persons. There was a plenty of cattle, the black natives were
always ill-nourished and hungry. The land belonged to *them.* The
whites had not bought it, and couldn't buy it; for the tribes had no
chiefs, nobody in authority, nobody competent to sell and convey; and
the tribes themselves had no comprehension of the idea of transferable
ownership of land. The ousted owners were despised by the white
interlopers, and this opinion was not hidden under a bushel. More
promising materials for a tragedy could not have been collated. Let
Mrs. Praed speak:

At Nie Nie station, one dark night, the unsuspecting hut-keeper, having, as he believed, secured himself against assault, was lying wrapped in his blankets sleeping profoundly. The Blacks crept stealthily down the chimney and battered in his skull while he slept.

One could guess the whole drama from that little text. The curtain was up. It would not fall until the mastership of one party or the other was determined—and permanently:

There was treachery on both sides. The Blacks killed the Whites when they found them defenseless, and the Whites slew the Blacks in a wholesale and promiscuous fashion which offended against my childish sense of justice. . . . They were regarded as little above the level of brutes, and in some cases *were destroyed like vermin.*

Here is an instance. A squatter, whose station was surrounded by Blacks, whom he suspected to be hostile and from whom he feared an attack, parleyed with them from his house-door. He told them it was Christmas-time—a time at which all men, black or white, feasted; that there were flour, sugar-plums, good things in plenty in the store, and that he would make for them such a pudding as they had never dreamed of—a great pudding of which all might eat and be filled. The Blacks listened and were lost. The pudding was made and distributed. Next morning there was howling in the camp, for it had been sweetened with sugar and arsenic!

The white man's spirit was right, but his method was wrong. His spirit was the spirit which the civilized white has always exhibited toward the savage, but the use of poison was a departure from custom. True, it was merely a technical departure, not a real one: still, it was a departure, and therefore a mistake, in my opinion. It was better, kinder, swifter, and much more humane than a number of the methods which have been sanctified by custom, but that does not justify its employment. That is, it does not wholly justify it. Its unusual nature makes it stand out and attract an amount of attention which it is not entitled to. It takes hold upon morbid imaginations and they work it up into a sort of exhibition of cruelty, and this smirches the good name of our civilization, whereas one of the old harsher methods would have had no such effect because usage has made those methods familiar to us and innocent. In many countries we have chained the savage and starved him to death; and this we do not care for, because custom has inured us to it; yet a quick death by poison is loving-kindness to it. In many countries we have burned the savage at the stake; and this we do not care for, because custom has inured us to it; yet a quick death is loving-kindness to it. In more than one country we have hunted the savage and his little children and their mother with dogs and guns through the woods and swamps for an afternoon's sport, and filled the region with happy laughter over their sprawling and stumbling flight, and their wild supplications for mercy; but this method we do not mind, because custom has inured us to it; yet a quick death by poison is loving-kindness to it. In many countries we have taken the savage's land from him, and made him our slave, and lashed him every day, and broken his pride, and made death his only friend, and overworked him till he dropped in his tracks; and this we do not care for, because custom has inured us to it; yet a quick death by poison is loving-kindness to it. In the Matabeleland to-day—why, there we are confining ourselves to sanctified custom, we Rhodes-Beit millionaires in South Africa and Dukes in London; and nobody cares, because we are used to the old holy customs, and all we ask is that no notice-inviting new ones shall be intruded upon the attention of our comfortable consciences. Mrs. Praed says of the poisoner, "That squatter deserves to have his name handed down to the contempt of posterity."

I am sorry to hear her say that. I myself blame him for one thing, and severely, but I stop there. I blame him for the indiscretion of introducing a novelty which was calculated to attract attention to our civilization. There was no occasion to do that. It was his duty, and it is every loyal man's duty, to protect that heritage in every way he can; and the best way to do that is to attract attention elsewhere. The squatter's judgment was bad—that is plain; but his heart was right. He is almost the only pioneering representative of civilization in history who has risen above the prejudices of his caste and his heredity and tried to introduce the element of mercy into the superior race's dealings with the savage. His name is lost, and it is a pity; for it deserves to be handed down to posterity with homage and reverence.

This paragraph is from a London journal:

To learn what France is doing to spread the blessings of civilization in her distant dependencies we may turn with advantage to New Caledonia. With a view to attracting free settlers to that penal colony, M. Feillet, the Governor, forcibly expropriated the Kanaka cultivators from the best of their plantations, with a derisory compensation, in spite of the protests of the Council General of the island. Such immigrants as could be induced to cross the seas thus found themselves in possession of thousands of coffee, cocoa, banana, and bread-fruit trees, the raising of which had cost the wretched natives years of toil, whilst the latter had a few five-franc pieces to spend in the liquor stores of Noumea.

You observe the combination? It is robbery, humiliation, and slow, slow murder, through poverty and the white man's whisky. The savage's gentle friend, the savage's noble friend, the only magnanimous and unselfish friend the savage has ever had, was not there with the merciful swift release of his poisoned pudding.

There are many humorous things in the world; among them the white man's notion that he is less savage than the other savages.

You notice that Mrs. Praed knows her art. She can place a thing before you so that you can see it. She is not alone in that. Australia is fertile in writers whose books are faithful mirrors of the life of the country and of its history. The materials were surprisingly rich, both in quality and in mass, and Marcus Clarke, Rolf Boldrewood, Gordon, Kendall, and the others, have built out of them a brilliant and vigorous literature, and one which must endure. Materials—there is no end to them! Why, a literature might be made out of the aboriginal all by himself, his character and ways are so freckled with varieties—varieties not staled by familiarity, but new to us. You do not need to invent any picturesquenesses; whatever you want in that line he can furnish you; and they will not be fancies and doubtful, but realities and authentic. In his history, as preserved by the white man's official records, he is everything—everything that a human creature can be. He covers the entire ground. He is a coward—there are a thousand facts to prove it. He is brave—there are a thousand facts to prove it. He is treacherous—oh, beyond imagination! He is faithful, loyal, true— the white man's records supply you with a harvest of instances of it that are noble, worshipful, and pathetically beautiful. He kills the starving stranger who comes begging for food and shelter—there is proof of it. He succors, and feeds, and guides to safety, to-day, the lost stranger who fired on him only yesterday—there is proof of it. He takes his reluctant bride by force, he courts her with a club, then loves her faithfully through a long life—it is of record. He gathers to himself another wife by the same processes, beats and bangs her as a daily diversion, and by and by lays down his life in defending her from some outside harm—it is of record. He will face a hundred hostiles to rescue one of his children, and will kill another of his children because the family is large enough without it. His delicate stomach turns, at certain details of the white man's food; but he likes over-ripe fish, and braised dog, and cat, and rat, and will eat his own uncle with relish. He is a sociable animal, yet he turns aside and hides behind his shield when his mother-in-law goes by. He is childishly afraid of ghosts and other trivialities that menace his soul, but dread of physical pain is a weakness which he is not acquainted with. He knows all the great and many of the little constellations, and has names for them; he has a symbol-writing by means of which he can convey messages far and wide among the tribes; he has a correct eye for form and expression, and draws a good picture; he can track a fugitive by delicate traces which the white man's eye cannot discern, and by methods which the finest white intelligence cannot master; he makes a missile which science itself cannot duplicate without the model—if with it; a missile whose secret baffled and defeated the searchings and theorizings of the white mathematicians for seventy years; and by an art all his own he performs miracles with it which the white man cannot approach untaught, nor parallel after teaching. Within certain limits this savage's intellect is the alertest and the brightest known to history or tradition; and yet the poor creature was never able to invent a counting system that would reach above five, nor a vessel that he could boil water in. He is the prize-curiosity of all the races. To all intents and purposes he is dead—in the body; but he has features that will live in literature.

THE SLAVE-CATCHING TRADE IN QUEENSLAND:

Civilization and the Kanakas*

In these past few days we are plowing through a mighty Milky Way of islands. They are so thick on the map that one would hardly expect

* *Following the Equator.*

to find room between them for a canoe; yet we seldom glimpse one. Once we saw the dim bulk of a couple of them, far away, spectral and dreamy things; members of the Horne—Alofa and Fortuna. On the larger one are two rival native kings—and they have a time together. They are Catholics; so are their people. The missionaries there are French priests.

From the multitudinous islands in these regions the "recruits" for the Queensland plantations were formerly drawn; are still drawn from them, I believe. Vessels fitted up like old-time slavers came here and carried off the natives to serve as laborers in the great Australian province. In the beginning it was plain, simple man-stealing, as per testimony of the missionaries. This has been denied, but not disproven. Afterward it was forbidden by law to "recruit" a native without his consent, and governmental agents were sent in all recruiting vessels to see that the law was obeyed—which they did, according to the recruiting people; and which they sometimes didn't, according to the missionaries. A man could be lawfully recruited for a three years' term of service; he could volunteer for another term if he so chose; when his time was up he could return to his island. And would also have the means to do it; for the government required the employer to put money in its hands for this purpose before the recruit was delivered to him.

Captain Wawn was a recruiting shipmaster during many years. From his pleasant book one gets the idea that the recruiting business was quite popular with the islanders, as a rule. And yet that did not make the business wholly dull and uninteresting; for one finds rather frequent little breaks in the monotony of it. . . .

The truth is, Captain Wawn furnishes such a crowd of instances of fatal encounters between natives and French and English recruiting crews (for the French are in the business for the plantations of New Caledonia), that one is almost persuaded that recruiting is not thoroughly popular among the islanders; else why this bristling string of attacks and blood-curdling slaughter? The captain lays it all to "Exeter Hall influence." But for the meddling philanthropists, the native fathers and mothers would be fond of seeing their children carted into exile and now and then the grave, instead of weeping about it and trying to kill the kind recruiters.

Captain Wawn is crystal-clear on one point. He does not approve of missionaries. They obstruct his business. They make "Recruiting," as he calls it ("Slave-Catching," as *they* call it in their frank way) a trouble when it ought to be just a picnic and a pleasure excursion. The missionaries have their opinion about the manner in which the Labor Traffic is conducted, and about the recruiter's evasions of the law of the Traffic, and about the Traffic itself: and it is distinctly uncomplimentary to the Traffic and to everything connected with it, including the law for its regulation. Captain Wawn's book is of very recent date; I have by me a pamphlet of still later date—hot from the press, in fact—by Rev. Wm. Gray, a missionary; and the book and the pamphlet taken together make exceedingly interesting reading, to my mind.

Interesting, and easy to understand—except in one detail, which I will mention presently. It is easy to understand why the Queensland sugar-planter should want the Kanaka recruit: he is cheap. Very cheap, in fact. These are the figures paid by the planter: £20 to the recruiter for getting the Kanaka—or "catching" him, as the missionary phrase goes; £3 to the Queensland government for "superintending" the importation; £5 deposited with the government for the Kanaka's passage home when his three years are up, in case he shall live that long; about £25 to the Kanaka himself for three years' wages and clothing; total payment for the use of a man three years, £53; or, including diet, £60. Altogether, a hundred dollars a year. One can understand why the recruiter is fond of the business; the recruit costs him a few cheap presents (given to the recruit's relatives, not to the recruit himself), and the recruit is worth £20 to the recruiter when delivered in Queensland. All this is clear enough; but the thing that is not clear is, what there is about it all to persuade the recruit. He is young and brisk; life at home in his beautiful island is one lazy, long holiday to him; or if he wants to work he can turn out a couple of bags of copra per week and sell it for four or five shillings a bag. In Queensland he must get up at dawn and work from eight to twelve hours a day in the cane-fields—in a much hotter climate than he is used to—and get less than four shillings a week for it.

I cannot understand his willingness to go to Queensland. It is a deep puzzle to me. Here is the explanation, from the planter's point of view; at least I gather from the missionary's pamphlet that it is the planter's:

When he comes from his home he is a savage, pure and simple. He feels no shame at his nakedness and want of adornment. When he returns home he does so well dressed, sporting a Waterbury watch, collars, cuffs, boots, and jewelry. He takes with him one or more boxes* well filled with clothing, a musical instrument or two, and perfumery and other articles of luxury he has learned to appreciate.

For just one moment we have a seeming flash of comprehension of the Kanaka's reason for exiling himself: he goes away to acquire *civilization.* Yes, he was naked and not ashamed, now he is clothed and knows how to be ashamed; he was unenlightened, now he has a Waterbury watch; he was unrefined, now he has jewelry, and something to make him smell good; he was a nobody, a provincial, now he has been to far countries and can show off.

It all looks plausible—for a moment. Then the missionary takes hold of this explanation and pulls it to pieces, and dances on it, and damages it beyond recognition.

Admitting that the foregoing description is the average one, the average sequel is this: The cuffs and collars, if used at all, are carried off by youngsters, who fasten them round the leg, just below the knee, as ornaments. The Waterbury, broken and dirty, finds its way to the trader, who gives a trifle for it; or the inside is taken out, the wheels strung on a thread and hung around the neck. Knives, axes, calico, and handkerchiefs are divided among friends, and there is hardly one of these apiece. The boxes, the keys often lost on the road home, can be bought for 2s.6d. They are to be seen rotting outside in almost any shore village on Tanna. (I speak of what I have seen.) A returned Kanaka has been furiously angry with me because I would not buy his trousers, which he declared were just my fit. He sold them afterward to one of my Aniwan teachers for 9d. worth of tobacco—a pair of trousers that probably cost him 8s. or 10s. in Queensland. A coat or shirt is handy for cold weather. The white handkerchiefs, the "senet" (perfumery), the umbrella, and perhaps the hat, are kept. The boots have to take their chance, if they do not happen to fit the copra trader. "Senet" on the hair, streaks of paint on the face, a dirty white handkerchief round the neck, strips of turtle-shell in the ears, a belt, a sheath and knife, and an umbrella constitute the rig of the returned Kanaka at home the day after landing.

* "Box" is English for trunk. (M.T.)

A hat, an umbrella, a belt, a neckerchief. Otherwise stark naked. All in a day the hard-earned "civilization" has melted away to this. And even these perishable things must presently go. Indeed, there is but a single detail of his civilization that can be depended on to stay by him: according to the missionary, he has learned to swear. This is art, and art is long, as the poet says.

In all countries the laws throw light upon the past. The Queensland law for the regulation of the Labor Traffic is a confession. It is a confession that the evils charged by the missionaries upon the traffic had existed in the past, and that they still existed when the law was made. The missionaries make a further charge: that the law is evaded by the recruiters, and that the Government Agent sometimes helps them to do it. Regulation thirty-one reveals two things: that sometimes a young fool of a recruit gets his senses back, after being persuaded to sign away his liberty for three years, and dearly wants to get out of the engagement and stay at home with his own people; and that threats, intimidation, and force are used to keep him on board the recruiting ship, and to hold him to his contract. Regulation thirty-one forbids these coercions. The law requires that he shall be allowed to go free; and another clause of it requires the recruiter to set him ashore—per boat, because of the prevalence of sharks. Testimony from Rev. Mr. Gray:

There are "wrinkles" for taking the penitent Kanaka. My first experience of the Traffic was a case of this kind in 1884. A vessel anchored just out of sight of our station, word was brought to me that some boys were stolen, and relatives wished me to go and get them back. The facts were, as I found, that six boys had recruited, had *rushed* into the boat, the Government Agent informed me. They had all "signed"; and, said the Government Agent, "on board they shall remain." I was assured that the six boys were of age and willing to go. Yet on getting ready to leave the ship I found four of the lads ready to come ashore in the boat! This I forbade. One of them jumped into the water and persisted in coming ashore in my boat. When appealed to, the Government Agent suggested that we go and leave him to be picked up by the ship's boat, a quarter-mile distant at the time!

The law and the missionaries feel for the repentant recruit—and properly, one may be permitted to think, for he is only a youth and ignorant and persuadable to his hurt—but sympathy for him is not kept in stock by the recruiter. Rev. Mr. Gray says:

> A captain many years in the Traffic explained to me how a penitent could be taken. "When a boy jumps overboard we just take a boat and pull ahead of him, then lie between him and the shore. If he has not tired himself swimming, and passes the boat, keep on heading him in this way. The dodge rarely fails. The boy generally tires of swimming, gets into the boat of his own accord, and goes quietly on board."

Yes, exhaustion is likely to make a boy quiet. If the distressed boy had been the speaker's son, and the captors savages, the speaker would have been surprised to see how differently the thing looked from the new point of view; however, it is not our custom to put ourselves in the other person's place. Somehow there is something pathetic about that disappointed young savage's resignation. I must explain, here, that in the traffic dialect, "boy" does not always mean boy; it means a youth above sixteen years of age. That is by Queensland law the age of consent, though it is held that recruiters allow themselves some latitude in guessing at ages.

Captain Wawn of the free spirit chafes under the annoyance of "cast-iron regulations." They and the missionaries have poisoned his life. He grieves for the good old days, vanished to come no more. See him weep; hear him cuss between the lines!

> For a long time we were allowed to apprehend and detain all deserters who had signed the agreement on board ship, but the "cast-iron" regulations of the Act of 1884 put a stop to that, allowing the Kanaka to sign the agreement for three years' service, travel about in the ship in receipt of the regular rations, cadge all he could, and leave when he thought fit, so long as he did not extend his pleasure trip to Queensland.

Rev. Mr. Gray calls this same restrictive cast-iron law a "farce." "There is as much cruelty and injustice done to natives by acts that are legal as by deeds unlawful. The regulations that exist are unjust and inadequate—unjust and inadequate they must ever be." He furnishes his reasons for his position, but they are too long for reproduction here.

However, if the most a Kanaka advantages himself by a three-year course in civilization in Queensland is a necklace and an umbrella and a showy imperfection in the art of swearing, it must be that *all* the profit of the traffic goes to the white man. This could be twisted into a plausible argument that the traffic ought to be squarely abolished.

However, there is reason for hope that that can be left alone to achieve itself. It is claimed that the traffic will depopulate its sources of supply within the next twenty or thirty years. Queensland is a very healthy place for white people—death-rate 12 in 1,000 of the population—but the Kanaka death-rate is away above that. The vital statistics for 1893 place it at 52; for 1894 (Mackay district), 68. The first six months of the Kanaka's exile are peculiarly perilous for him because of the rigors of the new climate. The death-rate among the new men has reached as high as 180 in the 1,000. In the Kanaka's native home his death-rate is 12 in time of peace, and 15 in time of war. Thus exile to Queensland—with the opportunity to acquire civilization, an umbrella, and a pretty poor quality of profanity—is twelve times as deadly for him as war. Common Christian charity, common humanity, does seem to require, not only that these people be returned to their homes, but that war, pestilence, and famine be introduced among them for their preservation.

Concerning these Pacific isles and their peoples an eloquent prophet spoke long years ago—five and fifty years ago. In fact, he spoke a little too early. Prophecy is a good line of business, but it is full of risks. This prophet was the Right Rev. M. Russell, LL.D., D.C.L., of Edinburgh:

> Is the tide of civilization to roll only to the foot of the Rocky Mountains, and is the sun of knowledge to set at last in the waves of the Pacific? No; the mighty day of four thousand years is drawing to its close; the sun of humanity has performed its destined course; but long ere its setting rays are extinguished in the west, its ascending beams have glittered on the isles of the eastern seas. . . . And now we see the race of Japhet setting forth to people the isles, and the seeds of another Europe and a second England sown in the region of the sun. But mark the words of the prophecy: "He shall dwell in the tents of Shem, and Canaan shall be his servant." It is not said Canaan shall be his *slave*. To the Anglo-Saxon race is given the scepter of the globe, but there is not given either the lash or the slave-driver or the

rack of the executioner. The East will not be stained with the same atrocities as the West; the frightful gangrene of an enthralled race is not to mar the destinies of the family of Japhet in the Oriental world; humanizing, not destroying, as they advance; uniting with, not enslaving, the inhabitants with whom they dwell, the British race may [etc., etc.].

And he closes his vision with an invocation from Campbell:

> Come, bright Improvement! on the car of Time,
> And rule the spacious world from clime to clime.

Very well, Bright Improvement has arrived, you see, with her civilization, and her Waterbury, and her umbrella, and her third-quality profanity, and her humanizing-not-destroying machinery, and her hundred-and-eighty death-rate, and everything is going along just as handsome!

PAGAN DRESS AND EUROPEAN CLOTHES:
Black Skin and White Skin*

The drive through the town and out to the Gallè Face by the seashore, what a dream it was of tropical splendors of bloom and blossom, and Oriental conflagrations of costume! The walking groups of men, women, boys, girls, babies—each individual was a flame, each group a house afire for color. And such stunning colors, such intensely vivid colors, such rich and exquisite minglings and fusings of rainbows and lightnings! And all harmonious, all in perfect taste; never a discordant note; never a color on any person swearing at another color on him or failing to harmonize faultlessly with the colors of any group the wearer might join. The stuffs were silk—thin, soft, delicate, clinging; and, as a rule, each piece a solid color: a splendid green, a splendid blue, a splendid yellow, a splendid purple, a splendid ruby, deep and rich with

* *Following the Equator.*

smoldering fires—they swept continuously by in crowds and legions and multitudes, glowing, flashing, burning, radiant; and every five seconds came a burst of blinding red that made a body catch his breath, and filled his heart with joy. And then, the unimaginable grace of those costumes! Sometimes a woman's whole dress was but a scarf wound about her person and her head, sometimes a man's was but a turban and a careless rag or two—in both cases generous areas of polished dark skin showing—but always the arrangement compelled the homage of the eye and made the heart sing for gladness.

I can see it to this day, that radiant panorama, that wilderness of rich color, that incomparable dissolving-view of harmonious tints, and lithe half-covered forms, and beautiful brown faces, and gracious and graceful gestures and attitudes and movements, free, unstudied, barren of stiffness and restraint, and—

Just then, into this dream of fairyland and paradise a grating dissonance was injected. Out of a missionary school came marching, two and two, sixteen prim and pious little Christian black girls, Europeanly clothed—dressed, to the last detail, as they would have been dressed on a summer Sunday in an English or American village. Those clothes— oh, they were unspeakably ugly! Ugly, barbarous, destitute of taste, destitute of grace, repulsive as a shroud. I looked at my women-folk's clothes—just full-grown duplicates of the outrages disguising those poor little abused creatures—and was ashamed to be seen in the street with them. Then I looked at my own clothes, and was ashamed to be seen in the street with myself.

However, we must put up with our clothes as they are—they have their reason for existing. They are on us to expose us—to advertise what we wear them to conceal. They are a sign; a sign of insincerity; a sign of suppressed vanity; a pretense that we despise gorgeous colors and the graces of harmony and form; and we put them on to propagate that lie and back it up. But we do not deceive our neighbor; and when we step into Ceylon we realize that we have not even deceived ourselves. We do love brilliant colors and graceful costumes; and at home we will turn out in a storm to see them when the procession goes by—and envy the wearers. We go to the theater to look at them and grieve that we can't be clothed like that. We go to the King's ball, when we get a chance, and are glad of a sight of the splendid uniforms and the glittering orders. When we are granted permission to attend an imperial drawing-room we shut ourselves up in private and parade around in the theatrical court-dress by the hour, and admire ourselves in the glass, and are utterly happy; and every member of every governor's staff in democratic America does the same with his grand new uniform—and if he is not watched he will get himself photographed in it, too. When I see the Lord Mayor's footman I am dissatisfied with my lot. Yes, our clothes are a lie, and have been nothing short of that these hundred years. They are insincere, they are the ugly and appropriate outward exposure of an inward sham and a moral decay.

The last little brown boy I chanced to notice in the crowds and swarms of Colombo had nothing on but a twine string around his waist, but in my memory the frank honesty of his costume still stands out in pleasant contrast with the odious flummery in which the little Sunday-school dowdies were masquerading.

I could have wished to start a rival exhibition there, of Christian hats and clothes. I would have cleared one side of the room of its Indian splendors and repacked the space with Christians drawn from America, England, and the Colonies, dressed in the hats and habits of now, and of twenty and forty and fifty years ago. It would have been a hideous exhibition, a thoroughly devilish spectacle. Then there would have been the added disadvantage of the white complexion. It is not an unbearably unpleasant complexion when it keeps to itself, but when it comes into competition with masses of brown and black the fact is betrayed that it is endurable only because we are used to it. Nearly all black and brown skins are beautiful, but a beautiful white skin is rare. How rare, one may learn by walking down a street in Paris, New York, or London on a week-day—particularly an unfashionable street—and keeping count of the satisfactory complexions encountered in the course of a mile. Where dark complexions are massed, they make the whites look bleached out, unwholesome, and sometimes frankly ghastly. I could notice this as a boy, down South in the slavery days before the war. The splendid black-satin skin of the South African Zulus of Durban seemed to me to come very close to perfection. I can see those Zulus yet—'rikisha athletes waiting in front of the hotel for custom; handsome and intensely black creatures, moderately clothed in loose summer stuffs whose snowy whiteness made the black all the blacker by contrast. Keeping that group in my mind, I can compare those complexions with the white ones which are streaming past this London window now. . . .

No end of people whose skins are dull and characterless modifications of the tint which we miscall white. Some of these faces are pimply; some exhibit other signs of diseased blood; some show scars of a tint out of harmony with the surrounding shades of color. The white man's complexion makes no concealments. It can't. It seems to have been designed as a catch-all for everything that can damage it. Ladies have to paint it, and powder it, and cosmetic it, and diet it with arsenic, and enamel it, and be always enticing it, and persuading it, and pestering it, and fussing at it, to make it beautiful; and they do not succeed. But these efforts show what they think of the natural complexion, as distributed. As distributed it needs these helps. The complexion which they try to counterfeit is one which nature restricts to the few—to the very few. To ninety-nine persons she gives a bad complexion, to the hundredth a good one. The hundredth can keep it—how long? Ten years, perhaps.

The advantage is with the Zulu, I think. He starts with a beautiful complexion, and it will last him through. And as for the Indian brown—firm, smooth, blemishless, pleasant and restful to the eye, afraid of no color, harmonizing with all colors and adding a grace to them all—I think there is no sort of chance for the average white complexion against that rich and perfect tint.

SLAVERY IN INDIA AND IN THE UNITED STATES*

In the region of Scandal Point—felicitous name—where there are handy rocks to sit on and a noble view of the sea on the one hand, and on the other the passing and repassing whirl and tumult of gay carriages, are great groups of comfortably off Parsee women—perfect flower-beds of brilliant color, a fascinating spectacle. Tramp, tramp, tramping along the road, in singles, couples, groups, and gangs, you

* *Following the Equator.*

have the working-man and the working-woman—but not clothed like ours. Usually the man is a nobly built great athlete, with not a rag on but his loin-handkerchief; his color a deep dark brown, his skin satin, his rounded muscles knobbing it as if it had eggs under it. Usually the woman is a slender and shapely creature, as erect as a lightning-rod, and she has but one thing on—a bright-colored piece of stuff which is wound about her head and her body down nearly half-way to her knees, and which clings like her own skin. Her legs and feet are bare, and so are her arms, except for her fanciful bunches of loose silver rings on her ankles and on her arms. She has jewelry bunched on the side of her nose also, and showy cluster-rings on her toes. When she undresses for bed she takes off her jewelry, I suppose. If she took off anything more she would catch cold. As a rule, she has a large shiny brass water-jar of graceful shape on her head, and one of her naked arms curves up and the hand holds it there. She is so straight, so erect, and she steps with such style, and such easy grace and dignity; and her curved arm and her brazen jar are such a help to the picture—indeed, our working-women cannot begin with her as a road decoration.

It is all color, bewitching color, enchanting color—everywhere—all around—all the way around the curving great opaline bay clear to Government House, where the turbaned big native *chuprassies* stand grouped in state at the door in their robes of fiery red, and do most properly and stunningly finish up the splendid show and make it theatrically complete. I wish I were a *chuprassy*. . . .

Even now, after the lapse of a year, the delirium of those days in Bombay has not left me, and I hope never will. It was all new, no detail of it hackneyed. And India did not wait for morning, it began at the hotel—straight away. The lobbies and halls were full of turbaned and fez'd and embroidered, cap'd, and barefooted, and cotton-clad dark natives, some of them rushing about, others at rest squatting, or sitting on the ground; some of them chattering with energy, others still and dreamy; in the dining-room every man's own private native servant standing behind his chair, and dressed for a part in the Arabian Nights.

Our rooms were high up, on the front. A white man—he was a burly German—went up with us, and brought three natives along to see to arranging things. About fourteen others followed in procession, with the hand-baggage; each carried an article—and only one; a bag, in some cases, in other cases less. One strong native carried my overcoat, another a parasol, another a box of cigars, another a novel, and the last man in the procession had no load but a fan. It was all done with earnestness and sincerity, there was not a smile in the procession from the head of it to the tail of it. Each man waited patiently, tranquilly, in no sort of hurry, till one of us found time to give him a copper, then he bent his head reverently, touched his forehead with his fingers, and went his way. They seemed a soft and gentle race, and there was something both winning and touching about their demeanor.

There was a vast glazed door which opened upon the balcony. It needed closing, or cleaning, or something, and a native got down on his knees and went to work at it. He seemed to be doing it well enough, but perhaps he wasn't, for the burly German put on a look that betrayed dissatisfaction, then without *explaining* what was wrong, gave the native a brisk cuff on the jaw and *then* told him where the defect was. It seemed such a shame to do that before us all. The native took it with meekness, saying nothing, and not showing in his face or manner any resentment. I had not seen the like of this for fifty years. It carried me back to my boyhood, and flashed upon me the forgotten fact that this was the *usual* way of explaining one's desires to a slave. I was able to remember that the method seemed right and natural to me in those days, I being born to it and unaware that elsewhere there were other methods; but I was also able to remember that those unresented cuffings made me sorry for the victim and ashamed for the punisher. My father was a refined and kindly gentleman, very grave, rather austere, of rigid probity, a sternly just and upright man, albeit he attended no church and never spoke of religious matters, and had no part nor lot in the pious joys of his Presbyterian family, nor ever seemed to suffer from this deprivation. He laid his hand upon me in punishment only twice in his life, and then not heavily; once for telling him a lie—which surprised me, and showed me how unsuspicious he was, for that was not my maiden effort. He punished me those two times only, and never any other member of the family at all; yet every now and then he cuffed our harmless slave-boy, Lewis, for trifling little blunders and awkwardnesses. My father had passed his life among the slaves from his cradle up, and his cuffings proceeded from the custom of the time, not from his nature. When I was ten years old I saw a man fling a lump of iron-ore at a slave-man in anger, for merely doing something awkwardly—as if that were a crime. It bounded from the man's skull, and the man fell and never spoke again. He was dead in an hour. I knew the man had a right to kill his slave if he wanted to, and yet it seemed a pitiful thing and somehow wrong, though why wrong I was not deep enough to explain if I had been asked to do it. Nobody in the village approved of that murder, but of course no one said much about it.

THE BOERS AND THE BLACKS,
THE BRITISH AND THE BLACKS*

I have been under the impression all along that I had an unpleasant paragraph about the Boers somewhere in my note-book, and also a pleasant one. I have found them now. The unpleasant one is dated at an interior village, and says:

Mr. Z called. He is an English Afrikander; is an old resident, and has a Boer wife. He speaks the language, and his professional business is with the Boers exclusively. He told me that the ancient Boer families in the great region of which this village is the commercial center are falling victims to their inherited indolence and dullness in the materialistic latter-day race and struggle, and are dropping one by one into the grip of the usurer—getting hopelessly in debt—and are losing their high place and retiring to second and lower. The Boer's farm does not go to another Boer when he loses it, but to a foreigner. Some have fallen so low that they sell their daughters to the blacks.

Under date of another South African town I find the note which is creditable to the Boers:

* *Following the Equator.*

Dr. X told me that in the Kafir war fifteen hundred Kafirs took refuge in a great cave in the mountains about ninety miles north of Johannesburg, and the Boers blocked up the entrance and smoked them to death. Dr. X has been in there and seen the great array of bleached skeletons—one a woman with the skeleton of a child hugged to her breast.

The great bulk of the savages must go. The white man wants their lands, and all must go excepting such percentage of them as he will need to do his work for him upon terms to be determined by himself. Since history has removed the element of guesswork from this matter and made it certainty, the humanest way of diminishing the black population should be adopted, not the old cruel ways of the past. Mr. Rhodes and his gang have been following the old ways. They are chartered to rob and slay, and they lawfully do it, but not in a compassionate and Christian spirit. They rob the Mashonas and the Matabeles of a portion of their territories in the hallowed old style of "purchase" for a song, and then they force a quarrel and take the rest by the strong hand. They rob the natives of their cattle under the pretext that all the cattle in the country belonged to the king whom they have tricked and assassinated. They issue "regulations" requiring the incensed and harassed natives to work for the white settlers, and neglect their own affairs to do it. This is slavery, and is several times worse than was the American slavery which used to pain England so much; for when this Rhodesian slave is sick, superannuated, or otherwise disabled, he must support himself or starve—his master is under no obligation to support him.

The reduction of the population by Rhodesian methods to the desired limit is a return to the old-time slow-misery and lingering-death system of a discredited time and a crude "civilization." We humanely reduce an overplus of dogs by swift chloroform; the Boer humanely reduced an overplus of blacks by swift suffocation; the nameless but right-hearted Australian pioneer humanely reduced his overplus of aboriginal neighbors by a sweetened swift death concealed in a poisoned pudding. All these are admirable, and worthy of praise; you and I would rather suffer either of these deaths thirty times over in thirty successive days than linger out one of the Rhodesian twenty-year deaths, with its daily burden of insult, humiliation, and forced labor for a man whose entire race the victim hates. Rhodesia is a happy name for that land of piracy and pillage, and puts the right stain upon it.

THE BOERS AND THE BLACKS IN SOUTH AFRICA*

I had been a gold-miner myself, in my day, and knew substantially everything that those people knew about it, except how to make money at it. But I learned a good deal about the Boers there, and that was a fresh subject. What I heard there was afterward repeated to me in other parts of South Africa. Summed up—according to the information thus gained—this is the Boer:

He is deeply religious, profoundly ignorant, dull, obstinate, bigoted, uncleanly in his habits, hospitable, honest in his dealings with the whites, a hard master to his black servant, lazy, a good shot, good horseman, addicted to the chase, a lover of political independence, a good husband and father, not fond of herding together in towns, but liking the seclusion and remoteness and solitude and empty vastness and silence of the veldt; a man of a mighty appetite, and not delicate about what he appeases it with—well satisfied with pork and Indian corn and biltong, requiring only that the quantity shall not be stinted; willing to ride a long journey to take a hand in a rude all-night dance interspersed with vigorous feeding and boisterous jollity, but ready to ride twice as far for a prayer-meeting; proud of his Dutch and Huguenot origin and its religious and military history; proud of his race's achievements in South Africa, its bold plunges into hostile and uncharted deserts in search of free solitudes unvexed by the pestering and detested English, also its victories over the natives and the British; proudest of all, of the direct and effusive personal interest which the Deity has always taken in its affairs. He cannot read, he cannot write; he has one or two newspapers, but he is apparently not aware of it; until latterly he had no schools, and taught his children nothing; news is a term which has no meaning to him, and the thing itself he cares

* *Following the Equator.*

nothing about. He hates to be taxed and resents it. He has stood stock-still in South Africa for two centuries and a half, and would like to stand still till the end of time, for he has no sympathy with Uitlander notions of progress. He is hungry to be rich, for he is human; but his preference has been for riches in cattle, not in fine clothes and fine houses and gold and diamonds. The gold and the diamonds have brought the godless stranger within his gates, also contamination and broken repose, and he wishes that they had never been discovered.

RACE AND IMPERIALISM:

Mr. Cecil Rhodes*

Before the middle of July we reached Cape Town, and the end of our African journeyings. And well satisfied; for, towering above us was Table Mountain—a reminder that we had now seen each and all of the great features of South Africa except Mr. Cecil Rhodes. I realize that that is a large exception. I know quite well that whether Mr. Rhodes is the lofty and worshipful patriot and statesman that multitudes believe him to be, or Satan come again, as the rest of the world account him, he is still the most imposing figure in the British Empire outside of England. When he stands on the Cape of Good Hope, his shadow falls to the Zambesi. He is the only colonial in the British dominions whose goings and comings are chronicled and discussed under all the globe's meridians, and whose speeches, unclipped, are cabled from the ends of the earth; and he is the only unroyal outsider whose arrival in London can compete for attention with an eclipse.

That he is an extraordinary man, and not an accident of fortune, not even his dearest South African enemies were willing to deny, so far as I heard them testify. The whole South African world seemed to stand in a kind of shuddering awe of him, friend and enemy alike. It was as if he were deputy God on the one side, deputy Satan on the other, pro-prietor of the people, able to make them or ruin them by his breath,

* *Following the Equator.*

worshiped by many, hated by many, but blasphemed by none among the judicious, and even by the indiscreet in guarded whispers only.

What is the secret of his formidable supremacy? One says it is his prodigious wealth—a wealth whose drippings in salaries and in other ways support multitudes and make them his interested and loyal vassals; another says it is his personal magnetism and his persuasive tongue, and that these hypnotize and make happy slaves of all that drift within the circle of their influence; another says it is his majestic ideas, his vast schemes for the territorial aggrandizement of England, his patriotic and unselfish ambition to spread her beneficent protection and her just rule over the pagan wastes of Africa and make luminous the African darkness with the glory of her name; and another says he wants the earth and wants it for his own, and that the belief that he will get it and let his friends in on the ground floor is *the* secret that rivets so many eyes upon him and keeps him in the zenith where the view is unobstructed.

One may take his choice. They are all the same price. One fact is sure: he keeps his prominence and a vast following, no matter what he does. He "deceives" the Duke of Fife—it is the Duke's word—but that does not destroy the Duke's loyalty to him. He tricks the Reformers into immense trouble with his Raid, but the most of them believe he meant well. He weeps over the harshly taxed Johannesburgers and makes them his friends; at the same time he taxes his Charter settlers fifty per cent., and so wins their affection and their confidence that they are squelched with despair at every rumor that the Charter is to be annulled. He raids and robs and slays and enslaves the Matabele and gets worlds of Charter-Christian applause for it. He has beguiled England into buying Charter waste-paper for Bank of England notes, ton for ton, and the ravished still burn incense to him as the Eventual God of Plenty. He has done everything he could think of to pull himself down to the ground; he has done more than enough to pull sixteen common-run great men down; yet there he stands, to this day, upon his dizzy summit under the dome of the sky, an apparent permanency, the marvel of the time, the mystery of the age, an Archangel with wings to half the world, Satan with a tail to the other half.

I admire him, I frankly confess it; and when his time comes I shall buy a piece of the rope for a keepsake.

BLACK SAVAGES AND WHITE SAVAGES
IN SOUTH AFRICA*

The black savage whom the Boer has driven out was brimming over with good nature and comradeship and friendliness, and he was the cheeriest soul, and had the easiest life in the world; and it was always on tap and ready. He went naked; he was dirty; he housed himself like a cow; he was indolent; he worshipped a fetich; he was a savage, and all his customs were savage; but he had a sunny spirit, and at bottom a good disposition.

He was replaced by the Boer, a white savage, who is dirty; houses himself like a cow; is indolent; worships a fetich; is grim, serious, solemn, and is always diligently fitting himself for heaven, probably suspecting that they couldn't stand him in the other place.

THE MOTLEY POPULATION OF
THE CHRISTIAN HEAVEN†

All of a sudden the whole region fairly rocked under the crash of eleven hundred and one thunder blasts, all let off at once, and Sandy says—

"There, that's for the barkeep."

I jumped up and says,—

"Then let's be moving along, Sandy; we don't want to miss any of this thing, you know."

---

* A. B. Paine, editor, *Mark Twain's Notebook* (Copyright 1935 by The Mark Twain Company, Harper and Brothers: New York, 1935).

† "Captain Stormfield's Visit to Heaven" in *The Mysterious Stranger, and Other Tales* (Copyright 1922 by The Mark Twain Company. Harper and Brothers: New York, 1922). Reprinted from Harper's Magazine, 1907–08.

"Keep your seat," he says; "he is only just telegraphed, that is all."

"How?"

"That blast only means that he has been sighted from the signal-station. He is off Sandy Hook. The committees will go down to meet him, now, and escort him in. There will be ceremonies and delays; they won't be coming up the Bay for a considerable time, yet. It is several billion miles away, anyway."

"*I* could have been a barkeeper and a hard lot just as well as not," says I, remembering the lonesome way I arrived, and how there wasn't any committee nor anything.

"I notice some regret in your voice," says Sandy, "and it is natural enough; but let bygones be bygones; you went according to your lights, and it is too late now to mend the thing."

"No, let it slide, Sandy, I don't mind. But you've got a Sandy Hook here, too, have you?"

"We've got everything here, just as it is below. All the States and Territories of the Union, and all the kingdoms of the earth and the islands of the sea are laid out here just as they are on the globe—all the same shape they are down there, and all graded to the relative size, only each State and realm and island is a good many billion times bigger here than it is below. There goes another blast."

"What is that one for?"

"That is only another fort answering the first one. They each fire eleven hundred and one thunder blasts at a single dash—it is the usual salute for an eleventh-hour guest; a hundred for each hour and an extra one for the guest's sex; if it was a woman we would know it by their leaving off the extra gun."

"How do we know there's eleven hundred and one, Sandy, when they all go off at once?—and yet we certainly do know."

"Our intellects are a good deal sharpened up, here, in some ways, and that is one of them. Numbers and sizes and distances are so great, here, that we have to be made so we can *feel* them—our old ways of counting and measuring and ciphering wouldn't ever give us an idea of them, but would only confuse us and oppress us and make our heads ache."

After some more talk about this, I says: "Sandy, I notice that I hardly ever see a white angel; where I run across one white angel, I strike as many as a hundred million copper-colored ones—people that can't speak English. How is that?"

"Well, you will find it the same in any State or Territory of the American corner of heaven you choose to go to. I have shot along, a whole week on a stretch, and gone millions and millions of miles, through perfect swarms of angels, without ever seeing a single white one, or hearing a word I could understand. You see, America was occupied a billion years and more, by Injuns and Aztecs, and that sort of folks, before a white man ever set his foot in it. During the first three hundred years after Columbus's discovery, there wasn't ever more than one good lecture audience of white people, all put together, in America —I mean the whole thing, British Possessions and all; in the beginning of our century there were only 6,000,000 or 7,000,000—say seven; 12,000,000 or 14,000,000 in 1825; say 23,000,000 in 1850; 40,000,-000 in 1875. Our death-rate has always been 20 in 1000 per annum. Well, 140,000 died the first year of the century; 280,000 the twenty-fifth year; 500,000 the fiftieth year; about a million the seventy-fifth year. Now I am going to be liberal about this thing, and consider that fifty million whites have died in America from the beginning up to to-day—make it sixty, if you want to; make it a hundred million—it's no difference about a few millions one way or t'other. Well, now, you can see, yourself, that when you come to spread a little dab of people like that over these hundreds of billions of miles of American territory here in heaven, it is like scattering a ten-cent box of homœpathic pills over the Great Sahara and expecting to find them again. You can't expect us to amount to anything in heaven, and we *don't*—now that is the simple fact, and we have got to do the best we can with it. The learned men from other planets and other systems come here and hang around a while, when they are touring around the Kingdom, and then go back to their own section of heaven and write a book of travels, and they give America about five lines in it. And what do they say about us? They say this wilderness is populated with a scattering few hundred thousand billions of red angels, with now and then a curiously complected *diseased* one. You see, they think we whites and the occasional nigger are Injuns that have been bleached out or blackened by some leprous disease or other—for some peculiarly rascally *sin*, mind you. It is a mighty sour pill for us all, my friend—even the modestest of us, let alone the other kind, that think they are going to be received like a long-lost government bond, and hug Abraham into the bargain. I haven't asked you any of the particulars, Captain, but I judge it goes without saying—if my experience is worth anything—that there wasn't much of a hooraw made over you when you arrived—now was there?"

"Don't mention it, Sandy," says I, coloring up a little; "I wouldn't have had the family see it for any amount you are a mind to name. Change the subject, Sandy, change the subject."

"Well, do you think of settling in the California department of bliss?"

"I don't know. I wasn't calculating on doing anything really definite in that direction till the family come. I thought I would just look around, meantime, in a quiet way, and make up my mind. Besides, I know a good many dead people, and I was calculating to hunt them up and swap a little gossip with them about friends, and old times, and one thing or another, and ask them how they like it here, as far as they have got. I reckon my wife will want to camp in the California range, though, because most all her departed will be there, and she likes to be with folks she knows."

"Don't you let her. You see what the Jersey district of heaven is, for whites; well, the California district is a thousand times worse. It swarms with a mean kind of leather-headed mud-colored angels—and your nearest white neighbors is likely to be a million miles away. *What a man mostly misses, in heaven, is company*—company of his own sort and color and language. I have come near settling in the European part of heaven once or twice on that account."

"Well, why didn't you, Sandy?"

"Oh, various reasons. For one thing, although you *see* plenty of whites there, you can't understand any of them hardly, and so you go about as hungry for talk as you do here. I like to look at a Russian or a German or an Italian—I even like to look at a Frenchman if I ever have the luck to catch him engaged in anything that ain't indelicate—but *looking* don't cure the hunger—what you want is talk."

"Well, there's England, Sandy—the English district of heaven."

"Yes, but it is not so very much better than this end of the heavenly domain. As long as you run across Englishmen born this side of three hundred years ago, you are all right; but the minute you get back of Elizabeth's time the language begins to fog up, and the further back you go the foggier it gets. I had some talk with one Langland and a man by the name of Chaucer—old-time poets—but it was no use, I couldn't quite understand them and they couldn't quite understand me. I have had letters from them since, but it is such broken English I can't make it out. Back of those men's time the English are just simply foreigners, nothing more, nothing less; they talk Danish, German, Norman French, and sometimes a mixture of all three; back of *them*, they talk Latin, and ancient British, Irish, and Gaelic; and then back of these come billions and billions of pure savages that talk a gibberish that Satan himself couldn't understand. The fact is, where you strike one man in the English settlements that you can understand, you wade through awful swarms that talk something you can't make head nor tail of. You see, every country on earth has been overlaid so often, in the course of a billion years, with different kinds of people and different sorts of languages, that this sort of mongrel business was bound to be the result in heaven."

"Sandy," says I, "did you see a good many of the great people history tells about?"

"Yes—plenty. I saw kings and all sorts of distinguished people."

"Do the kings rank just as they did below?"

"No; a body can't bring his rank up here with him. Divine right is a good-enough earthly romance, but it don't go, here. Kings drop down to the general level as soon as they reach the realms of grace. I knew Charles the Second very well—one of the most popular comedians in the English section—draws first rate. There are better, of course—people that were never heard of on earth—but Charles is making a very good reputation indeed, and is considered a rising man. Richard the Lion-hearted is in the prize-ring, and coming into considerable favor. Henry the Eighth is a tragedian, and the scenes where he kills people are done to the very life. Henry the Sixth keeps a religious-book stand."

"Did you ever see Napoleon, Sandy?"

"Often—sometimes in the Corsican range, sometimes in the French. He always hunts up a conspicuous place, and goes frowning around with his arms folded and his field-glass under his arm, looking as grand, gloomy and peculiar as his reputation calls for, and very much bothered because he don't stand as high, here, for a soldier, as he expected to."

"Why, who stands higher?"

"Oh, a *lot* of people *we* never heard of before—the shoemaker and horse-doctor and knife-grinder kind, you know—clodhoppers from goodness knows where, that never handled a sword or fired a shot in their lives—but the soldiership was in them, though they never had a chance to show it. But here they take their right place, and Cæsar and Napoleon and Alexander have to take a back seat. The greatest military genius our world ever produced was a brick-layer from somewhere back of Boston—died during the Revolution—by the name of Absalom Jones. Wherever he goes, crowds flock to see him. You see, everybody knows that if he had had a chance he would have shown the world some generalship that would have made all generalship before look like child's play and 'prentice work. But he never got a chance; he tried heaps of times to enlist as a private, but he had lost both thumbs and a couple of front teeth, and the recruiting sergeant wouldn't pass him. However, as I say, everybody knows, now, what he *would* have been, and so they flock by the million to get a glimpse of him whenever they hear he is going to be anywhere. Cæsar, and Hannibal, and Alexander, and Napoleon are all on his staff, and ever so many more great generals; but the public hardly care to look at *them* when *he* is around. Boom! There goes another salute. The barkeeper's off quarantine now."

THANKSGIVING DAY AND THE INDIANS*

Thanksgiving Day originated in New England when the Puritans realized they had succeeded in exterminating their neighbors, the Indians, instead of getting exterminated by their neighbors, the Indians. Thanksgiving Day became a habit, for the reason that in the course of time, as the years drifted on, it was perceived that exterminating had ceased to be mutual and was all on the white man's side, consequently on the Lord's side; hence it was proper to thank the Lord for it and extend the usual annual compliments. . . . The original reason for Thanksgiving Day has long ceased to exist, since the Indians have long ago been comprehensively and satisfactorily exter-

* *Autobiography.*

minated and the account closed with the Lord, with the thanks due. But still the habit persists as a national holiday, and every year the American presidents and state governors set themselves the task to hunt up something to be thankful for, and then they put these thanks into a few crisp and reverent phrases, in the form of a proclamation, and this read from all the pulpits in the land, the national conscience is wiped clean with one swipe, and sin is resumed at the old stand.

EDITORIAL IN BUFFALO EXPRESS, AUGUST, 1869, ABOUT THE FACT THAT A SOUTHERN NEGRO WAS DISCOVERED TO BE INNOCENT OF A RAPE FOR WHICH HE HAD BEEN LYNCHED*

Ah, well! Too bad, to be sure! A little blunder in the administration of justice by Southern mob-law; but nothing to speak of. Only "a nigger" killed by mistake—that is all. Of course, every high-toned gentleman whose chivalric impulses were so unfortunately misled in this affair . . . is as sorry about it as a high-toned gentleman can be expected to be sorry about the unlucky fate of "a nigger." But mistakes will happen, even in the conduct of the best regulated and most high-toned mobs, and surely there is no good reason why Southern gentlemen should worry themselves with useless regrets, so long as only an innocent "nigger" is hanged, or roasted or knouted to death, now and then. What if the blunder of lynching the wrong man does happen once in four or five cases? Is that any fair argument against the cultivation and indulgence of those fine chivalric passions and that noble Southern spirit which will not brook the slow and cold formalities of regular law, when outraged white womanhood appeals for vengeance? Perish the thought so unworthy of a Southern soul! Leave it to the sentimentalism and humanitarianism of a cold-blooded Yankee civilization! What are the lives of a few "niggers" in comparison of the impetuous instincts of a proud and fiery race? Keep ready the halter, therefore, oh chivalry of

* *Mark Twain: Social Critic.*

Memphis! Keep the lash knotted; keep the brand and the faggots in waiting, for prompt work with the next "nigger" who may be suspected of any damnable crime! Wreak a swift vengeance upon him, for the satisfaction of the noble impulses that animate knightly hearts, and then leave time and accident to discover, if they will, whether he was guilty or no.

PERSECUTION OF THE CHINESE IN CALIFORNIA AND PASSAGE OF THE BURLINGAME TREATY TO PROTECT THEIR RIGHTS

New York Tribune, 1868*

They can never beat and bang and set the dogs on the Chinamen any more. These pastimes are lost to them forever. In San Francisco, a large part of the most interesting local news in the daily papers consists of gorgeous compliments to the 'able and efficient' Officer This and That for arresting Ah Foo, or Ching Wang, or Song Hi for stealing a chicken; but when some white brute breaks an unoffending China-man's head with a brick, the paper does not compliment any officer for arresting the assaulter, for the simple reason that the officer does not make the arrest; the shedding of Chinese blood only makes him laugh; he considers it fun of the most entertaining description. I have seen dogs almost tear helpless Chinamen to pieces in broad daylight in San Francisco, and I have seen hod-carriers who help to make Presidents stand around and enjoy the sport. I have seen troops of boys assault a Chinaman with stones when he was walking quietly along about his business, and send him bruised and bleeding home. I have seen China-men abused and maltreated in all the mean, cowardly ways possible to the invention of a degraded nature, but I never saw a Chinaman righted in a court of justice for wrongs thus done him. The California laws do not allow Chinamen to testify against white men. California is

* *Mark Twain: Social Critic.*

one of the most liberal and progressive States in the Union, and the best and worthiest of her citizens will be glad to know that the days of persecuting Chinamen are over, in California.

ANNEX THE HAWAIIAN ISLES!

New York Tribune, *1873**

We *must* annex those people. We can afflict them with our wise and beneficent government. We can introduce the novelty of thieves, all the way up from streetcar pick-pockets to municipal robbers and Government defaulters and show them how amusing it is to arrest them and try them and turn them loose—some for cash, and some for "political influence." We can make them ashamed of their simple and primitive justice . . . We can give them juries composed of the most simple and charming leather-heads. We can give them railway corporations who will buy their Legislatures like old clothes, and run over their best citizens. We can furnish them some Jay Goulds who will do away their old-time notions that stealing is not respectable . . . We can give them lecturers! I will go myself.

We can make that bunch of sleepy islands the hottest corner on earth, and array it in the moral splendor of our high and holy civilization. Annexation is what the poor islanders need. "Shall we to men benighted the lamp of life deny?"

* Reprinted in *Mark Twain on the Damned Human Race.*

PART TWO

Religion

CHRISTIANITY AND IMPERIALISM:

Greeting to the Twentieth Century, New York Herald, December 30, 1900*

A salutation-speech from the Nineteenth Century to the Twentieth, taken down in short-hand by Mark Twain:

"I bring you the stately matron named Christendom, returning bedraggled, besmirched, and dishonored from pirate-raids in Kiao-Chou, Manchuria, South Africa & the Philippines, with her soul full of meanness, her pocket full of boodle and her mouth full of pious hypocrisies. Give her soap and a towel, but hide the looking-glass."

THE WAR PRAYER†

It was a time of great and exalting excitement. The country was up in arms, the war was on, in every breast burned the holy fire of patriotism; the drums were beating, the bands playing, the toy pistols popping, the bunched firecrackers hissing and spluttering; on every hand and far down the receding and fading spread of roofs and balconies a fluttering wilderness of flags flashed in the sun; daily the young volunteers marched down the wide avenue gay and fine in their new uniforms, the proud fathers and mothers and sisters and sweet-

---

* *Mark Twain: Social Critic.*

† *Europe and Elsewhere.* (Dictated 1904–05). This was perhaps the single most famous and widely quoted of Twain's polemical pieces during the Vietnam War student protests of the nineteen-sixties, and was reprinted as a special volume with handsome illustrations. *Ed.*

hearts cheering them with voices choked with happy emotion as they swung by; nightly the packed mass meetings listened, panting, to patriot oratory which stirred the deepest deeps of their hearts, and which they interrupted at briefest intervals with cyclones of applause, the tears running down their cheeks the while; in the churches the pastors preached devotion to flag and country, and invoked the God of Battles, beseeching His aid in our good cause in outpourings of fervid eloquence which moved every listener. It was indeed a glad and gracious time, and the half dozen rash spirits that ventured to disapprove of the war and cast a doubt upon its righteousness straightway got such a stern and angry warning that for their personal safety's sake they quickly shrank out of sight and offended no more in that way.

Sunday morning came—next day the battalions would leave for the front; the church was filled; the volunteers were there, their young faces alight with martial dreams—visions of the stern advance, the gathering momentum, the rushing charge, the flashing sabers, the flight of the foe, the tumult, the enveloping smoke, the fierce pursuit, the surrender!—then home from the war, bronzed heroes, welcomed, adored, submerged in golden seas of glory! With the volunteers sat their dear ones, proud, happy, and envied by the neighbors and friends who had no sons and brothers to send forth to the field of honor, there to win for the flag, or, failing, die the noblest of noble deaths. The service proceeded; a war chapter from the Old Testament was read; the first prayer was said; it was followed by an organ burst that shook the building, and with one impulse the house rose, with glowing eyes and beating hearts, and poured out that tremendous invocation—

> "God the all-terrible! Thou who ordainest,
> Thunder thy clarion and lightning thy sword!"

Then came the "long" prayer. None could remember the like of it for passionate pleading and moving and beautiful language. The burden of its supplication was, that an ever-merciful and benignant Father of us all would watch over our noble young soldiers, and aid, comfort, and encourage them in their patriotic work; bless them, shield them in the day of battle and the hour of peril, bear them in His mighty hand, make them strong and confident, invincible in the bloody onset; help them to crush the foe, grant to them and to their flag and country imperishable honor and glory—

An aged stranger entered and moved with slow and noiseless step up the main aisle, his eyes fixed upon the minister, his long body clothed in a robe that reached to his feet, his head bare, his white hair descending in a frothy cataract to his shoulders, his seamy face unnaturally pale, pale even to ghastliness. With all eyes following him and wondering, he made his silent way; without pausing, he ascended to the preacher's side and stood there, waiting. With shut lids the preacher, unconscious of his presence, continued his moving prayer, and at last finished it with the words, uttered in fervent appeal, "Bless our arms, grant us the victory, O Lord our God, Father and Protector of our land and flag!"

The stranger touched his arm, motioned him to step aside—which the startled minister did—and took his place. During some moments he surveyed the spellbound audience with solemn eyes, in which burned an uncanny light; then in a deep voice he said:

"I come from the Throne—bearing a message from Almighty God!" The words smote the house with a shock; if the stranger perceived it he gave no attention. 'He has heard the prayer of His servant your shepherd, and will grant it if such shall be your desire after I, His messenger, shall have explained to you its import—that is to say, its full import. For it is like unto many of the prayers of men, in that it asks for more than he who utters it is aware of—except he pause and think.

"God's servant and yours has prayed his prayer. Has he paused and taken thought? Is it one prayer? No, it is two—one uttered, the other not. Both have reached the ear of Him Who heareth all supplications, the spoken and the unspoken. Ponder this—keep it in mind. If you would beseech a blessing upon yourself, beware! lest without intent you invoke a curse upon a neighbor at the same time. If you pray for the blessing of rain upon your crop which needs it, by that act you are possibly praying for a curse upon some neighbor's crop which may not need rain and can be injured by it.

"You have heard your servant's prayer—the uttered part of it. I am commissioned of God to put into words the other part of it—that part which the pastor—and also you in your hearts—fervently prayed silently. And ignorantly and unthinkingly? God grant that it was so! You heard these words: 'Grant us the victory, O Lord our God!' That is sufficient. The *whole* of the uttered prayer is compact into those pregnant words. Elaborations were not necessary. When you have prayed for victory, you have prayed for many unmentioned results which follow victory—*must* follow it, cannot help but follow it. Upon the listening spirit of God the Father fell also the unspoken part of the prayer. He commandeth me to put it into words. Listen!

"O Lord our Father, our young patriots, idols of our hearts, go forth to battle—be Thou near them! With them—in spirit—we also go forth from the sweet peace of our beloved firesides to smite the foe. O Lord our God, help us to tear their soldiers to bloody shreds with our shells; help us to cover their smiling fields with the pale forms of their patriot dead; help us to drown the thunder of the guns with the shrieks of their wounded, writhing in pain; help us to lay waste their humble homes with a hurricane of fire; help us to wring the hearts of their unoffending widows with unavailing grief; help us to turn them out roofless with their little children to wander unfriended the wastes of their desolated land in rags and hunger and thirst, sports of the sun flames of summer and the icy winds of winter, broken in spirit, worn with travail, imploring Thee for the refuge of the grave and denied it—for our sakes who adore Thee, Lord, blast their hopes, blight their lives, protract their bitter pilgrimage, make heavy their steps, water their way with their tears, stain the white snow with the blood of their wounded feet! We ask it, in the spirit of love, of Him Who is the Source of Love, and Who is the ever-faithful refuge and friend of all that are sore beset and seek His aid with humble and contrite hearts. Amen."

(*After a pause.*) "Ye have prayed it; if ye still desire it, speak! The messenger of the Most High waits."

It was believed afterward that the man was a lunatic, because there was no sense in what he said.

BIBLE TEACHING AND RELIGIOUS PRACTICE*

Religion had its share in the changes of civilization and national character, of course. What share? The lion's. In the history of the human race this has always been the case, will always be the case, to

* *Europe and Elsewhere.*

the end of time, no doubt; or at least until man by the slow processes of evolution shall develop into something really fine and high—some billions of years hence, say.

The Christian's Bible is a drug store. Its contents remain the same; but the medical practice changes. For eighteen hundred years these changes were slight—scarcely noticeable. The practice was allopathic —allopathic in its rudest and crudest form. The dull and ignorant physician day and night, and all the days and all the nights, drenched his patient with vast and hideous doses of the most repulsive drugs to be found in the store's stock; he bled him, cupped him, purged him, puked him, salivated him, never gave his system a chance to rally, nor nature a chance to help. He kept him religion sick for eighteen centuries, and allowed him not a well day during all that time. The stock in the store was made up of about equal portions of baleful and debilitating poisons, and healing and comforting medicines; but the practice of the time confined the physician to the use of the former; by consequence, he could only damage his patient, and that is what he did.

Not until far within our century was any considerable change in the practice introduced; and then mainly, or in effect only, in Great Britain and the United States. In the other countries to-day, the patient either still takes the ancient treatment or does not call the physician at all. In the English-speaking countries the changes observable in our century were forced by that very thing just referred to—the revolt of the patient against the system; they were not projected by the physician. The patient fell to doctoring himself, and the physician's practice began to fall off. He modified his method to get back his trade. He did it gradually, reluctantly; and never yielded more at a time than the pressure compelled. At first he relinquished the daily dose of hell and damnation, and administered it every other day only; next he allowed another day to pass; then another and presently another; when he had restricted it at last to Sundays, and imagined that now there would surely be a truce, the homœpath arrived on the field and made him abandon hell and damnation altogether, and administered Christ's love, and comfort, and charity and compassion in its stead. These had been in the drug store all the time, gold labeled and conspicuous among the long shelfloads of repulsive purges and vomits and poisons, and so the practice was to blame that they had remained unused, not the pharmacy. To the ecclesiastical physician of fifty years ago, his predecessor for eighteen centuries was a quack; to the ecclesiastical physician of to-day, his predecessor of fifty years ago was a quack. To the every-man-his-own-ecclesiastical-doctor of—when?—what will the ecclesiastical physician of to-day be? Unless evolution, which has been a truth ever since the globes, suns, and planets of the solar system were but wandering films of meteor dust, shall reach a limit and become a lie, there is but one fate in store for him.

The methods of the priest and the parson have been very curious, their history is very entertaining. In all the ages the Roman Church has owned slaves, bought and sold slaves, authorized and encouraged her children to trade in them. Long after some Christian peoples had freed their slaves the Church still held on to hers. If any could know, to absolute certainty, that all this was right, and according to God's will and desire, surely it was she, since she was God's specially appointed representative in the earth and sole authorized and infallible expounder of his Bible. There were the texts; there was no mistaking their meaning; she was right, she was doing in this thing what the Bible had mapped out for her to do. So unassailable was her position that in all the centuries she had no word to say against human slavery. Yet now at last, in our immediate day, we hear a Pope saying slave trading is wrong, and we see him sending an expedition to Africa to stop it. The texts remain: it is the practice that has changed. Why? Because the world has corrected the Bible. The Church never corrects it; and also never fails to drop in at the tail of the procession—and take the credit of the correction. As she will presently do in this instance.

Christian England supported slavery and encouraged it for two hundred and fifty years, and her Church's consecrated ministers looked on, sometimes taking an active hand, the rest of the time indifferent. England's interest in the business may be called a Christian interest, a Christian industry. She had her full share in its revival after a long period of inactivity, and this revival was a Christian monopoly; that is to say, it was in the hands of Christian countries exclusively. English parliaments aided the slave traffic and protected it; two English kings held stock in slave-catching companies. The first regular English slave hunter—John Hawkins, of still revered memory—made such successful havoc, on his second voyage, in the matter of surprising and burning villages, and maiming, slaughtering, capturing, and selling their un-offending inhabitants, that his delighted queen conferred the chivalric honor of knighthood on him—a rank which had acquired its chief esteem and distinction in other and earlier fields of Christian effort. The new knight, with characteristic English frankness and brusque simplicity, chose as his device the figure of a negro slave, kneeling and in chains. Sir John's work was the invention of Christians, was to remain a bloody and awful monopoly in the hands of Christians for a quarter of a millennium, was to destroy homes, separate families, enslave friendless men and women, and break a myriad of human hearts, to the end that Christian nations might be prosperous and comfortable, Christian churches be built, and the gospel of the meek and merciful Redeemer be spread abroad in the earth; and so in the name of his ship, unsuspected but eloquent and clear, lay hidden prophecy. She was called *The Jesus.*

But at last in England, an illegitimate Christian rose against slavery. It is curious that when a Christian rises against a rooted wrong at all, he is usually an illegitimate Christian, member of some despised and bastard sect. There was a bitter struggle, but in the end the slave trade had to go—and went. The Biblical authorization remained, but the practice changed.

Then—the usual thing happened; the visiting English critic among us began straightway to hold up his pious hands in horror at our slavery. His distress was unappeasable, his word full of bitterness and contempt. It is true we had not so many as fifteen hundred thousand slaves for him to worry about, while his England still owned twelve millions, in her foreign possessions; but that fact did not modify his wail any, or stay his tears, or soften his censure. The fact that every time we had tried to get rid of our slavery in previous generations, but had always been obstructed, balked, and defeated by England, was a matter of no consequence to him; it was ancient history, and not worth the telling.

Our own conversion came at last. We began to stir against slavery. Hearts grew soft, here, there, and yonder. There was no place in the land where the seeker could not find some small budding sign of pity for the slave. No place in all the land but one—the pulpit. It yielded at last; it always does. It fought a strong and stubborn fight, and then did what it always does, joined the procession—at the tail end. Slavery fell. The slavery text remained; the practice changed, that was all.

During many ages there were witches. The Bible said so. The Bible commanded that they should not be allowed to live. Therefore the Church, after doing its duty in but a lazy and indolent way for eight hundred years, gathered up its halters, thumbscrews, and firebrands, and set about its holy work in earnest. She worked hard at it night and day during nine centuries and imprisoned, tortured, hanged, and burned whole hordes and armies of witches, and washed the Christian world clean with their foul blood.

Then it was discovered that there was no such thing as witches, and never had been. One does not know whether to laugh or to cry. Who discovered that there was no such thing as a witch—the priest, the parson? No, these never discover anything. At Salem, the parson clung pathetically to his witch text after the laity had abandoned it in remorse and tears for the crimes and cruelties it has persuaded them to do. The parson wanted more blood, more shame, more brutalities; it was the unconsecrated laity that stayed his hand. In Scotland the parson killed the witch after the magistrate had pronounced her innocent; and when the merciful legislature proposed to sweep the hideous laws against witches from the statute book, it was the parson who came imploring, with tears and imprecations, that they be suffered to stand.

There are no witches. The witch text remains; only the practice has changed. Hell fire is gone, but the text remains. Infant damnation is gone, but the text remains. More than two hundred death penalties are gone from the law books, but the texts that authorized them remain.

Is it not well worthy of note that of all the multitude of texts through which man has driven his annihilating pen he has never once made the mistake of obliterating a good and useful one? It does certainly seem to suggest that if man continues in the direction of enlightenment, his religious practice may, in the end, attain some semblance of human decency.

PLYMOUTH ROCK AND THE PILGRIMS*

I rise to protest. I have kept still for years, but really I think there is no sufficient justification for this sort of thing. What do you want to

---

* Speech, 1881, to New England Society of Philadelphia. *Mark Twain's Speeches.* Copyright 1923 by Mark Twain Company (Harper and Brothers: New York).

celebrate those people for?—those ancestors of yours of 1620—the *Mayflower* tribe, I mean. What do you want to celebrate *them* for? Your pardon: the gentleman at my left assures me that you are not celebrating the Pilgrims themselves, but the landing of the Pilgrims at Plymouth Rock on the 22d of December. So you are celebrating their landing. Why, the other pretext was thin enough, but this is thinner than ever; the other was tissue, tinfoil, fish-bladder, but this is gold-leaf. Celebrating their landing! What was there remarkable about it, I would like to know? What can you be thinking of? Why, those Pilgrims had been at sea three or four months. It was the very middle of winter: it was as cold as death off Cape Cod there. Why shouldn't they come ashore? If they *hadn't* landed there would be some reason for celebrating the fact. It would have been a case of monumental leather-headedness which the world would not willingly let die. If it had been *you*, gentlemen, you probably wouldn't have landed, but you have no shadow of right to be celebrating, in your ancestors, gifts which they did not exercise, but only transmitted. Why, to be celebrating the mere landing of the Pilgrims—to be trying to make out that this most natural and simple and customary procedure was an extraordinary circumstance—a circumstance to be amazed at, and admired, aggrandized and glorified, at orgies like this for two hundred and sixty years—hang it, a horse would have known enough to land; a horse— Pardon again; the gentleman on my right assures me that it was not merely the landing of the Pilgrims that we are celebrating, but the Pilgrims themselves. So we have struck an inconsistency here—one says it was the landing, the other says it was the Pilgrims. It is an inconsistency characteristic of your intractable and disputatious tribe, for you never agree about anything but Boston. Well, then, what do you want to celebrate those Pilgrims for? They were a mighty hard lot—you know it. I grant you, without the slightest unwillingness, that they were a deal more gentle and merciful and just than were the people of Europe of that day; I grant you that they are better than their predecessors. But what of that?—that is nothing. People always progress. You are better than your fathers and grandfathers were (this is the first time I have ever aimed a measureless slander at the departed, for I consider such things improper). Yes, those among you who have not been in the penitentiary, if such there be, are better than your fathers and grandfathers were; but is that any sufficient reason for getting up annual dinners and celebrating you? No, by no means—by no means. Well, I repeat, those Pilgrims were a hard lot. They took good care of themselves, but they abolished everybody else's ancestors. I am a border-ruffian from the State of Missouri. I am a Connecticut Yankee by adoption. In me, you have Missouri morals, Connecticut culture; this, gentlemen, is the combination which makes the perfect man. But where are my ancestors? Whom shall I celebrate? Where shall I find the raw material?

My first American ancestor, gentlemen, was an Indian—an early Indian. Your ancestors skinned him alive, and I am an orphan. Later ancestors of mine were the Quakers William Robinson, Marmaduke Stevenson, *et al.* Your tribe chased them out of the country for their religion's sake; promised them death if they came back; for your ancestors had forsaken the homes they loved, and braved the perils of the sea, the implacable climate, and the savage wilderness, to acquire that highest and most precious of boons, freedom for every man on this broad continent to worship according to the dictates of his own conscience—and they were not going to allow a lot of pestiferous Quakers to interfere with it. Your ancestors broke forever the chains of political slavery, and gave the vote to every man in this wide land, excluding none!—none except those who did not belong to the orthodox church. Your ancestors—yes, they were a hard lot; but, nevertheless, they gave us religious liberty to worship as they required us to worship, and political liberty to vote as the church required; and so I the bereft one, I the forlorn one, am here to do my best to help you celebrate them right.

The Quaker woman Elizabeth Hooton was an ancestress of mine. Your people were pretty severe with her—you will confess that. But, poor thing! I believe they changed her opinions before she died, and took her into their fold; and so we have every reason to presume that when she died she went to the same place which your ancestors went to. It is a great pity, for she was a good woman. Roger Williams was an ancestor of mine. I don't really remember what your people did with him. But they banished him to Rhode Island, anyway. And then, I believe, recognizing that this was really carrying harshness to an unjustifiable extreme, they took pity on him and burned him. They were a hard lot! All those Salem witches were ancestors of mine! Your people made it tropical for them. Yes, they did; by pressure and the gallows they made such a clean deal with them that there hasn't been a witch and hardly a halter in our family from that day to this, and that is one hundred and eighty-nine years. The first slave brought into New England out of Africa by your progenitors was an ancestor of mine— for I am of a mixed breed, an infinitely shaded and exquisite Mongrel. I'm not one of your sham meerschaums that you can color in a week. No, my complexion is the patient art of eight generations. Well, in my own time, I had acquired a lot of my kin—by purchase, and swapping around, and one way and another—and was getting along very well. Then, with the inborn perversity of your lineage, you got up a war, and took them all away from me. And so, again am I bereft, again am I forlorn; no drop of my blood flows in the veins of any living being who is marketable.

O my friends, hear me and reform! I seek your good, not mine. You have heard the speeches. Disband these New England societies—nurseries of a system of steadily augmenting laudation and hosannaing, which, if persisted in uncurbed, may some day in the remote future beguile you into prevaricating and bragging. Oh, stop, stop, while you are still temperate in your appreciation of your ancestors! Hear me, I beseech you; get up an auction and sell Plymouth Rock! The Pilgrims were a simple and ignorant race. They never had seen any good rocks before, or at least any that were not watched, and so they were excusable for hopping ashore in frantic delight and clapping an iron fence around this one. But you, gentlemen, are educated; you are enlightened; you know that in the rich land of your nativity, opulent New England, overflowing with rocks, this one isn't worth, at the outside, more than thirty-five cents. Therefore, sell it, before it is injured by exposure, or at least throw it open to the patent-medicine advertisements, and let it earn its taxes.

Yes, hear your true friend—your only true friend—list to his voice. Disband these societies, hot beds of vice, of moral decay—perpetuators of ancestral superstition. Here on this board I see water, I see milk, I see the wild and deadly lemonade. These are but steps upon the downward path. Next we shall see tea, then chocolate, then coffee— hotel coffee. A few more years—all too few, I fear—mark my words, we shall have cider! Gentlemen, pause ere it be too late. You are on the broad road which leads to dissipation, physical ruin, moral decay, gory crime, and the gallows! I beseech you, I implore you, in the name of your anxious friends, in the name of your impending widows and orphans, stop ere it be too late. Disband these New England societies, renounce these soul-blistering saturnalia, cease from varnishing the rusty reputations of your long-vanished ancestors—the super-high-moral old iron-clads of Cape Cod, the pious buccaneers of Plymouth Rock—go home, and try to learn to behave!

PATRIOTISM AND CHRISTIANITY*

A man can be a Christian *or* a patriot, but he can't legally be a Christian *and* a patriot—except in the usual way: one of the two with the mouth, the other with the heart. The spirit of Christianity proclaims the brotherhood of the race and the meaning of that strong word has not been left to guesswork, but made tremendously definite—the Christian must forgive his brother man all crimes he can imagine and commit, and all insults he can conceive and utter—forgive these injuries how many times?—seventy times seven—another way of saying there shall be no limit to this forgiveness. That is the spirit and the law of Christianity. Well—patriotism has *its* law. And it also is a perfectly definite one, there are no vaguenesses about it. It commands that the brother over the border shall be sharply watched and brought to book every time he does us a hurt or offends us with an insult. Word it as softly as you please, the spirit of patriotism is the spirit of the dog and the wolf. The moment there is a misunderstanding about a boundary line or a hamper of fish or some other squalid matter, see patriotism rise, and hear him split the universe with his war-whoop. The spirit of patriotism being in its nature jealous and selfish, is just in man's line, it comes natural to him—he can live up to all its requirements to the letter; but the spirit of Christianity is not in its entirety possible to him.

The prayer concealed in what I have been saying is, not that patriotism should cease and not that the talk about universal brotherhood should cease, but that the incongruous firm be dissolved and each limb of it be required to transact business by itself, for the future.

* *Mark Twain's Notebook.*

CHRISTIAN PROGRESS THROUGH THE AGES

*Letter to Rev. J. H. Twitchell in Hartford**

Yes, oh yes, I am not overlooking the "steady progress from age to age of the coming of the kingdom of God and righteousness." "From age to age"—yes, it describes that giddy gait. I (and the rocks) will not live to see it arrive, but that is all right—it will arrive, it surely will. But you ought not to be always ironically apologizing for the Deity. If that thing is going to arrive, it is inferable that He wants it to arrive; and so it is not quite kind of you, and it hurts me, to see you flinging sarcasms at the gait of it. And yet it would not be fair in me not to admit that the sarcasms are deserved. When the Deity wants a thing, and after working at it for "ages and ages" can't show even a shade of progress toward its accomplishment, we—well, we don't laugh, but it is only because we dasn't. The source of "righteousness"—is in the heart? Yes. And engineered and directed by the brain? Yes. Well, history and tradition testify that the heart is just about what it was in the beginning; it has undergone no shade of change. Its good and evil impulses and their consequences are the same to-day that they were in Old Bible times, in Egyptian times, in Greek times, in Middle Age times, in Twentieth Century times. There has been no change.

Meantime, the brain has undergone no change. It is what it always was. There are a few good brains and a multitude of poor ones. It was so in Old Bible times and in all other times—Greek, Roman, Middle Ages and Twentieth Century. Among the savages—all the savages—the average brain is as competent as the average brain here or elsewhere. I will prove it to you, some time, if you like. And there are great brains among them, too. I will prove that also, if you like.

Well, the 19th century made progress—the first progress after "ages and ages"—colossal progress. In what? Materialities. Prodigious acquisitions were made in things which add to the comfort of many and

* *Mark Twain's Letters.*

make life harder for as many more. But the addition to righteousness? Is that discoverable? I think not. The materialities were not invented in the interest of righteousness; that there is more righteousness in the world because of them than there was before, is hardly demonstrable, I think. In Europe and America there is a vast change (due to them) in ideals—do you admire it? All Europe and all America are feverishly scrambling for money. Money is the supreme ideal—all others take tenth place with the great bulk of the nations named. Money-lust has always existed, but not in the history of the world was it ever a craze, a madness, until your time and mine. This lust has rotted these nations; it has made them hard, sordid, ungentle, dishonest, oppressive.

Did England rise against the infamy of the Boer war? No—rose in favor of it. Did America rise against the infamy of the Philippine war? No—rose in favor of it. Did Russia rise against the infamy of the present war? No—sat still and said nothing. Has the Kingdom of God advanced in Russia since the beginning of time?

Or in Europe and America, considering the vast backward step of the money-lust? Or anywhere else? If there has been any progress toward righteousness since the early days of Creation—which, in my ineradicable honesty, I am obliged to doubt—I think we must confine it to ten per cent of the populations of Christendom (but leaving Russia, Spain and South America entirely out). This gives us 320,000,-000 to draw the ten per cent from. That is to say, 32,000,000 have advanced toward righteousness and the Kingdom of God since the "ages and ages" have been flying along, the Deity sitting up there admiring. Well, you see it leaves 1,200,000,000 out of the race. They stand just where they have always stood, there has been no change.

N. B. No charge for these informations. Do come down soon, Joe.

THE BLESSINGS OF CHRISTIAN CIVILIZATION*

Next we had Egyptian wars, Greek wars, Roman wars, hideous drenchings of the earth with blood; and we saw the treacheries of the Romans toward the Carthaginians, and the sickening spectacle of the

* The Mysterious Stranger.

massacre of those brave people. Also we saw Cæsar invade Britain—
"not that those barbarians had done him any harm, but because he
wanted their land, and desired to confer the blessings of civilization
upon their widows and orphans," as Satan explained.

Next, Christianity was born. Then ages of Europe passed in review
before us, and we saw Christianity and Civilization march hand in
hand through those ages, "leaving famine and death and desolation in
their wake, and other signs of the progress of the human race," as
Satan observed.

And always we had wars, and more wars, and still other wars—all
over Europe, all over the world. "Sometimes in the private interest of
royal families," Satan said, "sometimes to crush a weak nation; but
never a war started by the aggressor for any clean purpose—there is no
such war in the history of the race."

"Now," said Satan, "you have seen your progress down to the
present, and you must confess that it is wonderful—in its way. We
must now exhibit the future."

He showed us slaughters more terrible in their destruction of life,
more devastating in their engines of war, than any we had seen.

"You perceive," he said, "that you have made continual progress.
Cain did his murder with a club; the Hebrews did their murders with
javelins and swords; the Greeks and Romans added protective armor
and the fine arts of military organization and generalship; the Christian has added guns and gunpowder; a few centuries from now he will
have so greatly improved the deadly effectiveness of his weapons of
slaughter that all men will confess that without Christian civilization
war must have remained a poor and trifling thing to the end of
time." . . .

Satan laughed his unkind laugh to a finish; then he said: "It is a
remarkable progress. In five or six thousand years five or six high
civilizations have risen, flourished, commanded the wonder of the
world, then faded out and disappeared; and not one of them except the
latest ever invented any sweeping and adequate way to kill people.
They all did their best—to kill being the chiefest ambition of the
human race and the earliest incident in its history—but only the Christian civilization has scored a triumph to be proud of. Two or three
centuries from now it will be recognized that all the competent killers
are Christians; then the pagan world will go to school to the Chris-

tian—not to acquire his religion, but his guns. The Turk and the Chinaman will buy those to kill missionaries and converts with."*

AN ANSWER TO A READER WHO HAD SENT MARK TWAIN A LIST OF THE ONE HUNDRED GREATEST MEN IN HISTORY†

To———, *Buffalo, N. Y.:*
Private.   REDDING, CONN., *Aug. 28, '08.*
   DEAR SIR,—By "private," I mean don't print any remarks of mine.

———

I like your list.
The *"largest visible influence."*
These terms *require* you to add Jesus. And they doubly and trebly require you to add Satan. From A.D. 350 to A.D. 1850 these gentlemen exercised a vaster influence over a fifth part of the human race than was exercised over that fraction of the race by all other influences combined. Ninety-nine hundredths of this influence proceeded from Satan, the remaining fraction of it from Jesus. During those 1500 years the fear of Satan and Hell made 99 Christians where love of God and Heaven landed *one*. During those 1500 years, Satan's influence was worth very nearly a hundred times as much to the business as was the influence of all the rest of the Holy Family put together.

   You have asked me a question, and I have answered it seriously and sincerely. You have put in Buddha—a god, with a following, at one time, greater than Jesus ever had: a god with perhaps a little better evidence of his godship than that which is offered for Jesus's. How then, in fairness, can you leave Jesus out? And if you put him in, how can you logically leave Satan out? Thunder is good, thunder is impressive; but it is the lightning that does the work.

———

   * Satan is the diabolical "teacher" and prophet in *The Mysterious Stranger,* and this particular prophecy came true sooner than he anticipated. *Ed.*
   † *Mark Twain's Letters.*

THE TWO TESTAMENTS*

The two Testaments are interesting, each in its own way. The Old one gives us a picture of these people's Deity as he was before he got religion, the other one gives us a picture of him as he appeared afterward. The Old Testament is interested mainly in blood and sensuality. The New one in Salvation. Salvation by fire.

The first time the Deity came down to earth, he brought life and death; when he came the second time, he brought hell.

Life was not a valuable gift, but death was. Life was a fever-dream made up of joys embittered by sorrows, pleasure poisoned by pain; a dream that was a nightmare-confusion of spasmodic and fleeting delights, ecstasies, exultations, happinesses, interspersed with long-drawn miseries, griefs, perils, horrors, disappointments, defeats, humiliations, and despairs—the heaviest curse devisable by divine ingenuity; but death was sweet, death was gentle, death was kind; death healed the bruised spirit and the broken heart, and gave them rest and forgetfulness; death was man's best friend; when man could endure life no longer, death came and set him free.

In time, the Deity perceived that death was a mistake; a mistake, in that it was insufficient; insufficient, for the reason that while it was an admirable agent for the inflicting of misery upon the survivor, it allowed the dead person himself to escape from all further persecution in the blessed refuge of the grave. This was not satisfactory. A way must be contrived to pursue the dead beyond the tomb.

The Deity pondered this matter during four thousand years unsuccessfully, but as soon as he came down to earth and became a Christian his mind cleared and he knew what to do. He invented hell, and proclaimed it.

Now here is a curious thing. It is believed by everybody that while he was in heaven he was stern, hard, resentful, jealous, and cruel; but that when he came down to earth and assumed the name Jesus Christ,

* Bernard DeVoto, editor, *Letters from the Earth* (Harper & Row: New York and Evanston, 1962).

he became the opposite of what he was before: that is to say, he became sweet, and gentle, merciful, forgiving, and all harshness disappeared from his nature and a deep and yearning love for his poor human children took its place. Whereas it was as Jesus Christ that he devised hell and proclaimed it!

Which is to say, that as the meek and gentle Savior he was a thousand billion times crueler than ever he was in the Old Testament—oh, incomparably more atrocious than ever he was when he was at his very worst in those old days!

Meek and gentle? By and by we will examine this popular sarcasm by the light of the hell which he invented.

While it is true that the palm for malignity must be granted to Jesus, the inventor of hell, he was hard and ungentle enough for all godlike purposes even before he became a Christian. It does not appear that he ever stopped to reflect that *he* was to blame when a man went wrong, inasmuch as the man was merely acting in accordance with the disposition he had afflicted him with. No, he punished the man, instead of punishing himself. Moreover the punishment usually oversized the offense. Often, too, it fell, not upon the doer of a misdeed, but upon somebody else—a chief man, the head of a community, for instance.

> And Israel abode in Shittim, and the people began to commit whoredom with the daughters of Moab.
>
> And the Lord said unto Moses, Take *all the heads of the people,* and hang them up before the Lord against the Sun, that the fierce anger of the Lord may be turned away from Israel.

Does that look fair to you? It does not appear that the "heads of the people" got any of the adultery, yet it is they that are hanged, instead of "the people."

If it was fair and right in that day it would be fair and right today, for the pulpit maintains that God's justice is eternal and unchangeable; also that he is the Fountain of Morals, and that his morals are eternal and unchangeable. Very well, then, we must believe that if the people of New York should begin to commit whoredom with the daughters of New Jersey, it would be fair and right to set up a gallows in front of the city hall and hang the mayor and the sheriff and the judges and the archbishop on it, although they did not get any of it. It does not look right to me.

Moreover, you may be quite sure of one thing: it couldn't happen. These people would not allow it. They are better than their Bible. *Nothing* would happen here, except some lawsuits, for damages, if the incident couldn't be hushed up; and even down South they would not proceed against persons who did not get any of it; they would get a rope and hunt for the corespondents, and if they couldn't find them they would lynch a nigger.

Things have greatly improved since the Almighty's time, let the pulpit say what it may.

GOD'S DELIGHT IN MAN*

"For ourselves we do throughly believe that man, as he lives just here on this tiny earth, is in essence and possibilities the most sublime existence in all the range of non-divine being—the chief love and delight of God."—Chicago *Interior* (Presbyterian)

Land, it is just for the world the way I feel about it myself, sometimes, even when dry. And when not dry, even those warm words are not nearly warm enough to get up to what I am feeling, when I am holding on to something, and blinking affectionately at myself in the glass, and recollecting that I'm it.

And when I am feeling historical, there is nothing that ecstatifies me like hunting the Chief Love and Delight of God around and around just here on this tiny earth and watching him perform. I watch him progressing and progressing—always progressing—always mounting higher and higher, sometimes by means of the Inquisition, sometimes by means of the Terror, sometimes by eight hundred years of witch-burning, sometimes by help of a St. Bartholomew's, sometimes by spreading hell and civilization in China, sometimes by preserving and elevating the same at home by a million soldiers and a thousand battle-ships; and when he gets down to today I still look at him spread out over a whole page of the morning paper, grabbing in Congress, grabbing in Albany, grabbing in New York and St. Louis and all around,

---

* *Mark Twain in Eruption.*

lynching the innocent, slobbering hypocrisies, reeking, dripping, unsavory, but always recognizable as the same old Most Sublime Existence in all the range of Non-Divine Being, the Chief Love and Delight
of God; and then I am more gladder than ever that I am it.

SIN AND REPENTANCE*

It is curious—the misassociation of certain words. For instance, the
word Repentance. Through want of reflection we associate it exclusively with Sin. We get the notion early, and keep it always, that we
repent of bad deeds only; whereas we do a formidably large business in
repenting of good deeds which we have done. Often when we repent of
a sin, we do it perfunctorily, from principle, coldly and from the head;
but when we repent of a good deed the repentance comes hot and bitter
and straight from the heart. Often when we repent of a sin, we can
forgive ourselves and drop the matter out of mind; but when we repent
of a good deed, we seldom get peace—we go on repenting to the end.
And the repentance is so perennially young and strong and vivid and
vigorous! A great benefaction conferred with your whole heart upon an
ungrateful man—with what immortal persistence and never-cooling
energy do you repent of that! Repentance of a sin is a pale, poor,
perishable thing compared with it.

I am quite sure that the average man is built just as I am; otherwise
I should not be making this revelation of my inside. I say the average
man and stop there; for I am quite certain that there are people who do
not repent of their good deeds when the return they get for them is
treachery and ingratitude. I think that these few ought to be in heaven;
they are in the way here. In my time I have committed several millions
of sins. Many of them I probably repented of—I do not remember
now; others I was partly minded to repent of, but it did not seem
worthwhile; all of them but the recent ones and a few scattering former
ones I have forgotten. In my time I have done eleven good deeds. I
remember all of them, four of them with crystal clearness. These four I
repent of whenever I think of them—and it is not seldomer than fifty-

* Letters from the Earth.

two times a year. I repent of them in the same old original furious way, undiminished, always. If I wake up away in the night, they are there, waiting and ready; and they keep me company till the morning. I have not committed any sin that has lasted me like this save one; and have not repented of any sin with the unmodifying earnestness and sincerity with which I have repented of these four gracious and beautiful good deeds.

Possibly you who are reading these paragraphs are of those few who have got mislaid and ought to be in heaven. In that case you will not understand what I have been saying and will have no sympathy with it; but your neighbor will, if he is fifty years old.

THE CHRISTIAN GOSPEL OF PEACE*

"The gospel of peace" is always making a deal of noise, always rejoicing in its progress but always neglecting to furnish statistics. There are no peaceful nations now. All Christendom is a soldier-camp. The poor have been taxed in some nations to the starvation point to support the giant armaments which Christian governments have built up, each to protect itself from the rest of the Christian brotherhood, and incidentally to snatch any scrap of real estate left exposed by a weaker owner. King Leopold II. of Belgium, the most intensely Christian monarch, since Alexander VI., that has escaped hell thus far, has stolen an entire kingdom in Africa, and in fourteen years of Christian endeavor there has reduced the population from thirty millions to fifteen by murder and mutilation and overwork, confiscating the labor of the helpless natives, and giving them nothing in return but salvation and a home in heaven, furnished at the last moment by the Christian priest.

Within the last generation each Christian power has turned the bulk of its attention to finding out newer and still newer and more and more effective ways of killing Christians, and, incidentally, a pagan now and then; and the surest way to get rich quickly in Christ's earthly

* Extract from Albert Bigelow Paine, *Mark Twain: A Biography* (Harper & Brothers: New York and London, 1912).

kingdom is to invent a kind of gun that can kill more Christians at one shot than any other existing kind. All the Christian nations are at it. The more advanced they are, the bigger and more destructive engines of war they create.

THE CHRISTIAN GOD AND THE SEXUAL
SERVITUDE OF WOMEN*

It is as I have said: every statute in the Bible and in the lawbooks is an attempt to defeat a law of God—in other words an unalterable and indestructible law of nature. These people's God has shown them by a million acts that he respects none of the Bible's statutes. He breaks every one of them himself, adultery and all.

The law of God, as quite plainly expressed in woman's construction, is this: There shall be no limit put upon your intercourse with the other sex sexually, at any time of life.

The law of God, as quite plainly expressed in man's construction, is this: During your entire life you shall be under inflexible limits and restrictions, sexually.

During twenty-three days in every month (in the absence of pregnancy) from the time a woman is seven years old till she dies of old age, she is ready for action, and *competent*. As competent as the candlestick is to receive the candle. Competent every day, competent every night. Also, she *wants* that candle—yearns for it, longs for it, hankers after it, as commanded by the law of God in her heart.

But man is only briefly competent; and only then in the moderate measure applicable to the word in *his* sex's case. He is competent from the age of sixteen or seventeen thenceforward for thirty-five years. After fifty his performance is of poor quality, the intervals between are wide, and its satisfactions of no great value to either party; whereas his great-grandmother is as good as new. There is nothing the matter with her plant. Her candlestick is as firm as ever, whereas his candle is increasingly softened and weakened by the weather of age, as the years

* Letters from the Earth.

go by, until at last it can no longer stand, and is mournfully laid to rest in the hope of a blessed resurrection which is never to come.

By the woman's make, her plant has to be out of service three days in the month and during a part of her pregnancy. These are times of discomfort, often of suffering. For fair and just compensation she has the high privilege of unlimited adultery all the other days of her life.

That is the law of God, as revealed in her make. What becomes of this high privilege? Does she live in the free enjoyment of it? No. Nowhere in the whole world. She is robbed of it everywhere. Who does this? Man. Man's statutes—if the Bible *is* the Word of God.

Now there you have a sample of man's "reasoning powers," as he calls them. He observes certain facts. For instance, that in all his life he never sees the day that he can satisfy one woman; also, that no woman ever sees the day that she can't overwork, and defeat, and put out of commission any ten masculine plants that can be put to bed to her.* He puts those strikingly suggestive and luminous facts together, and from them draws this astonishing conclusion: The Creator intended the woman to be restricted to one man.

So he concretes that singular conclusion into a *law*, for good and all.

And he does it without consulting the woman, although she has a thousand times more at stake in the matter than he has. His procreative competency is limited to an average of a hundred exercises per year for fifty years, hers is good for three thousand a year for that whole time—and as many years longer as she may live. Thus his life interest in the matter is five thousand refreshments, while hers is a hundred and fifty thousand; yet instead of fairly and honorably leaving the making of the law to the person who has an overwhelming interest at stake in it, this immeasurable hog, who has nothing at stake in it worth considering, makes it himself!

You have heretofore found out, by my teachings, that man is a fool; you are now aware that woman is a damned fool.

* In the Sandwich Islands in 1866 a buxom royal princess died. Occupying a place of distinguished honor at her funeral were thirty-six splendidly built young native men. In a laudatory song which celebrated the various merits, achievements and accomplishments of the late princess whose thirty-six stallions were called her *harem*, and the song said it had been her pride and boast that she kept the whole of them busy, and that several times it had happened that more than one of them had been able to charge overtime. (M.T.)

Now if you or any other really intelligent person were arranging the fairnesses and justices between man and woman, you would give the man a one-fiftieth interest in one woman, and the woman a harem. Now wouldn't you? Necessarily. I give you my word, this creature with the decrepit candle has arranged it exactly the other way. Solomon, who was one of the Deity's favorites, had a copulation cabinet composed of seven hundred wives and three hundred concubines. To save his life he could not have kept two of those young creatures satisfactorily re-freshed, even if he had had fifteen experts to help him. Necessarily almost the entire thousand had to go hungry years and years on a stretch. Conceive of a man hardhearted enough to look daily upon all that suffering and not be moved to mitigate it. He even wantonly added a sharp pang to that pathetic misery; for he kept within those women's sight, always, stalwart watchmen whose splendid masculine forms made the poor lassies' mouths water but who hadn't anything to solace a candlestick with, these gentry being eunuchs. A eunuch is a person whose candle has been put out. By art.

From time to time, as I go along, I will take up a Biblical statute and show you that it always violates a law of God, and then is imported into the lawbooks of the nations, where it continues its violations. But those things will keep; there is no hurry.

THE CHRISTIAN HEAVEN*

This is a strange place, an extraordinary place, and interesting. There is nothing resembling it at home. The people are all insane, the other animals are all insane, the earth is insane, Nature itself is insane. Man is a marvelous curiosity. When he is at his very very best he is a sort of low grade nickel-plated angel; at his worst he is unspeakable, unimaginable; and first and last and all the time he is a sarcasm. Yet he blandly and in all sincerity calls himself the "noblest work of God." This is the truth I am telling you. And this is not a new idea with him, he has talked it through all the ages, and believed it. Believed it, and found nobody among all his race to laugh at it.

* *Letters from the Earth.*

Moreover—if I may put another strain upon you—he thinks he is the Creator's pet. He believes the Creator is proud of him; he even believes the Creator loves him; has a passion for him; sits up nights to admire him; yes, and watch over him and keep him out of trouble. He prays to Him, and thinks He listens. Isn't it a quaint idea? Fills his prayers with crude and bald and florid flatteries of Him, and thinks He sits and purrs over these extravagancies and enjoys them. He prays for help, and favor, and protection, every day; and does it with hopefulness and confidence, too, although no prayer of his has ever been answered. The daily affront, the daily defeat, do not discourage him, he goes on praying just the same. There is something almost fine about this perseverance. I must put one more strain upon you: he thinks he is going to heaven!

He has salaried teachers who tell him that. They also tell him there is a hell, of everlasting fire, and that he will go to it if he doesn't keep the Commandments. What are the Commandments? They are a curiosity. I will tell you about them by and by.

"I have told you nothing about man that is not true." You must pardon me if I repeat that remark now and then in these letters; I want you to take seriously the things I am telling you, and I feel that if I were in your place and you in mine, I should need that reminder from time to time, to keep my credulity from flagging.

For there is nothing about man that is not strange to an immortal. He looks at nothing as we look at it, his sense of proportion is quite different from ours, and his sense of values is so widely divergent from ours, that with all our large intellectual powers it is not likely that even the most gifted among us would ever be quite able to understand it.

For instance, take this sample: he has imagined a heaven, and has left entirely out of it the supremest of all his delights, the one ecstasy that stands first and foremost in the heart of every individual of his race—and of ours—sexual intercourse!

It is as if a lost and perishing person in a roasting desert should be told by a rescuer he might choose and have all longed-for things but one, and he should elect to leave out water!

His heaven is like himself: strange, interesting, astonishing, grotesque. I give you my word, it has not a single feature in it that he *actually values*. It consists—utterly and entirely—of diversions which he cares next to nothing about, here in the earth, yet is quite sure he will like in heaven. Isn't it curious? Isn't it interesting? You must not think I am exaggerating, for it is not so. I will give you details.

Most men do not sing, most men cannot sing, most men will not stay where others are singing if it be continued more than two hours. Note that.

Only about two men in a hundred can play upon a musical instrument, and not four in a hundred have any wish to learn how. Set that down.

Many men pray, not many of them like to do it. A few pray long, the others make a short cut.

More men go to church than want to.

To forty-nine men in fifty the Sabbath Day is a dreary, dreary bore.

Of all the men in a church on a Sunday, two-thirds are tired when the service is half over, and the rest before it is finished.

The gladdest moment for all of them is when the preacher uplifts his hands for the benediction. You can hear the soft rustle of relief that sweeps the house, and you recognize that it is eloquent with gratitude.

All nations look down upon all other nations.

All nations dislike all other nations.

All white nations despise all colored nations, of whatever hue, and oppress them when they can.

White men will not associate with "niggers," nor marry them.

They will not allow them in their schools and churches.

All the world hates the Jew, and will not endure him except when he is rich.

I ask you to note all those particulars.

Further. All sane people detest noise.

All people, sane or insane, like to have variety in their life. Monotony quickly wearies them.

Every man, according to the mental equipment that has fallen to his share, exercises his intellect constantly, ceaselessly, and this exercise makes up a vast and valued and essential part of his life. The lowest intellect, like the highest, possesses a skill of some kind and takes a keen pleasure in testing it, proving it, perfecting it. The urchin who is his comrade's superior in games is as diligent and as enthusiastic in his

practice as are the sculptor, the painter, the pianist, the mathematician
and the rest. Not one of them could be happy if his talent were put
under an interdict.

Now then, you have the facts. You know what the human race
enjoys, and what it doesn't enjoy. It has invented a heaven, out of its
own head, all by itself: guess what it is like! In fifteen hundred eternities you couldn't do it. The ablest mind known to you or me in fifty
million aeons couldn't do it. Very well, I will tell you about it.

1. First of all, I recall to your attention the extraordinary fact with
which I began. To wit, that the human being, like the immortals,
naturally places sexual intercourse far and away above all other joys—
yet he has left it out of his heaven! The very thought of it excites him;
opportunity sets him wild; in this state he will risk life, reputation,
everything—even his queer heaven itself—to make good that opportunity and ride it to the overwhelming climax. From youth to middle
age all men and all women prize copulation above all other pleasures
combined, yet it is actually as I have said: it is not in their heaven;
prayer takes its place.

They prize it thus highly; yet, like all their so-called "boons," it is a
poor thing. At its very best and longest the act is brief beyond imagination—the imagination of an immortal, I mean. In the matter of repetition the man is limited—oh, quite beyond immortal conception. We
who continue the act and its supremest ecstasies unbroken and without
withdrawal for centuries, will never be able to understand or ade-
quately pity the awful poverty of these people in that rich gift which,
possessed as we possess it, makes all other possessions trivial and not
worth the trouble of invoicing.

2. In man's heaven *everybody sings!* The man who did not sing on
earth sings there; the man who could not sing on earth is able to do it
there. This universal singing is not casual, not occasional, not relieved
by intervals of quiet; it goes on, all day long, and every day, during a
stretch of twelve hours. And *everybody stays;* whereas in the earth the
place would be empty in two hours. The singing is of hymns alone.
Nay, it is of *one* hymn alone. The words are always the same, in
number they are only about a dozen, there is no rhyme, there is no
poetry: "Hosannah, hosannah, hosannah, Lord God of Sabaoth, 'rah!
'rah! 'rah! siss!—boom! . . . a-a-ah!"

3. Meantime, every person is playing on a harp—those millions and

millions!—whereas not more than twenty in the thousand of them could play an instrument in the earth, or ever wanted to.

Consider the deafening hurricane of sound—millions and millions of voices screaming at once and millions and millions of harps gritting their teeth at the same time! I ask you: is it hideous, is it odious, is it horrible?

Consider further: it is a *praise* service; a service of compliment, of flattery, of adulation! Do you ask who it is that is willing to endure this strange compliment, this insane compliment; and who not only endures it, but likes it, enjoys it, requires it, *commands* it? Hold your breath!

It is God! This race's God, I mean. He sits on his throne, attended by his four and twenty elders and some other dignitaries pertaining to his court, and looks out over his miles and miles of tempestuous worshipers, and smiles, and purrs, and nods his satisfaction northward, eastward, southward; as quaint and naïve a spectacle as has yet been imagined in this universe, I take it.

It is easy to see that the inventor of the heaven did not originate the idea, but copied it from the show-ceremonies of some sorry little sovereign State up in the back settlements of the Orient somewhere.

All sane white people hate noise; yet they have tranquilly accepted this kind of a heaven—without thinking, without reflection, without examination—and they actually want to go to it! Profoundly devout old gray-headed men put in a large part of their time dreaming of the happy day when they will lay down the cares of this life and enter into the joys of that place. Yet you can see how unreal it is to them, and how little it takes a grip upon them as being fact, for they make no practical preparation for the great change: you never see one of them with a harp, you never hear one of them sing.

As you have seen, that singular show is a service of praise: praise by hymn, praise by prostration. It takes the place of "church." Now then, in the earth these people cannot stand much church—an hour and a quarter is the limit, and they draw the line at once a week. That is to say, Sunday. One day in seven; and even then they do not look forward to it with longing. And so—consider what their heaven provides for them: "church" that lasts forever, and a Sabbath that has no end! They quickly weary of this brief hebdomadal Sabbath here, yet they long for that eternal one; they dream of it, they talk about it, they *think* they think they are going to enjoy it—with all their simple hearts they think they think they are going to be happy in it!

It is because they do not think at all; they only think they think. Whereas they can't think; not two human beings in ten thousand have anything to think with. And as to imagination—oh, well, look at their heaven! They accept it, they approve it, they admire it. That gives you their intellectual measure.

4. The inventor of their heaven empties into it all the nations of the earth, in one common jumble. All are on an equality absolute, no one of them ranking another; they have to be "brothers"; they have to mix together, pray together, harp together, hosannah together—whites, niggers, Jews, everybody—there's no distinction. Here in the earth all nations hate each other, and every one of them hates the Jew. Yet every pious person adores that heaven and wants to get into it. He really does. And when he is in a holy rapture he thinks he thinks that if he were only there he would take all the populace to his heart, and hug, and hug, and hug!

He is a marvel—man is! I would I knew who invented him.

5. Every man in the earth possesses some share of intellect, large or small; and be it large or be it small he takes a pride in it. Also his heart swells at mention of the names of the majestic intellectual chiefs of his race, and he loves the tale of their splendid achievements. For he is of their blood, and in honoring themselves they have honored him. Lo, what the mind of man can do! he cries; and calls the roll of the illustrious of all the ages; and points to the imperishable literatures they have given to the world, and the mechanical wonders they have invented, and the glories wherewith they have clothed science and the arts; and to them he uncovers, as to kings, and gives to them the profoundest homage, and the sincerest, his exultant heart can furnish—thus exalting intellect above all things else in his world, and enthroning it there under the arching skies in a supremacy unapproachable. And then he contrives a heaven that hasn't a rag of intellectuality in it anywhere!

Is it odd, is it curious, is it puzzling? It is exactly as I have said, incredible as it may sound. This sincere adorer of intellect and prodigal rewarder of its mighty services here in the earth has invented a religion and a heaven which pay no compliments to intellect, offer it no distinctions, fling to it no largess: in fact, never even mention it.

By this time you will have noticed that the human being's heaven has been thought out and constructed upon an absolutely definite plan; and that this plan is, that it shall contain, in labored detail, each and every imaginable thing that is repulsive to a man, and not a single thing he likes!

Very well, the further we proceed the more will this curious fact be apparent.

Make a note of it: in man's heaven there are no exercises for the intellect, nothing for it to live upon. It would rot there in a year—rot and stink. Rot and stink—and at that stage become holy. A blessed thing: for only the holy can stand the joys of that bedlam.

THE CHRISTIAN GOD*

The discomforts furnished by the Ark were many and various. The family had to live right in the presence of the multitudinous animals, and breathe the distressing stench they made and be deafened day and night with the thunder-crash of noise their roarings and screechings produced; and in addition to these intolerable discomforts it was a peculiarly trying place for the ladies, for they could look in no direction without seeing some thousands of the creatures engaged in multiplying and replenishing. And then, there were the flies. They swarmed everywhere, and persecuted the Family all day long. They were the first animals up, in the morning, and the last ones down, at night. But they must not be killed, they must not be injured, they were sacred, their origin was divine, they were the special pets of the Creator, his darlings.

By and by the other creatures would be distributed here and there about the earth—scattered: the tigers to India, the lions and the elephants to the vacant desert and the secret places of the jungle, the birds to the boundless regions of empty space, the insects to one or another climate, according to nature and requirement; but the fly? He is of no nationality; all the climates are his home, all the globe is his province,

* *Letters from the Earth.*

all creatures that breathe are his prey, and unto them all he is a scourge and a hell.

To man he is a divine ambassador, a minister plenipotentiary, the Creator's special representative. He infests him in his cradle; clings in bunches to his gummy eyelids; buzzes and bites and harries him, robbing him of his sleep and his weary mother of her strength in those long vigils which she devotes to protecting her child from this pest's persecutions. The fly harries the sick man in his home, in the hospital, even on his deathbed at his last gasp. Pesters him at his meals; previously hunts up patients suffering from loathsome and deadly diseases; wades in their sores, gaums its legs with a million death-dealing germs; then comes to that healthy man's table and wipes these things off on the butter and discharges a bowel-load of typhoid germs and excrement on his batter-cakes. The housefly wrecks more human constitutions and destroys more human lives than all God's multitude of misery-messengers and death-agents put together.

Shem was full of hookworms. It is wonderful, the thorough and comprehensive study which the Creator devoted to the great work of making man miserable. I have said he devised a special affliction-agent for each and every detail of man's structure, overlooking not a single one, and I said the truth. Many poor people have to go barefoot, because they cannot afford shoes. The Creator saw his opportunity. I will remark, in passing, that he always has his eye on the poor. Nine-tenths of his disease-inventions were intended for the poor, and they *get* them. The well-to-do get only what is left over. Do not suspect me of speaking unheedfully, for it is not so: the vast bulk of the Creator's affliction-inventions *are* specially designed for the persecution of the poor. You could guess this by the fact that one of the pulpit's finest and commonest names for the Creator is "The Friend of the Poor." Under no circumstances does the pulpit ever pay the Creator a compliment that has a vestige of truth in it. The poor's most inplacable and unwearying enemy is their Father in Heaven. The poor's only real friend is their fellow man. He is sorry for them, he pities them, and he shows it by his deeds. He does much to relieve their distresses; and in every case their Father in Heaven gets the credit of it.

Just so with diseases. If science exterminates a disease which has been working for God, it is God that gets the credit, and all the pulpits break into grateful advertising-raptures and call attention to how good he is!

Yes, *he* has done it. Perhaps he has waited a thousand years before doing it. That is nothing; the pulpit says he was thinking about it all the time. When exasperated men rise up and sweep away an age-long tyranny and set a nation free, the first thing the delighted pulpit does is to advertise it as God's work, and invite the people to get down on their knees and pour out their thanks to him for it. And the pulpit says with admiring emotion, "Let tyrants understand that the Eye that never sleeps is upon them; and let them remember that the Lord our God will not always be patient, but will loose the whirlwinds of his wrath upon them in his appointed day."

They forget to mention that he is the slowest mover in the universe; that his Eye that never sleeps, might as well, since it takes it a century to see what any other eye would see in a week; that in all history there is not an instance where he thought of a noble deed *first*, but always thought of it just a little after somebody else had thought of it and *done* it. He arrives then, and annexes the dividend.

*CHRISTIAN SCIENCE**

This last summer, when I was on my way back to Vienna from the Appetite Cure in the mountains, I fell over a cliff in the twilight and broke some arms and legs and one thing or another, and by good luck was found by some peasants who had lost an ass, and they carried me to the nearest habitation, which was one of those large, low, thatch-roofed farm-houses, with apartments in the garret for the family, and a cunning little porch under the deep gable decorated with boxes of bright-colored flowers and cats; on the ground-floor a large and light sitting-room, separated from the milch-cattle apartment by a partition; and in the front yard rose stately and fine the wealth and pride of the house, the manure-pile. That sentence is Germanic, and shows that I am acquiring that sort of mastery of the art and spirit of the language which enables a man to travel all day in one sentence without changing cars.

* *Christian Science* (Harper and Brothers: New York, 1907).

There was a village a mile away, and a horse-doctor lived there, but there was no surgeon. It seemed a bad outlook; mine was distinctly a surgery case. Then it was remembered that a lady from Boston was summering in that village, and she was a Christian Science doctor and could cure anything. So she was sent for. It was night by this time, and she could not conveniently come, but sent word that it was no matter, there was no hurry, she would give me "absent treatment" now, and come in the morning; meantime she begged me to make myself tranquil and comfortable and remember that there was nothing the matter with me. I thought there must be some mistake.

"Did you tell her I walked off a cliff seventy-five feet high?"

"Yes."

"And struck a boulder at the bottom and bounced?"

"Yes."

"And struck another one and bounced again?"

"Yes."

"And struck another one and bounced yet again?"

"Yes."

"And broke the boulders?"

"Yes."

"That accounts for it; she is thinking of the boulders. Why didn't you tell her I got hurt, too?"

"I did. I told her what you told me to tell her: that you were now but an incoherent series of compound fractures extending from your scalplock to your heels, and that the comminuted projections caused you to look like a hat-rack."

"And it was after this that she wished me to remember that there was nothing the matter with me?"

"Those were her words."

"I do not understand it. I believe she has not diagnosed the case with sufficient care. Did she look like a person who was theorizing, or did she look like one who has fallen off precipices herself and brings to the aid of abstract science the confirmations of personal experience?"

"*Bitte?*"

It was too large a contract for the *Stubenmädchen's* vocabulary; she couldn't call the hand. I allowed the subject to rest there, and asked for something to eat and smoke, and something hot to drink, and a basket to pile my legs in; but I could not have any of these things.

"Why?"

"She said you would need nothing at all."

"But I am hungry and thirsty, and in desperate pain."

"She said you would have these delusions, but must pay no attention to them. She wants you to particularly remember that there are no such things as hunger and thirst and pain."

"She does, does she?"

"It is what she said."

"Does she seem to be in full and functionable possession of her intellectual plant, such as it is?"

"*Bitte?*"

"Do they let her run at large, or do they tie her up?"

"Tie her up?"

"There, good night, run along; you are a good girl, but your mental *Geschirr* is not arranged for light and airy conversation. Leave me to my delusions."

It was a night of anguish, of course—at least, I supposed it was, for it had all the symptoms of it—but it passed at last, and the Christian Scientist came, and I was glad. She was middle-aged, and large and bony, and erect, and had an austere face and a resolute jaw and a Roman beak and was a widow in the third degree, and her name was Fuller. I was eager to get to business and find relief, but she was distressingly deliberate. She unpinned and unhooked and uncoupled her upholsteries one by one, abolished the wrinkles with a flirt of her hand, and hung the articles up; peeled off her gloves and disposed of them, got a book out of her hand-bag, then drew a chair to the bedside, descended into it without hurry, and I hung out my tongue. She said, with pity but without passion:

"Return it to its receptacle. We deal with the mind only, not with its dumb servants."

I could not offer my pulse, because the connection was broken; but she detected the apology before I could word it, and indicated by a negative tilt of her head that the pulse was another dumb servant that she had no use for. Then I thought I would tell her my symptoms and how I felt, so that she would understand the case; but that was another inconsequence, she did not need to know those things; moreover, my remark about how I felt was an abuse of language, a misapplication of terms.

"One does not *feel*," she explained; "there is no such thing as feeling: therefore, to speak of a non-existent thing as existent is a contradiction. Matter has no existence; nothing exists but mind; the mind cannot feel pain, it can only imagine it."

"But if it hurts, just the same—"

"It doesn't. A thing which is unreal cannot exercise the functions of reality. Pain is unreal; hence, pain cannot hurt."

In making a sweeping gesture to indicate the act of shooting the illusion of pain out of the mind, she raked her hand on a pin in her dress, said "Ouch!" and went tranquilly on with her talk. "You should never allow yourself to speak of how you feel, nor permit others to ask you how you are feeling; you should never concede that you are ill, nor permit others to talk about disease or pain or death or similar non-existences in your presence. Such talk only encourages the mind to continue its empty imaginings." Just at that point the *Stubenmädchen* trod on the cat's tail, and the cat let fly a frenzy of cat profanity. I asked, with caution:

"Is a cat's opinion about pain valuable?"

"A cat has no opinion; opinions proceed from mind only; the lower animals, being eternally perishable, have not been granted mind; without mind, opinion is impossible."

"She merely *imagined* she felt a pain—the cat?"

"She cannot imagine a pain, for imagining is an effect of mind; without mind, there is no imagination. A cat has no imagination."

"Then she had a *real* pain?"

"I have already told you there is no such *thing* as real pain."

"It is strange and interesting. I do wonder what was the matter with the cat. Because, there being no such thing as a real pain, and she not being able to imagine an imaginary one, it would seem that God in His pity has compensated the cat with some kind of a mysterious emotion usable when her tail is trodden on which, for the moment, joins cat and Christian in one common brotherhood of—"

She broke in with an irritated—

"Peace! The cat feels nothing, the Christian feels nothing. Your empty and foolish imaginings are profanation and blasphemy, and can do you an injury. It is wiser and better and holier to recognize and confess that there is no such thing as disease or pain or death."

"I am full of imaginary tortures," I said, "but I do not think I could be any more uncomfortable if they were real ones. What must I do to get rid of them?"

"There is no occasion to get rid of them, since they do not exist. They are illusions propagated by matter, and matter has no existence; there is no such thing as matter."

"It sounds right and clear, but yet it seems in a degree elusive; it seems to slip through, just when you think you are getting a grip on it."

"Explain."

"Well, for instance: if there is no such thing as matter, how can matter propagate things?"

In her compassion she almost smiled. She would have smiled if there were any such thing as a smile.

"It is quite simple," she said; "the fundamental propositions of Christian Science explain it, and they are summarized in the four following self-evident propositions: 1. God is All in all. 2. God is good. Good is Mind. 3. God, Spirit, being all, nothing is matter. 4. Life, God, omnipotent Good, deny death, evil, sin, disease. There—now you see."

It seemed nebulous; it did not seem to say anything about the difficulty in hand—how non-existent matter can propagate illusions. I said, with some hesitancy:

"Does—does it explain?"

"*Doesn't* it? Even if read backward it will do it."

With a budding hope, I asked her to do it backward.

"Very well. Disease sin evil death deny Good omnipotent God life matter is nothing all being Spirit God Mind is Good good is God all in All is God. There—do you understand now?"

"It—it—well, it is plainer than it was before; still—"

"Well?"

"Could you try it some more ways?"

"As many as you like; it always means the same. Interchanged in any way you please it cannot be made to mean anything different from what it means when put in any other way. Because it is perfect. You can jumble it all up, and it makes no difference: it always comes out the way it was before. It was a marvelous mind that produced it. As a mental *tour de force* it is without a mate, it defies alike the simple, the concrete, and the occult."

"It seems to be a corker."

I blushed for the word, but it was out before I could stop it.

"A what?"

"A—wonderful structure—combination, so to speak, of profound thoughts—unthinkable ones—un—"

"It is true. Read backward, or forward, or perpendicularly, or at any given angle, these four propositions will always be found to agree in statement and proof."

"Ah—proof. Now we are coming at it. The *statements* agree; they agree with—with—anyway, they agree; I noticed that; but what is it they prove—I mean, in particular?"

"Why, nothing could be clearer. They prove: 1. GOD—Principle, Life, Truth, Love, Soul, Spirit, Mind. Do you get that?"

"I—well, I seem to. Go on, please."

"2. MAN—God's universal idea, individual, perfect, eternal. Is it clear?"

"It—I think so. Continue."

"3. IDEA—An image in Mind; the immediate object of understanding. There it is—the whole sublime Arcana of Christian Science in a nutshell. Do you find a weak place in it anywhere?"

"Well—no; it seems strong."

"Very well. There is more. Those three constitute the Scientific Definition of Immortal Mind. Next, we have the Scientific Definition of Mortal Mind. Thus. FIRST DEGREE: *Depravity*. 1. Physical—Passions and appetites, fear, depraved will, pride, envy, deceit, hatred, revenge, sin, disease, death."

"Phantasms, madam—unrealities, as I understand it."

"Every one. SECOND DEGREE: *Evil Disappearing*. 1. Moral—Honesty, affection, compassion, hope, faith, meekness, temperance. Is it clear?"

"Crystal."

"THIRD DEGREE: *Spiritual Salvation*. 1. Spiritual—Faith, wisdom, power, purity, understanding, health, love. You see how searchingly and coordinately interdependent and anthropomorphous it all is. In this Third Degree, as we know by the revelations of Christian Science, mortal mind disappears."

"Not earlier?"

"No, not until the teaching and preparation for the Third Degree are completed."

"It is not until then that one is enabled to take hold of Christian Science effectively, and with the right sense of sympathy and kinship, as I understand you. That is to say, it could not succeed during the processes of the Second Degree, because there would still be remains of mind left; and therefore—but I interrupted you. You were about to further explain the good results proceeding from the erosions and disintegrations effected by the Third Degree. It is very interesting; go on, please."

"Yes, as I was saying, in this Third Degree mortal mind disappears. Science so reverses the evidence before the corporeal human senses as to make this scriptural testimony true in our hearts, 'the last shall be first and the first shall be last,' that God and His idea may be to us—what divinity really is, and must of necessity be—all-inclusive."

"It is beautiful. And with what exhaustive exactness your choice and arrangement of words confirm and establish what you have claimed for the powers and functions of the Third Degree. The Second could probably produce only temporary absence of mind; it is reserved to the Third to make it permanent. A sentence framed under the auspices of the Second could have a kind of meaning—a sort of deceptive semblance of it—whereas it is only under the magic of the Third that that defect would disappear. Also, without doubt, it is the Third Degree that contributes another remarkable specialty to Christian Science— viz., ease and flow and lavishness of words, and rhythm and swing and smoothness. There must be a special reason for this?"

"Yes—God-all, all-God, good God, non-Matter, Matteration, Spirit, Bones, Truth."

"That explains it."

"There is nothing in Christian Science that is not explicable; for God is one, Time is one, Individuality is one, and may be one of a series, one of many, as an individual man, individual horse; whereas God is one, not one of a series, but one alone and without an equal."

"These are noble thoughts. They make one burn to know more. How does Christian Science explain the spiritual relation of systematic duality to incidental deflection?"

"Christian Science reverses the seeming relation of Soul and body— as astronomy reverses the human perception of the movement of the solar system—and makes body tributary to the Mind. As it is the earth which is in motion, while the sun is at rest, though in viewing the sun rise one finds it impossible to believe the sun not to be really rising, so the body is but the humble servant of the restful Mind, though it seems otherwise to finite sense; but we shall never understand this while we admit that soul is in body, or mind in matter, and that man is included in non-intelligence. Soul is God, unchangeable and eternal; and man coexists with and reflects Soul, for the All-in-all is the Altogether, and the Altogether embraces the All-one, Soul-Mind, Mind-Soul, Love, Spirit, Bones, Liver, one of a series, alone and without an equal."

"What is the origin of Christian Science? Is it a gift of God, or did it just happen?"

"In a sense, it is a gift of God. That is to say, its powers are from Him, but the credit of the discovery of the powers and what they are for is due to an American lady."

"Indeed? When did this occur?"

"In 1866. That is the immortal date when pain and disease and death disappeared from the earth to return no more forever. That is, the fancies for which those terms stand disappeared. The things themselves had never existed; therefore, as soon as it was perceived that there were no such things, they were easily banished. The history and nature of the great discovery are set down in the book here, and—"

"Did the lady write the book?"

"Yes, she wrote it all, herself. The title is *Science and Health, with Key to the Scriptures*—for she explains the Scriptures; they were not understood before. Not even by the twelve Disciples. She begins thus— I will read it to you."

But she had forgotten to bring her glasses.

"Well, it is no matter," she said. "I remember the words—indeed, all Christian Scientists know the book by heart; it is necessary in our practice. We should otherwise make mistakes and do harm. She begins thus: 'In the year 1866 I discovered the Science of Metaphysical Healing, and named it Christian Science.' And she says—quite beautifully, I think—'Through Christian Science, religion and medicine are inspired with a diviner nature and essence, fresh pinions are given to faith and understanding, and thoughts acquaint themselves intelligently with God.' Her very words."

"It is elegant. And it is a fine thought, too—marrying religion to medicine, instead of medicine to the undertaker in the old way; for religion and medicine properly belong together, they being the basis of all spiritual and physical health. What kind of medicine do you give for the ordinary diseases, such as—"

"We never give medicine in *any* circumstances whatever! We—"

"But, madam, it *says*—"

"I don't care what it says, and I don't wish to talk about it."

"I am sorry if I have offended, but you see the mention seemed in some way inconsistent, and—"

"There *are* no inconsistencies in Christian Science. The thing is impossible, for the Science is absolute. It cannot be otherwise, since it proceeds directly from the All-in-all and the Everything-in-Which, also Soul, Bones, Truth, one of a series, alone and without equal. It is Mathematics purified from material dross and made spiritual."

"I can see that, but—"

"It rests upon the immovable basis of an Apodictical Principle."

The word flattened itself against my mind in trying to get in, and disordered me a little, and before I could inquire into its pertinency, she was already throwing the needed light:

"This Apodictical Principle is the absolute Principle of Scientific Mind-healing, the sovereign Omnipotence which delivers the children of men from pain, disease, decay, and every ill that flesh is heir to."

"Surely not every ill, every decay?"

"Every one; there are no exceptions; there is no such thing as decay—it is an unreality, it has no existence."

"But without your glasses your failing eyesight does not permit you to—"

"My eyesight cannot fail; nothing can fail; the Mind is master, and the Mind permits no retrogression."

She was under the inspiration of the Third Degree, therefore there could be no profit in continuing this part of the subject. I shifted to other ground and inquired further concerning the Discoverer of the Science.

"Did the discovery come suddenly, like Klondike, or after long study and calculation, like America?"

"The comparisons are not respectful, since they refer to trivialities— but let it pass. I will answer in the Discoverer's own words: 'God had been graciously fitting me, during many years, for the reception of a final revelation of the absolute Principle of Scientific Mind-healing.' "

"Many years. How many?"

"Eighteen centuries!"

"All-God, God good, good God, Truth, Bones, Liver, one of a series, alone and without equal—it is amazing!"

"You may well say it, sir. Yet it is but the truth. This American lady, our revered and sacred Founder, is distinctly referred to, and her coming prophesied, in the twelfth chapter of the Apocalypse; she could not have been more plainly indicated by St. John without actually mentioning her name."

"How strange, how wonderful!"

"I will quote her own words, from her *Key to the Scriptures:* 'The twelfth chapter of the Apocalypse *has a special suggestiveness in connection with this nineteenth century.*' There—do you note that? Think —note it well."

"But—what does it mean?"

"Listen, and you will know. I quote her inspired words again: 'In the opening of the Sixth Seal, typical of six thousand years since Adam, there is one distinctive feature *which has special reference to the present age.* Thus:

" 'Revelation xii. 1. And there appeared a great wonder in heaven— a *woman* clothed with the sun, and the moon under her feet, and upon her head a crown of twelve stars.'

"That is our Head, our Chief, our Discoverer of Christian Science— nothing can be plainer, nothing surer. And note this:

" 'Revelation xii. 6. And the woman fled into the wilderness, where she had a place prepared of God.' "

"That is Boston. I recognize it, madam. These are sublime things, and impressive; I never understood these passages before; please go on with the—with the—proofs."

"Very well. Listen:

" 'And I saw another mighty angel come down from heaven, clothed with a cloud; and a rainbow was upon his head, and his face was as it were the sun, and his feet as pillars of fire. And he held in his hand *a little book.*'

"A little book, merely a little book—could words be modester? Yet how stupendous its importance! Do you know what book that was?"

"Was it—"

"I hold it in my hand—Christian Science!"

"Love, Livers, Lights, Bones, Truth, Kidneys, one of a series, alone and without equal—it is beyond imagination for wonder!"

"Hear our Founder's eloquent words: 'Then will a voice from harmony cry, "Go and take the little book: take it and eat it up, and it shall make thy belly bitter; but it shall be in thy mouth sweet as honey." Mortal, obey the heavenly evangel. Take up Divine Science. Read it from beginning to end. Study it, ponder it. It will be, indeed, sweet at its first taste, when it heals you; but murmur not over Truth, if you find its digestion bitter.' You now know the history of our dear and holy Science, sir, and that its *origin* is not of this earth, but only its *discovery.* I will leave the book with you and will go, now; but give yourself no uneasiness—I will give you absent treatment from now till I go to bed."

Under the powerful influence of the near treatment and the absent treatment together, my bones were gradually retreating inward and disappearing from view. The good work took a brisk start, now, and went on swiftly. My body was diligently straining and stretching, this way and that, to accommodate the processes of restoration, and every minute or two I heard a dull click inside and knew that the two ends of a fracture had been successfully joined. This muffled clicking and gritting and grinding and rasping continued during the next three hours, and then stopped—the connections had all been made. All except dislocations; there were only seven of these: hips, shoulders, knees, neck; so that was soon over; one after another they slipped into their sockets with a sound like pulling a distant cork, and I jumped up as good as new, as to framework, and sent for the horse-doctor.

I was obliged to do this because I had a stomach-ache and a cold in the head, and I was not willing to trust these things any longer in the hands of a woman whom I did not know, and in whose ability to successfully treat mere disease I had lost all confidence. My position was justified by the fact that the cold and the ache had been in her charge from the first, along with the fractures, but had experienced not a shade of relief; and, indeed, the ache was even growing worse and worse, and more and more bitter, now, probably on account of the protracted abstention from food and drink.

The horse-doctor came, a pleasant man and full of hope and professional interest in the case. In the matter of smell he was pretty aromatic—in fact, quite horsy—and I tried to arrange with him for absent treatment, but it was not in his line, so, out of delicacy, I did not press it. He looked at my teeth and examined my hock, and said my age and general condition were favorable to energetic measures; therefore he would give me something to turn the stomach-ache into the botts and the cold in the head into the blind staggers; then he should be on his own beat and would know what to do. He made up a bucket of bran-mash, and said a dipperful of it every two hours, alternated with a drench with turpentine and axle-grease in it, would either knock my ailments out of me in twenty-four hours, or so interest me in other ways as to make me forget they were on the premises. He administered my first dose himself, then took his leave, saying I was free to eat and drink anything I pleased and in any quantity I liked. But I was not hungry any more, and did not care for food.

I took up the Christian Science book and read half of it, then took a dipperful of drench and read the other half. The resulting experiences were full of interest and adventure. All through the rumblings and grindings and quakings and effervescings accompanying the evolution of the ache into the botts and the cold into the blind staggers I could note the generous struggle for mastery going on between the mash and the drench and the literature; and often I could tell which was ahead, and could easily distinguish the literature from the others when the others were separate, though not when they were mixed; for when a bran-mash and an eclectic drench are mixed together they look just like the Apodictical Principle out on a lark, and no one can tell it from that. The finish was reached at last, the evolutions were complete, and a fine success, but I think that this result could have been achieved with fewer materials. I believe the mash was necessary to the conversion of the stomach-ache into the botts, but I think one could develop the blind staggers out of the literature by itself; also, that blind staggers produced in this way would be of a better quality and more lasting than any produced by the artificial processes of the horse-doctor.

For of all the strange and frantic and incomprehensible and uninterpretable books which the imagination of man has created, surely this one is the prize sample. It is written with a limitless confidence and complacency, and with a dash and stir and earnestness which often compel the effects of eloquence, even when the words do not seem to have any traceable meaning. There are plenty of people who imagine they understand the book; I know this, for I have talked with them; but in all cases they were people who also imagined that there were no such things as pain, sickness, and death, and no realities in the world; nothing actually existent but Mind. It seems to me to modify the value of their testimony. When these people talk about Christian Science they do as Mrs. Fuller did: they do not use their own language, but the book's; they pour out the book's showy incoherences, and leave you to find out later that they were not originating, but merely quoting; they seem to know the volume by heart, and to revere it as they would a Bible—another Bible, perhaps I ought to say. Plainly the book was written under the mental desolations of the Third Degree, and I feel sure that none but the membership of that Degree can discover meanings in it. When you read it you seem to be listening to a lively and aggressive and oracular speech delivered in an unknown tongue, a speech whose spirit you get but not the particulars; or, to change the figure, you seem to be listening to a vigorous instrument which is making a noise which it thinks is a tune, but which, to persons not members of the band, is only the martial tooting of a trombone, and merely stirs the soul through the noise, but does not convey a meaning.

The book's serenities of self-satisfaction do almost seem to smack of a heavenly origin—they have no blood-kin in the earth. It is more than human to be so placidly certain about things, and so finely superior, and so airily content with one's performance. Without ever presenting anything which may rightfully be called by the strong name of Evidence, and sometimes without even *mentioning* a reason for a deduction at all, it thunders out the startling words, "I have *Proved*" so and so. It takes the Pope and all the great guns of his Church in battery assembled to authoritatively settle and establish the meaning of a sole and single unclarified passage of Scripture, and this at vast cost of time and study and reflection, but the author of this work is superior to all that: she finds the whole Bible in an unclarified condition, and at small expense of time and no expense of mental effort she clarifies it from lid to lid, reorganizes and improves the meanings, then authoritatively settles and establishes them with formulas which you cannot tell from "Let there be light!" and "Here you have it!" It is the first time since the dawn-days of Creation that a Voice has gone crashing through space with such placid and complacent confidence and command.

"ABOUT SMELLS," AN ANSWER TO A BROOKLYN CLERGYMAN WHO WOULD NOT ALLOW WORKING MEN TO BE SEATED IN HIS CONGREGATION (1870)*

We have reason to believe that there will be laboring men in heaven; and also a number of Negroes, and Esquimaux, and Terra del Fuegans, and Arabs, and a few Indians, and possibly even some Spaniards and Portuguese. All things are possible with God. We shall have all these sorts of people in heaven; but alas! in getting them we shall lose the society of Dr. Talmage. Which is to say, we shall lose the company of one who could give more real "tone" to celestial society than any other contribution Brooklyn could furnish. And what would eternal happiness be without the Doctor? Blissful, unquestionably—we know that well enough—but would it be *distingué*, would it be *recherché* without him? St. Matthew without stockings or sandals; St. Jerome bareheaded, and with a coarse brown blanket robe dragging the

* *Mark Twain: Social Critic.*

ground; St. Sebastian with scarcely any raiment at all—these we should see, and should enjoy seeing them; but would we not miss a spike-tailed coat and kids, and turn away regretfully, and say to parties from the Orient: "These are well enough, but you ought to see Talmage of Brooklyn." I fear me that in the better world we shall not even have Dr. Talmage's "good Christian friend." For if he were sitting under the glory of the Throne, and the keeper of the keys admitted a Benjamin Franklin or other laboring man, that "friend," with his fine natural powers infinitely augmented by emancipation from hampering flesh, would detect him with a single sniff, and immediately take his hat and ask to be excused.

To all outward seeming, the Rev. T. De Witt Talmage is of the same material as that used in the construction of his early predecessors in the ministry; and yet one feels that there must be a difference somewhere between him and the Saviour's first disciples. It may be because here, in the nineteenth century, Dr. T. has had advantages which Paul and Peter and the others could not and did not have. There was a lack of polish about them, and a looseness of etiquette, and a want of exclusiveness, which one cannot help noticing. They healed the very beggars, and held intercourse with people of a villainous odor every day. If the subject of these remarks had been among the original Twelve Apostles, he would not have associated with the rest, because he could not have stood the fishy smell of some of his comrades who came from around the Sea of Galilee. He would have resigned his commission with some such remark as he makes . . . : "Master, if thou art going to kill the church thus with bad smells, I will have nothing to do with this work of evangelization." He is a disciple, and makes that remark to the Master; the only difference is, that he makes it in the nineteenth instead of the first century.

Is there a choir in Mr. T.'s church? And does it ever occur that they have no better manners than to sing that hymn which is so suggestive of laborers and mechanics:

> "Son of the Carpenter! receive
> This humble work of mine?"

Now, can it be possible that in a handful of centuries the Christian character has fallen away from an imposing heroism that scorned even the stake, the cross, and the axe, to a poor little effeminacy that withers and wilts under an unsavory smell? We are not prepared to believe so, the reverend Doctor and his friend to the contrary notwithstanding.

ON PITYING GOD*

The old man said: "When I think of the suffering which I see around me, and how it wrings my heart; and then I remember what a drop in the ocean this is, compared with measureless Atlantics of misery which God has to see every day, my resentment is roused against those thoughtless people who are so glib to glorify God, yet never have a word of pity for him."

If God is what people say there can be no one in the universe so unhappy as he; for he sees unceasingly myriads of his creatures suffering unspeakable miseries—and besides this foresees how they are going to suffer during the remainder of their lives. One might well say: "As unhappy as God."

LAST NOTEBOOK ENTRY, ON EDUCATION
AND RELIGION*

All schools, all colleges, have two great functions: to confer, and to conceal valuable knowledge. The Theological knowledge which they conceal cannot justly be regarded as less valuable than that which they reveal. That is, if, when man is buying a basket of strawberries, it can profit him to know that the bottom half of it is rotten. Nov. 5, 1908.

* *Mark Twain's Notebook.*

THE FATHER OF MERCY*

Human history in all ages is red with blood, and bitter with hate, and stained with cruelties; but not since Biblical times have these features been without a limit of some kind. Even the Church, which is credited with having spilt more innocent blood, since the beginning of its supremacy, than all the political wars put together have spilt, has observed a limit. A sort of limit. But you notice that when the Lord God of Heaven and Earth, adored Father of Man, goes to war, there is no limit. He is totally without mercy—he, who is called the Fountain of Mercy. He slays, slays, slays! All the men, all the beasts, all the boys, all the babies; also all the women and all the girls, except those that have not been deflowered.

He makes no distinction between innocent and guilty. The babies were innocent, the beasts were innocent, many of the men, many of the women, many of the boys, many of the girls were innocent, yet they had to suffer with the guilty. What the insane Father required was blood and misery; he was indifferent as to who furnished it.

The heaviest punishment of all was meted out to persons who could not by any possibility have deserved so horrible a fate—the 32,000 virgins. Their naked privacies were probed, to make sure that they still possessed the hymen unruptured; after this humiliation they were sent away from the land that had been their home, to be sold into slavery; the worst of slaveries and the shamefulest, the slavery of prostitution; bed-slavery, to excite lust, and satisfy it with their bodies; slavery to any buyer, be he gentleman or be he a coarse and filthy ruffian.

It was the Father that inflicted this ferocious and undeserved punishment upon those bereaved and friendless virgins, whose parents and kindred he had slaughtered before their eyes. And were they praying to him for pity and rescue, meantime? Without a doubt of it.

These virgins were "spoil," plunder, booty. He claimed his share and got it. What use had *he* for virgins? Examine his later history and you will know.

* *Letters from the Earth.*

His priests got a share of the virgins, too. What use could priests make of virgins? The private history of the Roman Catholic confessional can answer that question for you. The confessional's chief amusement has been seduction—in all the ages of the Church. Père Hyacinth testifies that of a hundred priests confessed by him, ninety-nine had used the confessional effectively for the seduction of married women and young girls. One priest confessed that of nine hundred girls and women whom he had served as father confessor in his time, none had escaped his lecherous embrace but the elderly and the homely. The official list of questions which the priest is required to ask will over-masteringly excite any woman who is not a paralytic.

There is nothing in either savage or civilized history that is more utterly complete, more remorselessly sweeping than the Father of Mercy's campaign among the Midianites. The official report does not furnish incidents, episodes, and minor details, it deals only in information in masses: *all* the virgins, *all* the men, *all* the babies, *all* "creatures *that breathe*," *all* houses, *all* cities; it gives you just one vast picture, spread abroad here and there and yonder, as far as eye can reach, of charred ruin and storm-swept desolation; your imagination adds a brooding stillness, an awful hush—the hush of death. But of course there were incidents. Where shall we get them?

Out of history of yesterday's date. Out of history made by the red Indian of America. He has duplicated God's work, and done it in the very spirit of God. In 1862 the Indians in Minnesota, having been deeply wronged and treacherously treated by the government of the United States, rose against the white settlers and massacred them; massacred all they could lay their hands upon, sparing neither age nor sex. Consider this incident:

Twelve Indians broke into a farmhouse at daybreak and captured the family. It consisted of the farmer and his wife and four daughters, the youngest aged fourteen and the eldest eighteen. They crucified the parents; that is to say, they stood them stark naked against the wall of the living room and nailed their hands to the wall. Then they stripped the daughters bare, stretched them upon the floor in front of their parents, and repeatedly ravished them. Finally they crucified the girls against the wall opposite the parents, and cut off their noses and their breasts. They also—but I will not go into that. There is a limit. There are indignities so atrocious that the pen cannot write them. One member of that poor crucified family—the father—was still alive when help came two days later.

Now you have one incident of the Minnesota massacre. I could give you fifty. They would cover all the different kinds of cruelty the brutal human talent has ever invented.

And now you know, by these sure indications, what happened under the personal direction of the Father of Mercies in his Midianite campaign. The Minnesota campaign was merely a duplicate of the Midianite raid. Nothing happened in the one that did not happen in the other.

No, that is not strictly true. The Indian was more merciful than was the Father of Mercies. He sold no virgins into slavery to minister to the lusts of the murderers of their kindred while their sad lives might last; he raped them, then charitably made their subsequent sufferings brief, ending them with the precious gift of death. He burned some of the houses, but not all of them. He carried off innocent dumb brutes, but he took the lives of none.

Would you expect this same conscienceless God, this moral bankrupt, to become a teacher of morals; of gentleness; of meekness; of righteousness; of purity? It looks impossible, extravagant; but listen to him. These are his own words:

> Blessed are the poor in spirit, for theirs is the kingdom of heaven.
> Blessed are they that mourn, for they shall be comforted.
> Blessed are the meek, for they shall inherit the earth.
> Blessed are they which do hunger and thirst after righteousness, for they shall be filled.
> *Blessed are the merciful,* for they shall obtain mercy.
> Blessed are the pure in heart, for they shall see God.
> *Blessed are the peace-makers,* for they shall be called *the children of God.*
> Blessed are they which are persecuted for righteousness' sake, for theirs is the kingdom of heaven.
> Blessed are ye when men shall revile you and persecute you, and say all manner of evil against you falsely for my sake.

The mouth that uttered these immense sarcasms, these giant hypocrisies, is the very same that ordered the wholesale massacre of the Midianitish men and babies and cattle; the wholesale destruction of house and city; the wholesale banishment of the virgins into a filthy and unspeakable slavery. This is the same person who brought upon the Midianites the fiendish cruelties which were repeated by the red Indians, detail by detail, in Minnesota eighteen centuries later. The Midianite episode filled him with joy. So did the Minnesota one, or he would have prevented it.

The Beatitudes and the chapters from Numbers and Deuteronomy ought always to be read from the pulpit together; then the congregation would get an all-round view of Our Father in Heaven. Yet not in a single instance have I ever known a clergyman to do this.

MARK TWAIN'S GOD*

If I were going to construct a God I would furnish Him with some ways and qualities and characteristics which the Present (Bible) One lacks.

He would not stoop to *ask* for any man's compliments, praises, flatteries; and He would be far above *exacting* them. I would have Him as self-respecting as the better sort of man in these regards.

He would not be a merchant, a trader. He would not buy these things. He would not sell, or offer to sell, temporary benefits or the joys of eternity for the product called worship. I would have Him as dignified as the better sort of men in this regard.

He would value no love but the love born of kindnesses conferred; not that born of benevolences contracted for. Repentance in a man's heart for a wrong done would cancel and annul that sin, and no verbal prayers for forgiveness be required or desired or expected of that man.

In His Bible there would be no Unforgivable Sin. He would recognize in Himself the Author and Inventor of Sin and Author and Inventor of the Vehicle and Appliances for its commission; and would place the whole responsibility where it would of right belong: upon Himself, the only Sinner.

He would not be a jealous God—a trait so small that even men despise it in each other.

* *Mark Twain's Notebook.*

He would not boast.

He would keep private His admirations of Himself; He would regard self-praise as unbecoming the dignity of His position.

He would not have the spirit of vengeance in His heart; then it could not issue from His lips.

There would not be any hell—except the one we live in from the cradle to the grave.

There would not be any heaven—of the kind described in the world's Bibles.

He would spend some of His eternities in trying to forgive Himself for making man unhappy when He could have made him happy with the same effort and He would spend the rest of them in studying astronomy.

MARK TWAIN'S GOD*

The Being who to me is the real God is the One who created this majestic universe and rules it. He is the only Originator, the only originator of thoughts; thoughts suggested from within not from without; the originator of colors and of all their possible combinations; of forces and the laws that govern them; of forms and shapes of *all* forms. Man has never invented a new one; He is the only Originator—He made the materials of all things; He made the laws by which and by which only, man may combine them into machines and other things which outside influence may suggest to him. He made character—man can portray it but not "create" it, for He is the only Creator.

He is the perfect artisan, the perfect artist. Everything which he has made is fine, everything which he has made is beautiful; nothing coarse, nothing ugly has ever come from His hand. Even His materials are all delicate, none of them is coarse. The materials of the leaf, the flower, the fruit; of the insect, the elephant, the man; of the earth, the crags and the ocean; of the snow, the hoarfrost and the ice—may be reduced to infinitesimal particles and they are still delicate, still faultless; whether He makes a gnat, a bird, a horse, a plain, a forest, a mountain range, a planet, a constellation, or a diatom whose form the

* *Mark Twain's Notebook.*

keenest eye in the world cannot perceive, it is all one—He makes it utterly and minutely perfect in form, and construction. The diatom which is invisible to the eye on the point of a needle is graceful and beautiful in form and in the minute exquisite elaboration of its parts it is a wonder. The contemplation of it moves one to something of the same awe and reverence which the march of the comets through their billion mile orbits compels.

This is indeed a God! He is not jealous, trivial, ignorant, revengeful—it is impossible. He has personal dignity—dignity answerable to his grandeur, his greatness, his might, his sublimity; He cares nothing for men's flatteries, compliments, praises, prayers; it is impossible that he should value them, impossible that he should listen to them, these mouthings of microbes. He is not ignorant, He does not mistake His myriad great suns, swimming in the measureless ocean of space for tallow candles hung in the roof to light this forgotten potato which we call the Earth, and name His footstool. He cannot see it except under His microscope. The shadow does not go back on His dial—it is against His law; His sun does not stand still on Gibeon to accommodate a worm out on a raid against other worms—it is against His law. His real character is written in plain words in His real Bible, which is Nature and her history; we read it every day, and we could understand it and trust in it if we would burn the spurious one and dig the remains of our insignificant reasoning faculties out of the grave where that and other man-made Bibles have buried them for 2,000 years and more.

The Bible of Nature tells us no word about any future life, but only about this present one. It does not promise a future life; it does not even vaguely indicate one. It is not intended as a message to us, any more than the scientist intends a message to surviving microbes when he boils the life out of a billion of them in a thimble. The microbes discover a message in it; this is certain—if they have a pulpit.

The Book of Nature tells us distinctly that God cares not a rap for us—nor for any living creature. It tells us that His laws inflict pain and suffering and sorrow, but it does not say that this is done in order that He may get pleasure out of this misery. We do not know what the object is, for the Book is not able to tell us. It may be mere indifference. Without a doubt He had an object, but we have no way of discovering what it was. The scientist has an object, but it is not the joy of inflicting pain upon the microbe.

PART THREE

R evolution

My privilege to write these sanguinary sentences in soft security was bought for me by rivers of blood poured upon many fields, in many lands, but I possess not one single little paltry right or privilege that come to me as a result of persuasion, agitation for reform, or any kindred method of procedure.

—Mark Twain's letter of 1890.

STATEMENT ABOUT REVOLUTION IN A NEWSPAPER

INTERVIEW OVER THE GORKI AFFAIR IN 1906*

I am said to be a revolutionist in my sympathies, by birth, by breeding and by principle. I am always on the side of the revolutionists, because there never was a revolution unless there were some oppressive and intolerable conditions against which to revolute.

ON THE BOXER REBELLION IN CHINA IN 1900*

Why shouldn't all the foreign powers withdraw from China and leave her free to attend to her own business?

It is the foreigners who are making all the trouble in China, and if they would only get out how pleasant everything would be!

As far as America is concerned we don't allow the Chinese to come here, and we would be doing the graceful thing to allow China to decide whether she will allow us to go there. China never wanted any foreigners, and when it comes to a settlement of this immigrant question I am with the Boxer every time.

The Boxer is a patriot; he is the only patriot China has, and I wish him success.

* *Mark Twain: Social Critic.*

THE BOXER REBELLION IN CHINA

Extract from a Letter to Rev. J. H. Twitchell, August 12, 1900*

It is all China, now, and my sympathies are with the Chinese. They have been villainously dealt with by the sceptred thieves of Europe, and I hope they will drive all the foreigners out and keep them out for good. I only wish it; of course I don't really expect it.†

STATEMENT ABOUT THE PEACE OF PORTSMOUTH
ENDING THE RUSSO-JAPANESE WAR IN 1905‡

Russia was on the high road to emancipation from an insane & intolerable slavery; I was hoping there would be no peace until Russian liberty was safe. I think that this was a holy war in the best & noblest sense of that abused term, & that no war was ever charged with a higher mission; I think there can be no doubt that that mission is now defeated and Russia's chains re-riveted, this time to stay. I think the Czar will now withdraw the small humanities that have been forced from him, & resume his medieval barbarisms with a relieved spirit & an immeasurable joy. I think Russian liberty has had its last chance, & has lost it. I think nothing has been gained by the peace that is remotely comparable to what has been sacrificed by it. One more battle would have abolished the waiting chains of billions and billions of unborn Russians, and I wish it could have been fought. I hope I am mistaken,

---

* *Mark Twain's Letters.*

† But in the end, Twain predicted elsewhere, China would rise up and free itself. And see the accounts of the Chinese and the missionaries, etc., in Part One. *Ed.*

‡ *Mark Twain: Social Critic.*

yet in all sincerity I believe that this peace is entitled to rank as the most conspicuous disaster in political history.

ON THE RUSSIAN REVOLUTION:

The Czar's Soliloquy, 1905*

After the Czar's morning bath it is his habit to meditate an hour before dressing himself.—*London Times Correspondence.*

(*Viewing himself in the pierglass.*) NAKED, what am I? A lank, skinny, spider-legged libel on the image of God! Look at the waxwork head—the face, with the expression of a melon—the projecting ears— the knotted elbows—the dished breast—the knife-edged shins—and then the feet, all beads and joints and bone-sprays, an imitation X-ray photograph! . . . Is it this that a hundred and forty million Russians kiss the dust before and worship? Manifestly not! . . . Then what is it? . . . Privately, none knows better than I: it is my clothes. . . .

There is no power without clothes. . . . Strip its chiefs to the skin, and no state could be governed; naked officials could exercise no authority; they would look (and be) like everybody else—commonplace, inconsequential. A policeman in plain clothes is one man; in his uniform he is ten. Clothes and title are the most potent thing, the most formidable influence, in the earth. They move the human race to willing and spontaneous respect for the judge, the general, the admiral, the bishop, the ambassador, the frivolous earl, the idiot duke, the sultan, the king, the emperor. . . . The king of the great Fan tribe wears a bit of leopard-skin on his shoulder—it is sacred to royalty; the rest of him is perfectly naked. Without his bit of leopard-skin to awe and impress the people, he would not be able to keep his job.

(*After a silence.*) A curious invention, an unaccountable invention—the human race! The swarming Russian millions have for centuries meekly allowed our family to rob them, insult them, trample them under foot, while they lived and suffered and died with no

* As abridged in *Mark Twain on the Damned Human Race.*

purpose and no function but to make that family comfortable! These people are horses—just that—horses with clothes and a religion. A horse with the strength of a hundred men will let one man beat him, starve him, drive him; the Russian millions allow a mere handful of soldiers to hold them in slavery—and these very soldiers are their own sons and brothers!

A strange thing, when one considers it: to wit, the world applies to Czar and system the same moral axioms that have vogue and acceptance in civilized countries! Because, in civilized countries, it is wrong to remove oppressors otherwise than by process of law, it is held that the same rule applies in Russia, where there is no such thing as law—except for our family. Laws are merely restraints—they have no other function. In civilized countries they restrain all persons, and restrain them all alike, which is fair and righteous; but in Russia such laws as exist make an exception—our family. We do as we please; we have done as we pleased for centuries. Our common trade has been crime, our common pastime murder, our common beverage blood—the blood of the nation. Upon our heads lie millions of murders. Yet the pious moralist says it is a crime to assassinate us. We and our uncles are a family of cobras set over a hundred and forty million rabbits, whom we torture and murder and feed upon all our days; yet the moralist urges that to kill us is a crime, not a duty.

It is not for me to say it aloud, but to one on the inside—like me—this is naïvely funny; on its face, illogical. Our family is above all law; there is no law that can reach us, restrain us, protect the people from us. Therefore, we are outlaws. Outlaws are a proper mark for anyone's bullet. Ah! what could our family do without the moralist? He has always been our stay, our support, our friend; today is our *only* friend. Whenever there has been dark talk of assassination, he has come forward and saved us with his impressive maxim, "Forbear: nothing politically valuable was ever yet achieved by violence." He probably believes it. It is because he has by him no child's book of world history to teach him that his maxim lacks the backing of statistics. All thrones have been established by violence; no regal tyranny has ever been overthrown except by violence; by violence my fathers set up our throne; by murder, treachery, perjury, torture, banishment, and the prison they have held it for four centuries, and by these same arts I hold it today. There is no Romanoff of learning and experience but would reverse the maxim and say: "Nothing politically valuable was ever yet achieved *except* by violence." The moralist realizes that today, for the first time in our history, my throne is in real peril and the nation waking up from its immemorial slave-lethargy; but he does not perceive that four deeds of violence are the reason for it: the assassination of the Finland Constitution by my hand; the slaughter, by revolutionary assassins, of Bobrikoff and Plehve, and my massacre of the unoffending innocents the other day. But the blood that flows in my veins—blood informed, trained, educated by its grim heredities, blood alert by its traditions, blood which has been to school four hundred years in the veins of professional assassins, my predecessors—*it* perceives, *it* understands! Those four deeds have set up a commotion in the inert and muddy deeps of the national heart such as no moral suasion could have accomplished; they have aroused hatred and hope in that long-atrophied heart; and, little by little, slowly but surely, that feeling will steal into every breast and possess it. In time, into even the *soldier's* breast—fatal day, day of doom, that! . . . By and by, there will be results! How little the academical moralist knows of the tremendous moral force of massacre and assassination! . . . Indeed there are going to be results! The nation is in labor; and by and by there will be a mighty birth—Patriotism! To put it in rude, plain, unpalatable words—*true* patriotism, real patriotism: loyalty, not to a family and a fiction, but loyalty to the nation itself!

. . . There are twenty-five million families in Russia. There is a man-child at every mother's knee. If these were twenty-five million patriotic mothers, they would teach these man-children daily, saying: "Remember this, take it to heart, live by it, die for it if necessary: that our patriotism is medieval, outworn, obsolete; that the modern patriotism, the true patriotism, the only rational patriotism, is *loyalty to the nation* ALL *the time, loyalty to the government when it deserves it.*" With twenty-five million taught and trained patriots in the land a generation from now, my successor would think twice before he would butcher a thousand helpless poor petitioners humbly begging for his kindness and justice, as I did the other day.

(*Reflective pause.*) Well, perhaps I have been affected by these depressing newspaper-clippings which I found under my pillow. I will read and ponder them again. (*Reads.*)

POLISH WOMEN KNOUTED.

Reservists' Wives Treated with Awful Brutality—At Least One Killed.

Special Cable to THE NEW YORK TIMES.

BERLIN, Nov. 27—Infuriated by the unwillingness of the Polish troops to leave their wives and children, the Russian authorities at Kutno, a town on the Polish frontier, have treated the people in a manner almost incredibly cruel.

It is known that *one woman has been knouted to death* and that a number of others have been injured. Fifty persons have been thrown into jail. Some of the prisoners were *tortured into unconsciousness.*

Details of the brutalities are lacking, but it seems that the Cossacks tore the reservists from the arms of their wives and children and then *knouted the women who followed their husbands into the streets.*

In cases where reservists could not be found *their wives were dragged by their hair into the streets and there beaten. The chief official of the district and the Colonel of a regiment are said to have looked on while this was being done.*

A girl who has assisted in distributing Socialist tracts was *treated in an atrocious manner.*

CZAR AS LORD'S ANOINTED.

People Spent Night in Prayer and Fasting Before His Visit to Novgorod.

LONDON TIMES—NEW TIMES.

Special Cablegram.

Copyright, 1904, THE NEW YORK TIMES

LONDON, July 27.—The London *Times*'s Russian correspondents say the following extract from the *Petersburger Zeitung,* describing the Czar's recent doings at Novgorod, affords a typical instance of the servile adulation which the subjects of the Czar deem it necessary to adopt:

"The blessing of the troops, *who knelt devoutly before his Majesty,* was a profoundly moving spectacle. His Majesty held the sacred ikon aloft and pronounced aloud a blessing in his own name and that of the Empress.

Thousands *wept with emotion and spiritual ecstasy.* Pupils of girls' schools scattered roses in the path of the monarch.

"People pressed up to the carriage in order to carry away an indelible memory of the *hallowed features of the Lord's Anointed.* Many old people had spent the night in prayer and fasting *in order to be worthy to gaze at his countenance with pure, undefiled souls.*

"The greatest enthusiasm prevails *at the happiness thus vouchsafed to the people.*"

(*Moved.*) . . . And it was I that got that grovelling and awe-smitten worship! *I*—this thing in the mirror—this carrot! With one hand I flogged unoffending women to death and tortured prisoners to unconsciousness; and with the other I held up the fetish toward my fellow deity in heaven and called down His blessing upon my adoring

animals whom, and whose forbears, with His holy approval, I and mine
have been instructing in the pains of hell for four lagging centuries. It
is a picture! To think that this thing in the mirror—this vegetable—is
an accepted deity to a mighty nation, an innumerable host, and nobody
laughs; and at the same time is a diligent and practical professional
devil, and nobody marvels, nobody murmurs about incongruities and
inconsistencies! Is the human race a joke? Was it devised and patched
together in a dull time when there was nothing important to do? Has it
no respect for itself? . . . I think my respect for it is drooping. sinking—and my respect for myself along with it. . . . There is but one
restorative—*Clothes!* I will put them on. . . .

THE RUSSIAN REVOLUTION AND THE USA*

Three days ago a neighbor brought the celebrated Russian revolutionist, Tchaykoffsky, to call upon me. He is grizzled, and shows age—
as to exteriors—but he has a Vesuvius, inside, which is a strong and
active volcano yet. He is so full of belief in the ultimate and almost
immediate triumph of the revolution and the destruction of the fiendish
autocracy, that he almost made me believe and hope with him. He has
come over here expecting to arouse a conflagration of noble sympathy
in our vast nation of eighty millions of happy and enthusiastic freemen. But honesty obliged me to pour some cold water down his crater.
I told him what I believed to be true: that our Christianity which we
have always been so proud of—not to say so vain of—is now nothing
but a shell, a sham. a hypocrisy; that we have lost our ancient sympathy with oppressed peoples struggling for life and liberty; that when
we are not coldly indifferent to such things we sneer at them, and that
the sneer is about the only expression the newspapers and the nation
deal in with regard to such things; that his mass meetings would not be
attended by people entitled to call themselves representative Americans, even if they may call themselves Americans at all; that his
audiences will be composed of foreigners who have suffered so recently
that they have not yet had time to become Americanized and their

* *Autobiography*, Paine Edition, 1924. Not in Charles Neider's edition of Mark
Twain's *Autobiography*, 1959.

hearts turned to stone in their breasts; that these audiences will be drawn from the ranks of the poor, not those of the rich; that they will give and give freely, but they will give from their poverty and the money result will not be large. I said that when our windy and flamboyant President conceived the idea, a year ago, of advertising himself to the world as the new Angel of Peace, and set himself the task of bringing about the peace between Russia and Japan and had the misfortune to accomplish his misbegotten purpose, no one in all this nation except Doctor Seaman and myself uttered a public protest against this folly of follies. That at that time I believed that that fatal peace had postponed the Russian nation's imminent liberation from its age-long chains indefinitely—probably for centuries; that I believed at that time that Roosevelt had given the Russian revolution its death-blow, and that I am of that opinion yet.

I will mention here, in parenthesis, that I came across Doctor Seaman last night for the first time in my life, and found that his opinion also remains to-day as he expressed it at the time that that infamous peace was consummated.

Tchaykoffsky said that my talk depressed him profoundly, and that he hoped I was wrong.

I said I hoped the same.

He said, "Why, from this very nation of yours came a mighty contribution only two or three months ago, and it made us all glad in Russia. You raised two millions of dollars in a breath—in a moment, as it were—and sent that contribution, that most noble and generous contribution, to suffering Russia. Does not that modify your opinion?"

"No," I said, "it doesn't. That money came not from Americans, it came from Jews; much of it from rich Jews, but the most of it from Russian and Polish Jews on the East Side—that is to say, it came from the very poor. The Jew has always been benevolent. Suffering can always move a Jew's heart and tax his pocket to the limit. He will be at your mass meetings. But if you find any Americans there put them in a glass case and exhibit them. It will be worthy fifty cents a head to go and look at that show and try to believe in it."

He asked me to come to last night's meeting and speak, but I had another engagement and could not do it. Then he asked me to write a line or two which could be read at the meeting, and I did that cheerfully.

THE RUSSIAN REVOLUTION

Letter to N. V. Tchaykoffsky, Spring, 1906*

DEAR MR. TCHAYKOFFSKY,—I thank you for the honor of the invitation, but I am not able to accept it, because on Thursday evening I shall be presiding at a meeting whose object is to find remunerative work for certain classes of our blind who would gladly support themselves if they had the opportunity.

My sympathies are with the Russian revolution, of course. It goes without saying. I hope it will succeed, and now that I have talked with you I take heart to believe it will. Government by falsified promises, by lies, by treacheries, and by the butcher-knife for the aggrandizement of a single family of drones and its idle and vicious kin has been borne quite long enough in Russia, I should think, and it is to be hoped that the roused nation, now rising in its strength, will presently put an end to it and set up the republic in its place. Some of us, even of the white headed, may live to see the blessed day when Czars and Grand Dukes will be as scarce there as I trust they are in heaven.

AN UNPUBLISHED LETTER ABOUT THE CZAR†

Onteora, *1890*.

TO THE EDITOR OF FREE RUSSIA,—I thank you for the compliment of your invitation to say something, but when I ponder the bottom paragraph on your first page, and then study your statement on your

---

* *Mark Twain's Letters.*

† *Ibid.* Clemens wrote this letter for the magazine *Free Russia*, but for whatever reasons never mailed it. Though he said as much or more about violence and revolution in "The Czar's Soliloquy," there are in this letter some remarkably fresh and penetrating historical observations. *Ed.*

third page, of the objects of the several Russian liberation-parties, I do not quite know how to proceed. Let me quote here the paragraph referred to:

"But men's hearts are so made that the sight of one voluntary victim for a noble idea stirs them more deeply than the sight of a crowd submitting to a dire fate they cannot escape. Besides, foreigners could not see so clearly as the Russians how much the Government was responsible for the grinding poverty of the masses; nor could they very well realize the moral wretchedness imposed by that Government upon the whole of educated Russia. But the atrocities committed upon the defenceless prisoners are there in all their baseness, concrete and palpable, admitting of no excuse, no doubt or hesitation, crying out to the heart of humanity against Russian tyranny. And the Czar's Government, stupidly confident in its apparently unassailable position, instead of taking warning from the first rebukes, seems to mock this humanitarian age by the aggravation of brutalities. Not satisfied with slowly killing its prisoners, and with burying the flower of our young generation in the Siberian deserts, the Government of Alexander III. resolved to break their spirit by deliberately submitting them to a regime of unheard-of brutality and degradation."

When one reads that paragraph in the glare of George Kennan's revelations, and considers how much it means; considers that all earthly figures fail to typify the Czar's government, and that one must descend into hell to find its counterpart, one turns hopefully to your statement of the objects of the several liberation-parties—and is disappointed. Apparently none of them can bear to think of losing the present hell entirely, they merely want the temperature cooled down a little.

I now perceive why all men are the deadly and uncompromising enemies of the rattlesnake: it is merely because the rattlesnake has not speech. Monarchy has speech, and by it has been able to persuade men that it differs somehow from the rattlesnake, has something valuable about it somewhere, something worth preserving, something even good and high and fine, when properly "modified," something entitling it to protection from the club of the first comer who catches it out of its hole. It seems a most strange delusion and not reconcilable with our superstition that man is a reasoning being. If a house is afire, we reason confidently that it is the first comer's plain duty to put the fire out in any way he can—drown it with water, blow it up with dynamite, use any and all means to stop the spread of the fire and save the rest of the city. What is the Czar of Russia but a house afire in the midst of a city of eighty millions of inhabitants? Yet instead of extinguishing him, together with his nest and system, the liberation-parties are all anxious to merely cool him down a little and keep him.

It seems to me that this is illogical—idiotic, in fact. Suppose you had this granite-hearted, bloody-jawed maniac of Russia loose in your house, chasing the helpless women and little children—your own. What would you do with him, supposing you had a shotgun? Well, he *is* loose in your house—Russia. And with your shotgun in your hand, you stand trying to think up ways to "modify" him.

Do these liberation-parties think that they can succeed in a project which has been attempted a million times in the history of the world and has never in one single instance been successful—the "modification" of a despotism by other means than bloodshed? They seem to think they can. My privilege to write these sanguinary sentences in soft security was bought for me by rivers of blood poured upon many fields, in many lands, but I possess not one single little paltry right or privilege that come to me as a result of petition, persuasion, agitation for reform, or any kindred method of procedure. When we consider that not even the most responsible English monarch ever yielded back a stolen public right until it was wrenched from them by bloody violence, is it rational to suppose that gentler methods can win privileges in Russia?

Of course I know that the properest way to demolish the Russian throne would be by revolution. But it is not possible to get up a revolution there; so the only thing left to do, apparently, is to keep the throne vacant by dynamite until a day when candidates shall decline with thanks. Then organize the Republic. And on the whole this method has some large advantages; for whereas a revolution destroys some lives which cannot well be spared, the dynamite way doesn't. Consider this: the conspirators against the Czar's life are caught in every rank of life, from the low to the high. And consider: if so many take an active part, where the peril is so dire, is this not evidence that the sympathizers who keep still and do not show their hands, are countless for multitudes? Can you break the hearts of thousands of families with the awful Siberian exodus every year for generations and not eventually cover all Russia from limit to limit with bereaved fathers and mothers and brothers and sisters who secretly hate the perpetrator of this prodigious crime and hunger and thirst for his life? Do you not believe that if your wife or your child or your father was exiled to the mines of Siberia for some trivial utterances wrung from a smarting spirit by the Czar's intolerable tyranny, and you got a chance to kill him and did not do it, that you would always be ashamed to be in your own society the rest of your life? Suppose that that refined and lovely Russian lady who was lately stripped bare before a brutal soldiery and whipped to death by the Czar's hand in the person of the Czar's creature had been your wife, or your daughter or your sister, and to-day the Czar should pass within reach of your hand, how would you feel—and what would you do? Consider, that all over vast Russia, from boundary to boundary, a myriad of eyes filled with tears when that piteous news came, and through those tears that myriad of eyes saw, not that poor lady, but lost darlings of their own whose fate her fate brought back with new access of grief out of a black and bitter past never to be forgotten or forgiven.

If I am a Swinburnian—and clear to the marrow I am—I hold human nature in sufficient honor to believe there are eighty million mute Russians that are of the same stripe, and only one Russian family that isn't.

MONARCHY AND REVOLUTION

A Letter to Sylvester Baxter of the Boston Herald *Concerning the Collapse of the Brazilian Monarchy in 1889.* *

DEAR MR. BAXTER,—Another throne has gone down, and I swim in oceans of satisfaction. I wish I might live fifty years longer; I believe I should see the thrones of Europe selling at auction for old iron. I believe I should really see the end of what is surely the grotesquest of all the swindles ever invented by man—monarchy. It is enough to make

* *Mark Twain's Letters.*

a graven image laugh, to see apparently rational people, away down here in this wholesome and merciless slaughter-day for shams, still mouthing empty reverence for those moss-backed frauds and scoundrelisms, hereditary kingship and so-called "nobility." It is enough to make the monarchs and nobles themselves laugh—and in private they do; there can be no question about that. I think there is only one funnier thing, and that is the spectacle of these bastard Americans—these Hamersleys and Huntingtons and such—offering cash, encumbered by themselves, for rotten carcasses and stolen titles. When our great brethren the disenslaved Brazilians frame their Declaration of Independence, I hope they will insert this missing link: "We hold these truths to be self-evident: that all monarchs are usurpers, and descendants of usurpers; for the reason that no throne was ever set up in this world by the will, freely exercised, of the only body possessing the legitimate right to set it up—the numerical mass of the nation."

You already have the advance sheets of my forthcoming book in your hands. If you will turn to about the five hundredth page, you will find a state paper of my Connecticut Yankee in which he announces the dissolution of King Arthur's monarchy and proclaims the English Republic. Compare it with the state paper which announces the downfall of the Brazilian monarchy and proclaims the Republic of the United States of Brazil, and stand by to defend the Yankee from plagiarism. There is merely a resemblance of ideas, nothing more. The Yankee's proclamation was already in print a week ago. This is merely one of those odd coincidences which are always turning up. Come, protect the Yank from that cheapest and easiest of all charges—plagiarism. Otherwise, you see, he will have to protect himself by charging approximate and indefinite plagiarism upon the official servants of our majestic twin down yonder, and then there might be war, or some similar annoyance.

Have you noticed the rumor that the Portuguese throne is unsteady, and that the Portuguese slaves are getting restive? Also, that the head slave-driver of Europe, Alexander III, has so reduced his usual monthly order for chains that the Russian foundries are running on only half time now? Also that other rumor that English nobility acquired an added stench the other day—and had to ship it to India and the continent because there wasn't any more room for it at home? Things are working. By and by there is going to be an emigration, maybe. Of course we shall make no preparation; we never do. In a few years from now we shall have nothing but played-out kings and dukes on the police, and driving the horse-cars, and whitewashing fences, and in fact over-crowding all the avenues of unskilled labor; and then we shall wish, when it is too late, that we had taken common and reasonable precautions and drowned them at Castle Garden.

THEFT, CRIME, AND VIOLENCE AT THE
BASE OF CIVILIZATION:
Land-Grabbing and Modern Imperialism*

To such as believe that the quaint product called French civilization would be an improvement upon the civilization of New Guinea and the like, the snatching of Madagascar and the laying on of French civilization there will be fully justified. But why did the English allow the French to have Madagascar? Did she respect a theft of a couple of centuries ago? Dear me, robbery by European nations of each other's territories has never been a sin, is not a sin to-day. To the several cabinets the several political establishments of the world are clothes-lines; and a large part of the official duty of these cabinets is to keep an eye on each other's wash and grab what they can of it as opportunity offers. All the territorial possessions of all the political establishments in the earth—including America, of course—consist of pilferings from other people's wash. No tribe, howsoever insignificant, and no nation, howsoever mighty, occupies a foot of land that was not stolen. When the English, the French, and the Spaniards reached America, the Indian tribes had been raiding each other's territorial clothes-lines for ages, and every acre of ground in the continent had been stolen and restolen five hundred times. The English, the French, and the Span-iards went to work and stole it all over again; and when that was satisfactorily accomplished they went diligently to work and stole it from each other. In Europe and Asia and Africa every acre of ground

---

* *Following the Equator.* Twain was right about everything but the last observation here, where he did not anticipate how soon the oppressed "savages" would revolt against the march of civilization in our own period. *Ed.*

has been stolen several millions of times. A crime persevered in a thousand centuries ceases to be a crime, and becomes a virtue. This is the law of custom, and custom supersedes all other forms of law. Christian governments are as frank to-day, as open and aboveboard, in discussing projects for raiding each other's clothes-lines as ever they were before the Golden Rule came smiling into this inhospitable world and couldn't get a night's lodging anywhere. In one hundred and fifty years England has beneficently retired garment after garment from the Indian lines, until there is hardly a rag of the original wash left dangling anywhere. In eight hundred years an obscure tribe of Muscovite savages has risen to the dazzling position of Land-Robber-in-Chief; she found a quarter of the world hanging out to dry on a hundred parallels of latitude, and she scooped in the whole wash. She keeps a sharp eye on a multitude of little lines that stretch along the northern boundaries of India, and every now and then she snatches a hip-rag or a pair of pajamas. It is England's prospective property, and Russia knows it; but Russia cares nothing for that. In fact, in our day, land-robbery, claim-jumping, is become a European governmental frenzy. Some have been hard at it in the borders of China, in Burma, in Siam, and the islands of the sea; and *all* have been at it in Africa. Africa has been as coolly divided up and portioned out among the gang as if they had bought it and paid for it. And now straightway they are beginning the old game again—to steal each other's grabbings. Germany found a vast slice of Central Africa with the English flag and the English missionary and the English trader scattered all over it, but with certain formalities neglected—no signs up, "Keep off the grass," "Trespassers forbidden," etc.—and she stepped in with a cold calm smile and put up the signs herself, and swept those English pioneers promptly out of the country.

There is a tremendous point there. It can be put into the form of a maxim: Get your formalities right—never mind about the moralities.

It was an impudent thing; but England had to put up with it. Now, in the case of Madagascar, the formalities had originally been observed, but by neglect they had fallen into desuetude ages ago. England should have snatched Madagascar from the French clothes-line. Without an effort she could have saved those harmless natives from the calamity of French civilization, and she did not do it. Now it is too late.

The signs of the times show plainly enough what is going to happen. All the savage lands in the world are going to be brought under subjection to the Christian governments of Europe. I am not sorry, but glad. This coming fate might have been a calamity to those savage peoples two hundred years ago; but now it will in some cases be a benefaction. The sooner the seizure is consummated, the better for the savages. The dreary and dragging ages of bloodshed and disorder and oppression will give place to peace and order and the reign of law.

PATRIOTISM AND ROBBERY*

Talking of patriotism what humbug it is; it is a word which always commemorates a robbery. There isn't a foot of land in the world which doesn't represent the ousting and re-ousting of a long line of successive "owners," who each in turn, as "patriots," with proud swelling hearts defended it against the next gang of "robbers" who came to steal it and *did*—and became swelling-hearted patriots in *their* turn. And this Transvaal, now, is full of patriots, who by the help of God, who is always interested in these things, stole the land from the feeble blacks, and then re-stole it from the English robber and has put up the monument—which the next robber will pull down and keep as a curiosity.

RUSSIA AND THE CONGO AGAIN†

A Connecticut Yankee in King Arthur's Court was an attempt to imagine, and after a fashion set forth, the hard conditions of life for the laboring and defenseless poor in bygone times in England, and incidentally contrast these conditions with those under which the civil and ecclesiastical pets of privilege and high fortune lived in those

* *Mark Twain's Notebook.*
† *Mark Twain in Eruption.* (Written in 1906.)

times. I think I was purposing to contrast that English life, not just the English life of Arthur's day but the English life of the whole of the Middle Ages, with the life of modern Christendom and modern civilization—to the advantage of the latter, of course. That advantage is still claimable and does creditably and handsomely exist everywhere in Christendom—if we leave out Russia and the royal palace of Belgium.

The royal palace of Belgium is still what it has been for fourteen years, the den of a wild beast, King Leopold II, who for money's sake mutilates, murders, and starves half a million of friendless and helpless poor natives in the Congo State every year, and does it by the silent consent of all the Christian powers except England, none of them lifting a hand or a voice to stop these atrocities, although thirteen of them are by solemn treaty pledged to the protecting and uplifting of those wretched natives. In fourteen years Leopold has deliberately destroyed more lives than have suffered death on all the battlefields of this planet for the past thousand years. In this vast statement I am well within the mark, several millions of lives within the mark. It is curious that the most advanced and most enlightened century of all the centuries the sun has looked upon should have the ghastly distinction of having produced this moldy and piety-mouthing hypocrite, this bloody monster whose mate is not findable in human history anywhere, and whose personality will surely shame hell itself when he arrives there— which will be soon, let us hope and trust.

The conditions under which the poor lived in the Middle Ages were hard enough, but those conditions were heaven itself as compared with those which have obtained in the Congo State for these past fourteen years. I have mentioned Russia. Cruel and pitiful as was life throughout Christendom in the Middle Ages, it was not as cruel, not as pitiful, as is life in Russia today. In Russia, for three centuries, the vast population has been ground under the heels, and for the sole and sordid advantage, of a procession of crowned assassins and robbers who have all deserved the gallows. Russia's hundred and thirty millions of miserable subjects are much worse off today than were the poor of the Middle Ages whom we so pity. We are accustomed now to speak of Russia as medieval and as standing still in the Middle Ages but that is flattery. Russia is way back of the Middle Ages; the Middle Ages are a long way in front of her and she is not likely to catch up with them so long as the Czardom continues to exist.

THE FRENCH REVOLUTION

Letter to William Dean Howells, August 22, 1887*

How stunning are the changes which age makes in man while he sleeps! When I finished Carlyle's *French Revolution* in 1871 I was a Girondin; every time I have read it since I have read it differently— being influenced & changed, little by little, by life & environment (& Taine & St. Simon); & now I lay the book down once more, & recognize that I am a Sansculotte!—And not a pale, characterless Sansculotte, but a Marat. Carlyle teaches no such gospel, so the change is in *me*—in my vision of the evidences.

FEUDAL SLAVERY AND THE FRENCH REVOLUTION:

The Two Reigns of Terror†

We were off before sunrise . . . In half an hour we came upon a group of ragged poor creatures who had assembled to mend the thing which was regarded as a road. They were as humble as animals to me; and when I proposed to breakfast with them, they were so flattered, so overwhelmed by this extraordinary condescension of mine that at first they were not able to believe that I was in earnest. My lady put up her scornful lip and withdrew to one side; she said in their hearing that she would as soon think of eating with the other cattle—a remark which embarrassed these poor devils merely because it referred to them, and not because it insulted or offended them, for it didn't. And yet they were not slaves, not chattels. By a sarcasm of law and phrase they were freemen. Seven-tenths of the free population of the country were of just

---

* *Mark Twain's Letters.*
  † *A Connecticut Yankee in King Arthur's Court* (Harper and Brothers: New York, 1889).

their class and degree: small "independent" farmers, artisans, etc.; which is to say, they were the nation, the actual Nation; they were about all of it that was useful, or worth saving, or really respectworthy, and to subtract them would have been to subtract the Nation and leave behind some dregs, some refuse, in the shape of a king, nobility and gentry, idle, unproductive, acquainted mainly with the arts of wasting and destroying, and of no sort of use of value in any rationally constructed world. And yet, by ingenious contrivance, this gilded minority, instead of being in the tail of the procession where it belonged, was marching head up and banners flying, at the other end of it; had elected itself to be the Nation, and these innumerable clams had permitted it so long that they had come at last to accept it as a truth; and not only that, but to believe it right and as it should be. The priests had told their fathers and themselves that this ironical state of things was ordained of God; and so, not reflecting upon how unlike God it would be to amuse himself with sarcasms, and especially such poor transparent ones as this, they had dropped the matter there and become respectfully quiet.

The talk of these meek people had a strange enough sound in a formerly American ear. They were freemen, but they could not leave the estates of their lord or their bishop without his permission; they could not prepare their own bread, but must have their corn ground and their bread baked at his mill and his bakery, and pay roundly for the same; they could not sell a piece of their own property without paying him a handsome percentage of the proceeds, nor buy a piece of somebody else's without remembering him in cash for the privilege; they had to harvest his grain for him gratis, and be ready to come at a moment's notice, leaving their own crop to destruction by the threatened storm; they had to let him plant fruit trees in their fields, and then keep their indignation to themselves when his heedless fruit-gatherers trampled the grain around the trees; they had to smother their anger when his hunting-parties galloped through their fields laying waste the result of their patient toil; they were not allowed to keep doves themselves, and when the swarms from my lord's dovecote settled on their crops they must not lose their temper and kill a bird, for awful would the penalty be; when the harvest was at last gathered, then came the procession of robbers to levy their blackmail upon it: first the Church carted off its fat tenth, then the king's commissioner took his twentieth, then my lord's people made a mighty inroad upon the remainder; after which, the skinned freeman had liberty to bestow the remnant in his barn, in case it was worth the trouble; there were taxes, and taxes, and taxes, and more taxes, and taxes again, and yet other taxes—upon this free and independent pauper, but none upon his lord the baron or the bishop, none upon the wasteful nobility or the all-devouring Church; if the baron would sleep unvexed, the freeman must sit up all night after his day's work and whip the ponds to keep the frogs quiet; if the freeman's daughter—but no, that last infamy of monarchical government is unprintable; and finally, if the freeman, grown desperate with his tortures, found his life unendurable under such conditions, and sacrificed it and fled to death for mercy and refuge, the gentle Church condemned him to eternal fire, the gentle law buried him at midnight at the crossroads with a stake through his back, and his master the baron or the bishop confiscated all his property and turned his widow and his orphans out of doors.

And here were these freemen assembled in the early morning to work on their lord the bishop's road three days each—gratis; every head of a family, and every son of a family, three days each, gratis, and a day or so added for their servants. Why, it was like reading about France and the French, before the ever memorable and blessed Revolution, which swept a thousand years of such villainy away in one swift tidal wave of blood—one: a settlement of that hoary debt in the proportion of half a drop of blood for each hogshead of it that had been pressed by slow tortures out of that people in the weary stretch of ten centuries of wrong and shame and misery the like of which was not to be mated but in hell. There were two "Reigns of Terror," if we would but remember it and consider it; the one wrought murder in hot passion, the other in heartless cold blood; the one lasted mere months, the other had lasted a thousand years; the one inflicted death upon ten thousand persons, the other upon a hundred millions; but our shudders are all for the "horrors" of the minor Terror, the momentary Terror, so to speak; whereas, what is the horror of swift death by the ax compared with lifelong death from hunger, cold, insult, cruelty, and heartbreak? What is swift death by lightning compared with death by slow fire at the stake? A city cemetery could contain the coffins filled by that brief Terror which we have all been so diligently taught to shiver at and mourn over; but all France could hardly contain the coffins filled by that older and real

Terror—that unspeakably bitter and awful Terror which none of us has been taught to see in its vastness or pity as it deserves.

These poor ostensible freemen who were sharing their breakfast and their talk with me, were as full of humble reverence for their king and Church and nobility as their worst enemy could desire. There was something pitifully ludicrous about it. I asked them if they supposed a nation of people ever existed, who, with a free vote in every man's hand, would elect that a single family and its descendants should reign over it forever, whether gifted or boobies, to the exclusion of all other families—including the voter's; and would also elect that a certain hundred families should be raised to dizzy summits of rank, and clothed on with offensive transmissible glories and privileges to the exclusion of the rest of the nation's families—*including his own.*

They all looked unhit, and said they didn't know; that they had never thought about it before, and it hadn't ever occurred to them that a nation could be so situated that every man *could* have a say in the government. I said I had seen one—and that it would last until it had an Established Church. Again they were all unhit—at first. But presently one man looked up and asked me to state that proposition again; and state it slowly, so it could soak into his understanding. I did it; and after a little he had the idea, and he brought his fist down and said *he* didn't believe a nation where every man had a vote would voluntarily get down in the mud and dirt in any such way; and that to steal from a nation its will and preference must be a crime and the first of all crimes. I said to myself:

"This one's a man. If I were backed by enough of his sort, I would make a strike for the welfare of this country, and try to prove myself its loyalest citizen by making a wholesome change in its system of government."

You see my kind of loyalty was loyalty to one's country, not to its institutions or its office-holders. The country is the real thing, the substantial thing, the eternal thing; it is the thing to watch over, and care for, and be loyal to; institutions are extraneous, they are its mere clothing, and clothing can wear out, become ragged, cease to be comfortable, cease to protect the body from winter, disease, and death. To be loyal to rags, to shout for rags, to worship rags, to die for rags—that is a loyalty of unreason, it is pure animal; it belongs to monarchy, was invented by monarchy; let monarchy keep it. I was from Connecticut, whose Constitution declares "that all political power is inherent in the people, and all free governments are founded on their authority and instituted for their benefit; and that they have *at all times* an undeniable and indefeasible right to *alter their form of government* in such a manner as they may think expedient."

Under that gospel, the citizen who thinks he sees that the commonwealth's political clothes are worn out, and yet holds his peace and does not agitate for a new suit, is disloyal; he is a traitor. That he may be the only one who thinks he sees this decay, does not excuse him; it is his duty to agitate anyway.

SLAVERY AND REVOLUTION*

It was a curious situation; yet it is not on that account that I have made room for it here, but on account of a thing which seemed to me still more curious. To wit, that this dreadful matter brought from these downtrodden people no outburst of rage against these oppressors. They had been heritors and subjects of cruelty and outrage so long that nothing could have startled them but a kindness. Yes, here was a curious revelation, indeed, of the depth to which this people had been sunk in slavery. Their entire being was reduced to a monotonous dead level of patience, resignation, dumb uncomplaining acceptance of whatever might befall them in this life. Their very imagination was dead. When you can say that of a man, he has struck bottom, I reckon; there is no lower deep for him.

I rather wished I had gone some other road. This was not the sort of experience for a statesman to encounter who was planning out a peaceful revolution in his mind. For it could not help bringing up the ungetaroundable fact that, all gentle cant and philosophizing to the contrary notwithstanding, no people in the world ever did achieve their freedom by goody-goody talk and moral suasion: it being immutable law that all revolutions that will succeed must *begin* in blood, whatever may answer afterward. If history teaches anything, it teaches that.† What

---

* *A Connecticut Yankee in King Arthur's Court.*

† The same thesis was elaborated on in the 1960s by the leading theoretician of the revolutionary third world, Frantz Fanon, in such books as *The Wretched of the*

this folk needed, then, was a Reign of Terror and a guillotine, and I was the wrong man for them.

*ROYALTY AND REVOLUTION**

The kingly office is entitled to no respect. It was originally procured by the highwayman's methods; it remains a perpetuated crime, can never be anything but the symbol of a crime. It is no more entitled to respect than is the flag of a pirate. A monarch when good is entitled to the consideration which we accord to a pirate who keeps Sunday School between crimes; when bad he is entitled to none at all. But if you cross a king with a prostitute the resulting mongrel perfectly satisfies the English idea of nobility. The ducal houses of Great Britain of today are mainly derived from this gaudy combination. . . .

There are shams and shams; there are frauds and frauds, but the transparentest of all is the sceptered one. We see monarchs meet and go through solemn ceremonies, farces, with straight countenances; but it is not possible to imagine them meeting in private and not laughing in each other's faces.

The system has for its end the degradation of the many to exalt the few, the misery of the many for the happiness of the few, the cold and hunger and overworking of the useful that the useless may live in luxury and idleness.

The system of our Indians is high and juster, for only merit makes a man chief, and his son cannot take the place if there is another man better fitted for it.

Observe how monarchies and nobilities are sprung upon a heedless and ignorant people. Chiefs rise by the one divine right—capacity, merit. One of these shows merit for war and government above all the rest, he conspires with a faction of the chiefs and is made king. The body of the people ignored, allowed no vote, their desires in the matter held to be of no consequence by these upstarts. The conspirators make the succession permanent in this king's family, and the crime is com-

---

Earth and *Black Skin White Masks;* and indeed by such prominent black American revolutionary figures as Malcolm X and Eldridge Cleaver. *Ed.*

* *Mark Twain's Notebook.*

plete. It is the same sort of crime that surprise and seizure of a weak community's property by a robber gang, and the conversion of the community itself into slaves, is. All monarchies have been so built; there was never a throne which did not represent a crime; there is no throne today which does not represent a crime. A monarchy is perpetuated piracy. In its escutcheon should always be the skull and cross-bones.

REBELLION AGAINST CHURCH AND STATE*

Europe has lived a life of hypocrisy for ages; it is so ingrained in flesh and blood that sincere speech is impossible to these people, when speaking of hereditary power. "God Save the King" is uttered millions of times a day in Europe, and issues nearly always from just the mouth, neither higher nor lower.

The first gospel of all monarchies should be Rebellion; the second should be Rebellion; and the third and all gospels and the only gospel in any monarchy should be Rebellion against Church and State.

TWO LETTERS ON THE BOER WAR, THE CONQUEST OF THE PHILIPPINES, AND CHRISTIAN CIVILIZATION†

To W. D. Howells, in Boston:

January 25, 1900

Dear Howells,—Privately speaking, this is a sordid and criminal war, and in every way shameful and excuseless. Every day I write (in my head) bitter magazine articles about it, but I have to stop with that. For England must not fall; it would mean an inundation of Russian

* *Mark Twain's Notebook.*

† *Mark Twain's Letters.* While Twain was "ambivalent" about the Boer War and England, let it be noted that he was ambivalent on the side of the Boers in their struggle for freedom, and on the side of Blacks in their struggle against the Boers. *Ed.*

and German political degradations which would envelop the globe and steep it in a sort of Middle-Age night and slavery which would last till Christ comes again. Even wrong—and she is wrong—England must be upheld. He is an enemy of the human race who shall speak against her now. Why *was* the human race created? Or at least why wasn't something creditable created in place of it? God had his opportunity. He could have made a reputation. But no, He must commit this grotesque folly—a lark which must have cost him a regret or two when He came to think it over and observe effects. For a giddy and unbecoming caprice there has been nothing like it till this war. I talk the war with both sides—always waiting until the other man introduces the topic. Then I say "My head is with the Briton, but my heart and such rags of morals as I have are with the Boer—now we will talk, unembarrassed and without prejudice." And so we discuss, and have no trouble.

January 26

It was my intention to make some disparaging remarks about the human race; and so I kept this letter open for that purpose, and for the purpose of telling my dream, wherein the Trinity were trying to guess a conundrum, but I can do better—for I can snip out of the "Times" various samples and side-lights which bring the race down to date, and expose it as of yesterday. If you will notice, there is seldom a telegram in a paper which fails to show up one or more members and beneficiaries of our Civilization as promenading in his shirt-tail, with the rest of his regalia in the wash.

I love to see the holy ones air their smug pieties and admire them and smirk over them, and at the same moment frankly and publicly show their contempt for the pieties of the Boer—confidently expecting the approval of the country and the pulpit, and getting it.

I notice that God is on both sides in this war; thus history repeats itself. But I am the only person who has noticed this; everybody here thinks He is playing the game for this side, and for this side only.

To Rev. J. H. Twitchell, in Hartford:

LONDON, *January 27, 1900.*

DEAR JOE,—Apparently we are not proposing to set the Filipinos free and give their islands to them; and apparently we are not proposing to hang the priests and confiscate their property. If these things are so, the war out there has no interest for me.

I have just been examining chapter LXX of "Following the Equator," to see if the Boer's old military effectiveness is holding out. It reads curiously as if it had been written about the present war.

I believe that in the next chapter my notion of the Boer was rightly conceived. He is popularly called uncivilized, I do not know why. Happiness, food, shelter, clothing, wholesale labor, modest and rational ambitions, honesty, kindliness, hospitality, love of freedom and limitless courage to fight for it, composure and fortitude in time of disaster, patience in time of hardship and privation, absence of noise and brag in time of victory, contentment with a humble and peaceful life void of insane excitements—if there is a higher and better form of civilization than this, I am not aware of it and do not know where to look for it. I suppose we have the habit of imagining that a lot of artistic, intellectual and other artificialities must be added, or it isn't complete. We and the English have these latter; but as we lack the great bulk of these others, I think the Boer civilization is the best of the two. My idea of our civilization is that it is a shabby poor thing and full of cruelties, vanities, arrogancies, meannesses, and hypocrisies. As for the word, I hate the sound of it, for it conveys a lie; and as for the thing itself, I wish it was in hell . . .

GUERRILLA WARFARE IN THE TRANSVAAL*

After the seizure of the Transvaal and the suppression of the Boer Government by England in 1877, the Boers fretted for three years, and made several appeals to England for a restoration of their liberties, but without result. Then they gathered themselves together in a great mass-meeting at Krugersdorp, talked their troubles over, and resolved to fight for their deliverance from the British yoke. (Krugersdorp—the place where the Boers interrupted the Jameson raid.) The little handful of farmers rose against the strongest empire in the world. They proclaimed martial law and the re-establishment of their Republic. They organized their forces and sent them forward to intercept the British

* Following the Equator.

battalions. This, although Sir Garnet Wolseley had but lately made proclamation that "so long as the sun shone in the heavens," the Transvaal would be and remain English territory. And also in spite of the fact that the commander of the Ninety-fourth Regiment—already on the march to suppress this rebellion—had been heard to say that "the Boers would turn tail at the first beat of the big drum."

Four days after the flag-raising, the Boer force which had been sent forward to forbid the invasion of the English troops met them at Bronkhorst Spruit—two hundred and forty-six men of the Ninety-fourth Regiment, in command of a colonel, the big drum beating, the band playing—and the first battle was fought. It lasted ten minutes. Result:

British loss, more than 150 officers and men, out of the 246. Surrender of the remnant.

Boer loss—if any—not stated.

They are fine marksmen, the Boers. From the cradle up, they live on horseback and hunt wild animals with the rifle. They have a passion for liberty and the Bible, and care for nothing else.

"General Sir George Colley, Lieutenant-Governor and Commander-in-Chief in Natal, felt it his duty to proceed at once to the relief of the loyalists and soldiers beleaguered in the different towns of the Transvaal." He moved out with one thousand men and some artillery. He found the Boers encamped in a strong and sheltered position on high ground at Laing's Nek—every Boer behind a rock. Early in the morning of the 28th of January, 1881, he moved to the attack "with the Fifty-eighth Regiment, commanded by Colonel Deane, a mounted squadron of seventy men, the Sixtieth Rifles, the Naval Brigade with three rocket tubes, and the Artillery with six guns." He shelled the Boers for twenty minutes, then the assault was delivered, the Fifty-eighth marching up the slope *in solid column.* The battle was soon finished, with this result, according to Russell:

British loss in killed and wounded, 174.

Boer loss, "trifling."

Colonel Deane was killed, and apparently every officer above the grade of lieutenant was killed or wounded, for the Fifty-eighth retreated to its camp *in command of a lieutenant.*

That ended the second battle.

On the 7th of February General Colley discovered that the Boers were flanking his position. The next morning he left his camp at Mount Pleasant and marched out and crossed the Ingogo River with two hundred and seventy men, started up the Ingogo heights, and there fought a battle which lasted from noon till nightfall. He then retreated, leaving his wounded with his military chaplain, and in recrossing the now swollen river lost some of his men by drowning. That was the third Boer victory. Result, according to Mr. Russell:

British loss, 150 out of 270 engaged.

Boer loss, 8 killed, 9 wounded—17.

There was a season of quiet, now, but at the end of about three weeks Sir George Colley conceived the idea of climbing, with an infantry and artillery force, the steep and rugged mountain of Amajuba in the night—a bitter hard task, but he acomplished it. On the way he left about two hundred men to guard a strategic point, and took about four hundred up the mountain with him. When the sun rose in the morning, there was an unpleasant surprise for the Boers; yonder were the English troops visible on top of the mountain two or three miles away, and now their own position was at the mercy of the English artillery. The Boer chief resolved to retreat—up that mountain. He asked for volunteers, and got them.

The storming party crossed the swale and began to creep up the steeps, "and from behind rocks and bushes they shot at the soldiers on the sky-line as if they were stalking deer," says Mr. Russell. There was "continuous musketry fire, steady and fatal on the one side, wild and ineffectual on the other." The Boers reached the top, and began to put in their ruinous work. Presently the British "broke and fled for their lives down the rugged steep." The Boers had won the battle. Result in killed and wounded, including among the killed the British general:

British loss, 226 out of 400 engaged.

Boer loss, 1 killed, 5 wounded.

That ended the war. England listened to reason, and recognized the Boer Republic—a government which has never been in any really awful danger since, until Jameson started after it with his five hundred "raw young fellows." To recapitulate:

The Boer farmers and British soldiers fought four battles, and the Boers won them all. Result of the four, in killed and wounded:

British loss, 700 men.

Boer loss, so far as known, 23 men.

THE SLAVE HOLDERS AND THE POOR WHITES
IN THE CIVIL WAR*

The painful thing observable about all this business was the alacrity with which this oppressed community had turned their cruel hands against their own class in the interest of the common oppressor. This man and woman seemed to feel that in a quarrel between a person of their own class and his lord, it was the natural and proper and rightful thing for that poor devil's whole caste to side with the master and fight his battle for him, without ever stopping to inquire into the rights or wrongs of the matter. This man had been out helping to hang his neighbors, and had done his work with zeal, and yet was aware that there was nothing against them but a mere suspicion, with nothing back of it describable as evidence, still neither he nor his wife seemed to see anything horrible about it.

This was depressing—to a man with the dream of a republic in his head. It reminded me of a time thirteen centuries away, when the "poor whites" of our South who were always despised and frequently insulted by the slave-lords around them, and who owed their base condition simply to the presence of slavery in their midst, were yet pusillanimously ready to side with the slave-lords in all political moves for the upholding and perpetuating of slavery, and did also finally shoulder their muskets and pour out their lives in an effort to prevent the destruction of that very institution which degraded them. And there was only one redeeming feature connected with that pitiful piece of history; and that was, that secretly the "poor white" did detest the slave-lord, and did feel his own shame. That feeling was not brought to the surface, but the fact that it was there and could have been brought out, under favoring circumstances, was something—in fact, it was enough; for it showed that a man is at bottom a man, after all, even if it doesn't show on the outside. . . .

There it was, you see. A man *is* a man, at bottom. Whole ages of

* *A Connecticut Yankee in King Arthur's Court.*

abuse and oppression cannot crush the manhood clear out of him. Whoever thinks it a mistake is himself mistaken. Yes, there is plenty good enough material for a republic in the most degraded people that ever existed—even the Russians; plenty of manhood in them—even in the Germans—if one could but force it out of its timid and suspicious privacy, to overthrow and trample in the mud any throne that ever was set up and any nobility that ever supported it. We should see certain things yet, let us hope and believe. First, a modified monarchy, till Arthur's days were done, then the destruction of the throne, nobility abolished, every member of it bound out to some useful trade, universal suffrage instituted, and the whole government placed in the hands of the men and women of the nation there to remain. Yes, there was no occasion to give up my dream yet awhile . . .

There is no use in stringing out the details. The earl put us up and sold us at auction. This same infernal law had existed in our own South in my own time, more than thirteen hundred years later, and under it hundreds of freemen who could not prove that they were freemen had been sold into life-long slavery without the circumstance making any particular impression upon me; but the minute law and the auction block came into my personal experience, a thing which had been merely improper before became suddenly hellish. Well, that's the way we are made.

THE BEHEADING OF KING CHARLES I*

Saturday, January 3, '97. The pedestal of the bronze, beruffled Charles I, is well clothed in wreaths of white flowers, with mottoes. This is a lament by irreconcilable English 'legitimists,' to commemorate what they think was a calamity—the beheading of Charles, January 21, 1649. They celebrate tomorrow (that apparently standing for January 21 O.S.). Charles' back is toward Nelson, in the sky on his column top; he looks down Whitehall, past the Palace where he was executed and past the Horse Guards and Downing Street, political executive center of the vast British Empire, and his bronze glance strikes the great tower of Parliament, further down—the legislative center of the B.E.

* Mark Twain's Notebook.

In Hartford there is a family of American donkeys who shut themselves up January 21 and snivel over Charles' death.

PATRIOTISM AGAIN*

In the North, before the War, the man who opposed slavery was despised and ostracized, and insulted. By the "Patriots." Then, by and by, the "Patriots" went over to his side, and thenceforth his attitude became patriotism.

There are two kinds of patriotism—monarchical patriotism and republican patriotism. In the one case the government and the king may rightfully furnish you their notions of patriotism; in the other, neither the government nor the entire nation is privileged to dictate to any individual what the form of his patriotism shall be. The Gospel of the Monarchical Patriotism is: "The King can do no wrong." We have adopted it with all its servility, with an unimportant change in the wording: "Our country, right *or* wrong!"

We have thrown away the most valuable asset we have—the individual right to oppose both flag and country when he (just *he* by himself) believes them to be in the wrong. We have thrown it away; and with it all that was really respectable about that grotesque and laughable word, Patriotism.

RIGHT AND MIGHT*

Man has not a single right which is the product of anything but might.

Not a single right is indestructible: a new might can at any time abolish it, hence, man possesses not a single *permanent* right.

God is Might (and He is shifty, malicious, and uncertain).

* *Mark Twain's Notebook.*

PART FOUR

–And R̨elated Matters

NATURE'S GIFT TO MAN*

It is strange and fine—Nature's lavish generosities to her creatures. At least to all of them except man. For those that fly she has provided a home that is nobly spacious—a home which is forty miles deep and envelops the whole globe, and has not an obstruction in it. For those that swim she has provided a more than imperial domain—a domain which is miles deep and covers four-fifths of the globe. But as for man, she has cut him off with the mere odds and ends of the creation. She has given him the thin skin, the meager skin which is stretched over the remaining one-fifth—the naked bones stick up through it in most places. On the one-half of this domain he can raise snow, ice, sand, rocks, and nothing else. So the valuable part of his inheritance really consists of but a single fifth of the family estate; and out of it he has to grub hard to get enough to keep him alive and provide kings and soldiers and powder to extend the blessings of civilization with. Yet man, in his simplicity and complacency and inability to cipher, thinks Nature regards him as the important member of the family—in fact, her favorite. Surely, it must occur to even his dull head, sometimes, that she has a curious way of showing it.

* Following the Equator.

193

MORALS AND INSTINCTS

Letter to J. Howard Moore, February 2, 1907*

There is one thing that always puzzles me: as inheritors of the mentality of our reptile ancestors we have improved the inheritance by a thousand grades; but in the matter of the morals which they left us we have gone backward as many grades. That evolution is strange, and to me unaccountable and unnatural. Necessarily we started equipped with their perfect and blemishless morals; now we are wholly destitute; we have no real morals, but only artificial ones—morals created and preserved by the forced suppression of natural and hellish instincts. Yet we are dull enough to be vain of them. Certainly we are a sufficiently comical invention, we humans.

WORLD PEACE AND DISARMAMENT

Letters to William T. Stead of the Review of Reviews in London, January 1899.†

VIENNA, *January 9.*

DEAR MR. STEAD,—The Czar is ready to disarm: *I* am ready to disarm. Collect the *others*, it should not be much of a task now.

DEAR MR. STEAD,—Peace by compulsion. That seems a better idea than the other. Peace by persuasion has a pleasant sound, but I think

---

* *Mark Twain's Letters.*

† *Ibid.* The second letter, with its schematic description of the military overkill existing among the nations in 1899, seems even more relevant today, in the age of nuclear weapons, when the balance of "power," or of terror, presently maintained between Russia and the US must soon be extended to China. *Ed.*

we should not be able to work it. We should have to tame the human race first, and history seems to show that that cannot be done. Can't we reduce the armaments little by little—on a pro rata basis—by concert of the powers? Can't we get four great powers to agree to reduce their strength 10 per cent a year and thrash the others into doing likewise? For, of course, we cannot expect all of the powers to be in their right minds at one time. It has been tried. We are not going to try to get all of them to go into the scheme peaceably, are we? In that case I must withdraw my influence; because, for business reasons, I must preserve the outward signs of sanity. Four is enough if they can be securely harnessed together. They can compel peace, and peace without compulsion would be against nature and not operative. A sliding scale of reduction of 10 per cent a year has a sort of plausible look, and I am willing to try that if three other powers will join. I feel sure that the armaments are now many times greater than necessary for the requirements of either peace or war. Take war-time for instance. Suppose circumstances made it necessary for us to fight another Waterloo, and that it would do what it did before—settle a large question and bring peace. I will guess that 400,000 men were on hand at Waterloo (I have forgotten the figures). In five hours they disabled 50,000 men. It took them that tedious, long time because the firearms delivered only two or three shots a minute. But we would do the work now as it was done at Omdurman, with shower guns, raining 600 balls a minute. Four men to a gun—is that the number? A hundred and fifty shots a minute per man. Thus a modern soldier is 149 Waterloo soldiers in one. Thus, also, we can now retain one man out of each 150 in service, disband the others, and fight our Waterloos just as effectively as we did eighty-five years ago. We should do the same beneficent job with 2,800 men now that we did with 400,000 then. The allies could take 1,400 of the men, and give Napoleon 1,400 and then whip him.

But instead what do we see? In war-time in Germany, Russia and France, taken together we find about 8 million men equipped for the field. Each man represents 149 Waterloo men, in usefulness and killing capacity. Altogether they constitute about 350 million Waterloo men, and there are not quite that many grown males of the human race now on this planet. Thus we have this insane fact—that whereas those three countries could arm 18,000 men with modern weapons and make them the equals of 3 million men of Napoleon's day, and accomplish with them all necessary war work, they waste their money and their prosperity creating forces of their populations in piling together 349,982,000 extra Waterloo equivalents which they would have no sort of use for if they would only stop drinking and sit down and cipher a little.

Perpetual peace we cannot have on any terms, I suppose; but I hope we can gradually reduce the war strength of Europe till we get it down to where it ought to be—20,000 men, properly armed. Then we can have all the peace that is worth while, and when we want a war anybody can afford it.

VIENNA, *January 9.*

P. S.—In the article I sent the figures are wrong—"350 million" ought to be 450 million; "349,982,000" ought to be 449,982,000, and the remark about the sum being a little more than the present number of males on the planet—that is wrong, of course; it represents really one and a half the existing males.

WOMEN'S LIBERATION*

We easily perceive that the peoples furtherest from civilization are the ones where equality between man and woman are furthest apart—and we consider this one of the signs of savagery. But we are so stupid that we can't see that we thus plainly admit that no civilization can be perfect until exact equality between man and woman is included.

THE POPULATION EXPLOSION†

. . . When the population reached five billions the earth was heavily burdened to support it. But wars, pestilences and famines brought relief, from time to time, and in some degree reduced the prodigious pressure. The memorable benefaction of the year 508,

* *Mark Twain's Notebook.*
† *Letters from the Earth.*

which was a famine reinforced by a pestilence, swept away sixteen hundred millions of people in nine months.

It was not much, but it was something. The same is all that can be said of its successors of later periods. The burden of population grew heavier and heavier and more and more formidable, century by century, and the gravity of the situation created by it was steadily and proportionately increased.

After the age of infancy, few died. The average of life was six hundred years. The cradles were filling, filling, filling—always, always, always; the cemeteries stood comparatively idle, the undertakers had but little traffic, they could hardly support their families. The death rate was 2,250 in the million. To the thoughtful this was portentous; to the light-witted it was matter for brag! These latter were always comparing the population of one decade with that of the previous one and hurrahing over the mighty increase—as if that were an advantage to the world; a world that could hardly scratch enough out of the earth to keep itself from starving.

And yet, worse was to come! Necessarily our true hope did not and could not lie in spasmodic famine and pestilence, whose effects could be only temporary, but in war and the physicians, whose help is constant. Now then, let us note what has been happening. In the past fifty years science has reduced the doctor's effectiveness by half. He uses but one deadly drug now, where formerly he used ten. Improved sanitation has made whole regions healthy which were previously not so. It has been discovered that the majority of the most useful and fatal diseases are caused by microbes of various breeds; very well, they have learned how to render the efforts of those microbes innocuous. As a result, yellow fever, black plague, cholera, diphtheria, and nearly every valuable distemper we had are become but entertainments for the idle hour, and are of no more value to the State than is the stomach-ache. Marvelous advances in surgery have been added to our disasters. They remove a diseased stomach, now, and the man gets along better and cheaper than he did before. If a man loses a faculty, they bore into his skull and restore it. They take off his legs and arms, and refurnish him from the mechanical junk shop, and he is as good as new. They give him a new nose if he needs it; new entrails; new bones; new teeth; glass eyes; silver tubes to swallow through; in a word, they take him to pieces and make him over again, and he can stand twice as much wear and tear as he could before. They do these things by help of antiseptics and anesthesia, and there is no gangrene and no pain. Thus war has become nearly valueless; out of a hundred wounded that would formerly have died, ninety-nine are back in the ranks again in a month.

What, then, is the grand result of all this microbing and sanitation and surgery? This—which is appalling: the death rate has *been reduced to 1,200 in the million.* And foolish people rejoice at it and boast about it! It is a serious matter. It promises to double the globe's population every twelve months. In time there will not be room in the world for the people to stand, let alone sit down.

Remedy? I know of none. The span of life is too long, the death rate is too trifling. The span should be thirty-five years—a mere moment of Time—the death rate should be 20,000 or 30,000 in the *million.* Even then the population would double in thirty-five years, and by and by even this would be a burden again and make the support of life difficult.

Honor to whom honor is due: the physician failed us, war has saved us. Not that the killed and wounded amount to anything as a relief, for they do not; but the poverty and desolation caused by war sweep myriads away and make space for immigrants. War is a rude friend, but a kind one. It keeps us down to sixty billion and saves the hard-grubbing world alive. It is all that the globe can support. . . .

*ELINOR GLYN AND THE PASSIONS**

Two or three weeks ago Elinor Glyn called on me one afternoon and we had a long talk, of a distinctly unusual character, in the library. It may be that by the time this chapter reaches print she may be less well known to the world than she is now, therefore I will insert here a word

* *Mark Twain in Eruption.* (Written in 1908.) Among major artists it is interesting to notice how often social rebellion is accompanied by sexual rebellion; it is possible that sexual rebellion is a primary cause of social rebellion (against social repression of any kind). Twain was no exception to this rule, as we have already seen, despite much commentary about his "censorship" and timidity in this area. In the end, Twain comes out as one of the most openly sexual writers of the Victorian period (and in American letters). This interview with Elinor Glyn is relevant, apart from the hilarious description of *Three Weeks*, for Twain's stress on the dominance of the passions. *Ed.*

or two of information about her. She is English. She is an author. The newspapers say she is visiting America with the idea of finding just the right kind of a hero for the principal character in a romance which she is purposing to write. She has come to us upon the stormwind of a vast and suddenly notoriety.

The source of this notoriety is a novel of hers called *Three Weeks*. In this novel the hero is a fine and gifted and cultivated young English gentleman of good family, who imagines he has fallen in love with the ungifted, uninspired, commonplace daughter of the rector. He goes to the Continent on an outing, and there he happens upon a brilliant and beautiful young lady of exceedingly foreign extraction, with a deep mystery hanging over her. It transpires later that she is the childless wife of a king or kinglet, a coarse and unsympathetic animal whom she does not love.

She and the young Englishman fall in love with each other at sight. The hero's feeling for the rector's daughter was pale, not to say color- less, and it is promptly consumed and extinguished in the furnace fires of his passion for the mysterious stranger—passion is the right word, passion is what the pair of strangers feel for each other, what they recognize as real love—the only real love, the only love worthy to be called by that great name—whereas the feeling which the young man had for the rector's daughter is perceived to have been only a passing partiality.

The queenlet and the Englishman flit away privately to the moun- tains and take up sumptuous quarters in a remote and lonely house there—and then business begins. They recognize that they were highly and holily created for each other and that their passion is a sacred thing, that it is their master by divine right, and that its commands must be obeyed. They get to obeying them at once and they keep on obeying them and obeying them, to the reader's intense delight and disapproval, and the process of obeying them is described, several times, almost exhaustively, but not quite—some little rag of it being left to the reader's imagination, just at the end of each infraction, the place where his imagination is to take up and do the finish being indicated by stars.

The unstated argument of the book is that the laws of Nature are paramount and properly take precedence of the interfering and im- pertinent restrictions obtruded upon man's life by man's statutes.

Mme. Glyn called, as I have said, and she was a picture! Slender, young, faultlessly formed and incontestably beautiful—a blonde with blue eyes, the incomparable English complexion, and crowned with a glory of red hair of a very peculiar, most rare, and quite ravishing tint. She was clad in the choicest stuffs and in the most perfect taste. There she is, just a beautiful girl; yet she has a daughter fourteen years old. She isn't winning; she has no charm but the charm of beauty, and youth, and grace, and intelligence and vivacity; she *acts* charm, and does it well, exceedingly well in fact, but it does not convince, it doesn't stir the pulse, it doesn't go to the heart, it leaves the heart serene and unemotional. Her English hero would have prodigiously admired her; he would have loved to sit and look at her and hear her talk, but he would have been able to get away from that lonely house with his purity in good repair, if he wanted to.

I talked with her with daring frankness, frequently calling a spade a spade instead of coldly symbolizing it as a snow shovel; and on her side she was equally frank. It was one of the damnedest conversations I have ever had with a beautiful stranger of her sex, if I do say it myself that shouldn't. She wanted my opinion of her book and I furnished it. I said its literary workmanship was excellent, and that I quite agreed with her view that in the matter of the sexual relation man's statutory regulations of it were a distinct interference with a higher law, the law of Nature. I went further and said I couldn't call to mind a written law of any kind that had been promulgated in any age of the world in any statute book or any Bible for the regulation of man's conduct in *any* particular, from assassination all the way up to Sabbath-breaking, that wasn't a violation of the law of Nature, which I regarded as the highest of laws, the most peremptory and absolute of all laws—Nature's laws being in my belief plainly and simply the laws of God, since He instituted them, He and no other, and the said laws, by authority of this divine origin taking precedence of all the statutes of man. I said that her pair of indelicate lovers were obeying the law of their make and disposition; that therefore they were obeying the clearly enunciated law of God, and in His eyes must manifestly be blameless.

Of course what she wanted of me was support and defense—I knew that but I said I couldn't furnish it. I said we were the servants of convention; that we could not subsist, either in a savage or a civilized state, without conventions; that we must accept them and stand by

them, even when we disapproved of them; that while the laws of
Nature, that is to say the laws of God, plainly made every human being
a law unto himself, we must steadfastly refuse to obey those laws, and
we must as steadfastly stand by the conventions which ignore them,
since the statutes furnish us peace, fairly good government, and stabil-
ity, and therefore are better for us than the laws of God, which would
soon plunge us into confusion and disorder and anarchy, if we should
adopt them. I said her book was an assault upon certain old and well-
established and wise conventions, and that it would not find many
friends, and indeed would not deserve many.

She said I was very brave, the bravest person she had ever met
(gross flattery which could have beguiled me when I was very very
young), and she implored me to publish these views of mine, but I
said, "No, such a thing is unthinkable." I said that if I, or any other
wise, intelligent, and experienced person, should suddenly throw down
the walls that protect and conceal his *real* opinions on almost any
subject under the sun, it would at once be perceived that he had lost his
intelligence and his wisdom and ought to be sent to the asylum. I said I
had been revealing to her my private sentiments, *not* my public ones;
that I, like all the other human beings, expose to the world only my
trimmed and perfumed and carefully barbered public opinions and
conceal carefully, cautiously, wisely, my private ones.

I explained that what I meant by that phrase "public opinions" was
published opinions, opinions spread broadcast in print. I said I was in
the common habit, in private conversation with friends, of revealing
every private opinion I possessed relating to religion, politics, and
men, but that I should never dream of *printing* one of them, because
they are individually and collectively at war with almost everybody's
public opinion, while at the same time they are in happy agreement
with almost everybody's private opinion. As an instance, I asked her if
she had ever encountered an intelligent person who privately believed
in the Immaculate Conception—which of course she hadn't; and I also
asked her if she had ever seen an intelligent person who was daring
enough to publicly deny his belief in that fable and print the denial. Of
course she hadn't encountered any such person.

I said I had a large cargo of most interesting and important private
opinions about every great matter under the sun, but that they were
not for print. I reminded her that we all break over the rule two or

three times in our lives and fire a disagreeable and unpopular private opinion of ours into print, but we never do it when we can help it, we never do it except when the desire to do it is too strong for us and overrides and conquers our cold, calm, wise judgment. She mentioned several instances in which I had come out publicly in defense of unpopular causes, and she intimated that what I had been saying about myself was not perhaps in strict accordance with the facts; but I said they were merely illustrations of what I had just been saying, that when I publicly attacked the American missionaries in China and some other iniquitous persons and causes, I did not do it for any reason but just the one: that the inclination to do it was stronger than my diplomatic instincts, and I had to obey and take the consequences. But I said I was not moved to defend her book in public; that it was not a case where inclination was overpowering and unconquerable, and that therefore I could keep diplomatically still and should do it.

The lady was young enough, and inexperienced enough, to imagine that whenever a person has an unpleasant opinion in stock which could be of educational benefit to Tom, Dick, and Harry, it is his *duty* to come out in print with it and become its champion. I was not able to get that juvenile idea out of her head. I was not able to convince her that we never do *any* duty for the duty's sake but only for the mere personal satisfaction we get out of doing that duty. The fact is, she was brought up just like the rest of the world, with the ingrained and stupid superstition that there is such a thing as *duty for duty's sake,* and so I was obliged to let her abide in her darkness. She believed that when a man held a private unpleasant opinion of an educational sort, which would get him hanged if he published it, he ought to publish it anyway and was a coward if he didn't. Take it all around, it was a very pleasant conversation, and glaringly unprintable, particularly those considerable parts of it which I haven't had the courage to more than vaguely hint at in this account of our talk.

Some days afterward I met her again for a moment, and she gave me the startling information that she had written down every word I had said, just as I had said, it, without any softening and purifying modifications, and that it was "just splendid, just wonderful." She said she had sent it to her husband, in England. Privately I didn't think that that was a very good idea, and yet I believed it would interest him. She begged me to let her publish it and said it would do infinite good in the

world, but I said it would damn me before my time and I didn't wish to
be useful to the world on such expensive conditions.

PATRIOTISM, THE CONSENSUS, GOOD AND EVIL*

As Regards Patriotism

It is agreed, in this country, that if a man can arrange his religion so
that it perfectly satisfies his conscience, it is not incumbent upon him
to care whether the arrangement is satisfactory to anyone else or not.

In Austria and some other countries this is not the case. There the
state arranges a man's religion for him, he has no voice in it himself.

Patriotism is merely a religion—love of country, worship of country,
devotion to the country's flag and honor and welfare.

In absolute monarchies it is furnished from the throne, cut and
dried, to the subject; in England and America it is furnished, cut and
dried, to the citizen by the politician and the newspaper.

The newspaper-and-politician-manufactured Patriot often gags in
private over his dose; but he takes it, and keeps it on his stomach the
best he can. Blessed are the meek.

Sometimes, in the beginning of an insane shabby political upheaval,
he is strongly moved to revolt but he doesn't do it—he knows better.
He knows that his maker would find out—the maker of his Patriotism, the windy and incoherent six-dollar subeditor of his village newspaper—and would bray out in print and call him a Traitor. And how
dreadful that would be. It makes him tuck his tail between his legs and
shiver. We all know—the reader knows it quite well—that two or three
years ago nine-tenths of the human tails in England and America
performed just that act. Which is to say, nine tenths of the Patriots in
England and America turned traitor to keep from being called traitor.
Isn't it true? You know it to be true. Isn't it curious?

Yet it was not a thing to be very seriously ashamed of. A man can
seldom—very, very seldom—fight a winning fight against his training;

* *Europe and Elsewhere.*

the odds are too heavy. For many a year—perhaps always—the training of the two nations had been dead against independence in political thought, persistently inhospitable toward Patriotism manufactured on a man's own premises, Patriotism reasoned out in the man's own head and fire-assayed and tested and proved in his own conscience. The resulting Patriotism was a shop-worn product procured at second hand. The Patriot did not know just how or when or where he got his opinions, neither did he care, so long as he was with what seemed the majority—which was the main thing, the safe thing, the comfortable thing. Does the reader believe he knows three men who have actual reasons for their pattern of Patriotism—and can furnish them? Let him not examine, unless he wants to be disappointed. He will be likely to find that his men got their Patriotism at the public trough, and had no hand in its preparation themselves.

Training does wonderful things. It moved the people of this country to oppose the Mexican War; then moved them to fall in with what they supposed was the opinion of the majority—majority Patriotism is the customary Patriotism—and go down there and fight. Before the Civil War it made the North indifferent to slavery and friendly to the slave interest; in that interest it made Massachusetts hostile to the American flag, and she would not allow it to be hoisted on her State House—in her eyes it was the flag of a faction. Then by and by training swung Massachusetts the other way, and she went raging South to fight under that very flag and against that aforetime protected interest of hers.

There is nothing that training cannot do. Nothing is above its reach or below it. It can turn bad morals to good, good morals to bad; it can destroy principles, it can recreate them; it can debase angels to men and lift men to angelship. And it can do any one of these miracles in a year—even in six months.

Then men can be trained to manufacture their own Patriotism. They can be trained to labor it out in their own heads and hearts and in the privacy and independence of their own premises. It can train them to stop taking it by command, as the Austrian takes his religion.

Dr. Loeb's Incredible Discovery

Experts in biology will be apt to receive with some skepticism the announcement of Dr. Jacques Loeb of the University of California as to the creation of life by chemical agencies. . . . Doctor Loeb is a very bright and ingenious experimenter, but *a consensus of opinion among biologists* would show that he is voted rather as a man of lively imagination than an inerrant investigator of natural phenomena. —New York *Times*, March 2.

I wish I could be as young as that again. Although I seem so old, now, I was once as young as that. I remember, as if it were but thirty or forty years ago, how a paralyzing Consensus of Opinion accumulated from Experts a-setting around, about brother experts who had patiently and laboriously cold-chiseled their way into one or another of nature's safe-deposit vaults and were reporting that they had found something valuable was a plenty for me. It settled it.

But it isn't so now—no. Because, in the drift of the years I by and by found out that a Consensus examines a new thing with its feelings rather oftener than with its mind. You know, yourself, that that is so. Do those people examine with feelings that are friendly to evidence? You know they don't. It is the other way about. They do the examining by the light of their prejudices—now isn't that true?

With curious results, yes. So curious that you wonder the Consensuses do not go out of the business. Do you know of a case where a Consensus won a game? You can go back as far as you want to and you will find history furnishing you this (until now) unwritten maxim for your guidance and profit: Whatever new thing a Consensus coppers (colloquial for "bets against"), bet your money on that very card and do not be afraid.

There was that primitive steam engine—ages back, in Greek times: a Consensus made fun of it. There was the Marquis of Worcester's steam engine, 250 years ago: a Consensus made fun of it. There was Fulton's steamboat of a century ago: a French Consensus, including the Great Napoleon, made fun of it. There was Priestley, with his oxygen: a Consensus scoffed at him, mobbed him, burned him out, banished him. While a Consensus was proving, by statistics and things, that a steamship could not cross the Atlantic, a steamship did it. A Consensus consisting of all the medical experts in Great Britain made fun of Jenner and inoculation. A Consensus consisting of all the medical experts in France made fun of the stethoscope. A Consensus of all the medical experts in Germany made fun of that young doctor (his name?

forgotten by all but doctors, now, revered now by doctors alone) who discovered and abolished the cause of that awful disease, puerperal fever; made fun of him, reviled him, hunted him, persecuted him, broke his heart, killed him. Electric telegraph, Atlantic cable, telephone, all "toys," and of no practical value—verdict of the Consensuses. Geology, palæontology, evolution—all brushed into space by a Consensus of theological experts, comprising all the preachers in Christendom, assisted by the Duke of Argyle and (at first) the other scientists. And do look at Pasteur and his majestic honor roll of prodigious benefactions! Damned—each and every one of them in its turn—by frenzied and ferocious Consensuses of medical and chemical Experts comprising, for years, every member of the tribe in Europe; damned without even a casual *look* at what he was doing—and he pathetically imploring them to come and take at least one little look before making the damnation eternal. They shortened his life by their malignities and persecutions; and thus robbed the world of the further and priceless services of a man who—along certain lines and within certain limits— had done more for the human race than any other one man in all its long history: a man whom it had taken the Expert brotherhood ten thousand years to produce, and whose mate and match the brotherhood may possibly not be able to bring forth and assassinate in another ten thousand. The preacher has an old and tough reputation for bullheaded and unreasoning hostility to new light; why, he is not "in it" with the doctor! Nor, perhaps, with some of the other breeds of Experts that sit around and get up the Consensuses and squelch the new things as fast as they come from the hands of the plodders, the searchers, the inspired dreamers, the Pasteurs that come bearing pearls to scatter in the Consensus sty.

This is warm work! It puts my temperature up to 106 and raises my pulse to the limit. It always works just so when the red rag of a Consensus jumps my fence and starts across my pasture. I have been a Consensus more than once myself, and I know the business—and its vicissitudes. I am a compositor-expert, of old and seasoned experience; nineteen years ago I delivered the final-and-for-good verdict that the linotype would never be able to earn its own living nor anyone else's: it takes fourteen acres of ground, now, to accommodate its factories in England. Thirty-five years ago I was an expert precious-metal quartz-miner. There was an outcrop in my neighborhood that assayed $600 a ton—gold. But every fleck of gold in it was shut up tight and fast in an intractable and impersuadable base-metal shell. Acting as a Consensus, I delivered the finality verdict that no human ingenuity would ever be able to set free two dollars' worth of gold out of a ton of that rock. The fact is, I did not foresee the cyanide process. Indeed, I have been a Consensus ever so many times since I reached maturity and approached the age of discretion, but I call to mind no instance in which I won out.

These sorrows have made me suspicious of Consensuses. Do you know, I tremble and the goose flesh rises on my skin every time I encounter one, now. I sheer warily off and get behind something, saying to myself, "It looks innocent and all right, but no matter, ten to one there's a cyanide process under that thing somewhere."

Now as concerns this "creation of life by chemical agencies." Reader, take my advice: don't you copper it. I don't say bet on it; no, I only say, don't you copper it. As you see, there is a Consensus out against it. If you find that you can't control your passions; if you feel that you have *got* to copper something and can't help it, copper the Consensus. It is the safest way—all history confirms it. If you are young, you will, of course, have to put up, on one side or the other, for you will not be able to restrain yourself; but as for me, I am old, and I am going to wait for a new deal.

P.S.—In the same number of the *Times* Doctor Funk says: "Man may be as badly fooled by believing too little as by believing too much; the hard-headed skeptic Thomas was the only disciple who was cheated." Is that the right and rational way to look at it? I will not be sure, for my memory is faulty, but it has always been my impression that Thomas was the only one who made an examination and proved a fact, while the others were accepting, or discounting, the fact on trust—like any other Consensus. If that is so, Doubting Thomas removed a doubt which must otherwise have confused and troubled the world until now. Including Doctor Funk. It seems to me that we owe that hard-headed—or sound-headed—witness something more than a slur. Why does Doctor Funk *examine* into spiritism, and then throw stones at Thomas? Why doesn't he take it on trust? Has inconsistency become a jewel in Lafayette Place?

Old-Man-Afraid-of-the-Consensus

Extract from Adam's Diary.—Then there was a Consensus about it. It was the very first one. It sat six days and nights. It was then delivered of the verdict that a world could not be made out of nothing; that such small things as sun and moon and stars might, maybe, but it would take years and years, if there was considerable many of them. Then the Consensus got up and looked out of the window, and there was the whole outfit spinning and sparkling in space! You never saw such a disappointed lot.

his

ADAM—i—mark

The Dervish and the Offensive Stranger

The Dervish: I will say again, and yet again, and still again, that a good deed—

The Offensive Stranger: Peace, and, O man of narrow vision! There is no such thing as a good *deed*—

The Dervish: O shameless blasphe—

The Offensive Stranger: And no such thing as an evil deed. There are good *impulses,* there are evil impulses, and that is all. Half of the results of a good intention are evil; half the results of an evil intention are good. No man can command the results, nor allot them.

The Dervish: And so—

The Offensive Stranger: And so you shall praise men for their good intentions, and not blame them for the evils resulting; you shall blame men for their evil intentions, and not praise them for the good resulting.

The Dervish: O maniac! will you say—

The Offensive Stranger: Listen to the law: From *every* impulse, whether good or evil, flow two streams; the one carries health, the other carries poison. From the beginning of time this law has not changed, to the end of time it will not change.

The Dervish: If I should strike thee dead in anger—

The Offensive Stranger: Or kill me with a drug which you hoped would give me new life and strength—

The Dervish: Very well. Go on.

The Offensive Stranger: In either case the results would be the same. Age-long misery of mind for you—an evil result; peace, repose, the end of sorrow for me—a good result. Three hearts that hold me dear would break; three pauper cousins of the third removed would get my riches and rejoice; you would go to prison and your friends would grieve, but your humble apprentice-priest would step into your shoes and your fat sleek life and be happy. And are these all the goods and all the evils that would flow from the well-intended or ill-intended act that cut short my life, O thoughtless one, O purblind creature? The good and evil results that flow from *any* act, even the smallest, breed on and on, century after century, forever and ever and ever, creeping by inches around the globe, affecting all its coming and going populations until the end of time, until the final cataclysm!

The Dervish: Then, there being no such thing as a good deed—

The Offensive Stranger: Don't I tell you there are good *intentions,* and evil ones, and there an end? The *results* are not foreseeable. They are of both kinds, in all cases. It is the law. Listen: this is far-Western history:

VOICES OUT OF UTAH

The White Chief (to his people): This wide plain was a desert. By our Heaven-blest industry we have dammed the river and utilized its waters and turned the desert into smiling fields whose fruitage makes prosperous and happy a thousand homes where poverty and hunger dwelt before. How noble, how beneficent, is Civilization!

Indian Chief (to his people): This wide plain, which the Spanish priests taught our fathers to irrigate, was a smiling field, whose fruitage made our homes prosperous and happy. The white American has dammed our river, taken away our water for his own valley, and turned our field into a desert; wherefore we starve.

The Dervish: I perceive that the good intention did really bring forth good and evil results in equal measure. But a single case cannot prove the rule. Try again.

The Offensive Stranger: Pardon me, *all* cases prove it. Columbus discovered a new world and gave to the plodding poor and the landless of Europe farms and breathing space and plenty and happiness—

The Dervish: A good result.

The Offensive Stranger: And they hunted and harried the original owners of the soil, and robbed them, beggared them, drove them from their homes, and exterminated them, root and branch.

The Dervish: An evil result, yes.

The Offensive Stranger: The French Revolution brought desolation to the hearts and homes of five million families and drenched the country with blood and turned its wealth to poverty.

The Dervish: An evil result.

The Offensive Stranger: But every great and precious liberty enjoyed by the nations of continental Europe to-day are the gift of that Revolution.

The Dervish: A good result, I concede it.

The Offensive Stranger: In our well-meant effort to lift up the Filipino to our own moral altitude with a musket, we have slipped on the ice and fallen down to his.

The Dervish: A large evil result.

The Offensive Stranger: But as an offset we are a World Power.

The Dervish: Give me time. I must think this one over. Pass on.

The Offensive Stranger: By help of three hundred thousand soldiers and eight hundred million dollars England has succeeded in her good purpose of lifting up the unwilling Boers and making them better and purer and happier than they could ever have become by their own devices.

The Dervish: Certainly that is a good result.

The Offensive Stranger: But there are only eleven Boers left now.

The Dervish: It has the appearance of an evil result. But I will think it over before I decide.

The Offensive Stranger: Take yet one more instance. With the best intentions the missionary has been laboring in China for eighty years.

The Dervish: The evil result is—

The Offensive Stranger: That nearly a hundred thousand Chinamen have acquired our Civilization.

The Dervish: And the good result is—

The Offensive Stranger: That by the compassion of God four hundred millions have escaped it.

LIES AND CIVILIZATION*

As I understand it, what you desire is information about "my first lie, and how I got out of it." I was born in 1835; I am well along, and my memory is not as good as it was. If you had asked about my first truth it would have been easier for me and kinder of you, for I remember that fairly well; I remember it as if it were last week. The family think it was week before, but that is flattery and probably has a selfish project back of it. When a person has become seasoned by experience and has reached the age of sixty-four, which is the age of discretion, he likes a family compliment as well as ever, but he does not lose his head over it as in the old innocent days.

I do not remember my first lie, it is too far back; but I remember my second one very well. I was nine days old at the time, and had noticed that if a pin was sticking in me and I advertised it in the usual fashion, I was lovingly petted and coddled and pitied in a most agreeable way and got a ration between meals besides. It was human nature to want to get these riches, and I fell. I lied about the pin—advertising one when there wasn't any. You would have done it; George Washington did it; anybody would have done it. During the first half of my life I never knew a child that was able to rise above that temptation and keep from telling that lie. Up to 1867 all the civilized children that were ever born into the world were liars—including George. Then the safety-pin came in and blocked the game. But is that reform worth anything? No; for it is reform by force and has no virtue in it; it merely stops that form of lying; it doesn't impair the disposition to lie, by a shade. It is the cradle application of conversion by fire and sword, or of the temperance principle through prohibition.

* *The Man That Corrupted Hadleyburg and Other Tales* (Harper and Brothers: New York, 1900).

To return to that early lie. They found no pin, and they realized that another liar had been added to the world's supply. For by grace of a rare inspiration, a quite commonplace but seldom noticed fact was borne in upon their understandings—that almost all lies are acts, and speech has no part in them. Then, if they examined a little further they recognized that all people are liars from the cradle onward, without exception, and that they begin to lie as soon as they wake up in the morning, and keep it up, without rest or refreshment, until they go to sleep at night. If they arrived at that truth it probably grieved them— did, if they had been heedlessly and ignorantly educated by their books and teachers; for why should a person grieve over a thing which by the eternal law of his make he cannot help? He didn't invent the law; it is merely his business to obey it and keep still; join the universal con- spiracy and keep so still that he shall deceive his fellow-conspirators into imagining that he doesn't know that the law exists. It is what we all do—we that know. I am speaking of the lie of silent assertion; we can tell it without saying a word, and we all do it—we that know. In the magnitude of its territorial spread it is one of the most majestic lies that the civilizations make it their sacred and anxious care to guard and watch and propagate.

For instance: it would not be possible for a humane and intelligent person to invent a rational excuse for slavery; yet you will remember that in early days of the emancipation agitation in the North, the agitators got but small help or countenance from any one. Argue and plead and pray as they might, they could not break the universal still- ness that reigned, from pulpit and press all the way down to the bottom of society—the clammy stillness created and maintained by the lie of silent assertion—the silent assertion that there wasn't anything going on in which humane and intelligent people were interested.

From the beginning of the Dreyfus case to the end of it, all France, except a couple of dozen moral paladins, lay under the smother of the silent-assertion lie that no wrong was being done to a persecuted and unoffending man. The like smother was over England lately, a good half of the population silently letting on that they were not aware that Mr. Chamberlain was trying to manufacture a war in South Africa and was willing to pay fancy prices for the materials.

Now there we have instances of three prominent ostensible civiliza- tions working the silent-assertion lie. Could one find other instances in the three countries? I think so. Not so very many, perhaps. but say a billion—just so as to keep within bounds. Are those countries working that kind of lie, day in and day out, in thousands and thousands of varieties, without ever resting? Yes, we know that to be true. The universal conspiracy of the silent-assertion lie is hard at work always and everywhere, and always in the interest of a stupidity or a sham, never in the interest of a thing fine or respectable. Is it the most timid and shabby of all lies? It seems to have the look of it. For ages and ages it has mutely labored in the interest of despotisms and aristocracies and chattel slaveries, and military slaveries, and religious slaveries, and has kept them alive; keeps them alive yet, here and there and yonder, all about the globe; and will go on keeping them alive until the silent-assertion lie retires from business—the silent assertion that nothing is going on which fair and intelligent men are aware of and are engaged by their duty to try to stop.

What I am arriving at is this: when whole races and peoples conspire to propagate gigantic mute lies in the interest of tyrannies and shams, why should we care anything about the trifling lies told by individuals? Why should we try to make it appear that abstention from lying is a virtue? Why should we want to beguile ourselves in that way? Why should we without shame help the nation lie, and then be ashamed to do a little lying on our own account? Why shouldn't we be honest and honorable, and lie every time we get a chance? That is to say, why shouldn't we be consistent, and either lie all the time or not at all? Why should we help the nation lie the whole day long and then object to telling one little individual private lie in our own interest to go to bed on? Just for the refreshment of it, I mean, and to take the rancid taste out of our mouth. . . .

To sum up, on the whole I am satisfied with things the way they are. There is a prejudice against the spoken lie, but none against any other, and by examination and mathematical computation I find that the proportion of the spoken lie to the other varieties is as 1 to 22,894. Therefore the spoken lie is of no consequence, and it is not worth while to go around fussing about it and trying to make believe that it is an important matter. The silent colossal National Lie that is the support and confederate of all the tyrannies and shams and inequalities and unfairnesses that afflict the peoples—that is the one to throw bricks and sermons at. But let us be judicious and let somebody else begin.

CORN-PONE OPINIONS*

Fifty years ago, when I was a boy of fifteen and helping to inhabit a Missourian village on the banks of the Mississippi, I had a friend whose society was very dear to me because I was forbidden by my mother to partake of it. He was a gay and impudent and satirical and delightful young black man—a slave—who daily preached sermons from the top of his master's woodpile, with me for sole audience. He imitated the pulpit style of the several clergymen of the village, and did it well, and with fine passion and energy. To me he was a wonder. I believed he was the greatest orator in the United States and would some day be heard from. But it did not happen; in the distribution of rewards he was overlooked. It is the way, in this world.

He interrupted his preaching, now and then, to saw a stick of wood; but the sawing was a pretense—he did it with his mouth; exactly imitating the sound the bucksaw makes in shrieking its way through the wood. But it served its purpose; it kept his master from coming out to see how the work was getting along. I listened to the sermons from the open window of a lumber room at the back of the house. One of his texts was this:

"You tell me whar a man gits his corn-pone, en I'll tell you what his 'pinions is."

I can never forget it. It was deeply impressed upon me. By my mother. Not upon my memory, but elsewhere. She had slipped in upon me while I was absorbed and not watching. The black philosopher's idea was that a man is not independent, and cannot afford views which might interfere with his bread and butter. If he would prosper, he must train with the majority; in matters of large moment, like politics and religion, he must think and feel with the bulk of his neighbors, or suffer damage in his social standing and in his business prosperities. He must restrict himself to corn-pone opinions—at least on the surface. He must get his opinions from other people; he must reason out none for himself; he must have no first-hand views.

* *Europe and Elsewhere.* (Written in 1900.)

I think Jerry was right, in the main, but I think he did not go far enough.

1. It was his idea that a man conforms to the majority view of his locality by calculation and intention.

This happens, but I think it is not the rule.

2. It was his idea that there is such a thing as a first-hand opinion; an original opinion; an opinion which is coldly reasoned out in a man's head, by a searching analysis of the facts involved, with the heart unconsulted, and the jury room closed against outside influences. It may be that such an opinion has been born somewhere, at some time or other, but I suppose it got away before they could catch it and stuff it and put it in the museum.

I am persuaded that a coldly-thought-out and independent verdict upon a fashion in clothes, or manners, or literature, or politics, or religion, or any other matter that is projected into the field of our notice and interest, is a most rare thing—if it has indeed ever existed.

A new thing in costume appears—the flaring hoopskirt, for example—and the passers-by are shocked, and the irreverent laugh. Six months later everybody is reconciled; the fashion has established itself; it is admired, now, and no one laughs. Public opinion resented it before, public opinion accepts it now, and is happy in it. Why? Was the resentment reasoned out? Was the acceptance reasoned out? No. The instinct that moves to conformity did the work. It is our nature to conform; it is a force which not many can successfully resist. What is its seat? The inborn requirement of self-approval. We all have to bow to that; there are no exceptions. Even the woman who refuses from first to last to wear the hoopskirt comes under that law and is its slave; she could not wear the skirt and have her own approval; and that she *must* have, she cannot help herself. But as a rule our self-approval has its source in but one place and not elsewhere—the approval of other people. A person of vast consequences can introduce any kind of novelty in dress and the general world will presently adopt it—moved to do it, in the first place, by the natural instinct to passively yield to that vague something recognized as authority, and in the second place by the human instinct to train with the multitude and have its approval. An empress introduced the hoopskirt, and we know the result. A nobody introduced the bloomer, and we know the result. If Eve should come again, in her ripe renown, and reintroduce her quaint styles—well, we know what would happen. And we should be cruelly embarrassed, along at first.

The hoopskirt runs its course and disappears. Nobody reasons about it. One woman abandons the fashion; her neighbor notices this and follows her lead; this influences the next woman; and so on and so on, and presently the skirt has vanished out of the world, no one knows how nor why; nor cares, for that matter. It will come again, by and by; and in due course will go again.

Twenty-five years ago, in England, six or eight wine glasses stood grouped by each person's plate at a dinner party, and they were used, not left idle and empty; to-day there are but three or four in the group, and the average guest sparingly uses about two of them. We have not adopted this new fashion yet, but we shall do it presently. We shall not think it out; we shall merely conform, and let it go at that. We get our notions and habits and opinions from outside influences; we do not have to study them out.

Our table manners, and company manners, and street manners change from time to time, but the changes are not reasoned out; we merely notice and conform. We are creatures of outside influences; as a rule we do not think, we only imitate. We cannot invent standards that will stick; what we mistake for standards are only fashions, and perishable. We may continue to admire them, but we drop the use of them. We notice this in literature. Shakespeare is a standard, and fifty years ago we used to write tragedies which we couldn't tell from—from somebody else's; but we don't do it any more, now. Our prose standard, three-quarters of a century ago, was ornate and diffuse; some authority or other changed it in the direction of compactness and simplicity, and conformity followed, without argument. The historical novel starts up suddenly, and sweeps the land. Everybody writes one, and the nation is glad. We had historical novels before; but nobody read them, and the rest of us conformed—without reasoning it out. We are conforming in the other way, now, because it is another case of everybody.

The outside influences are always pouring in upon us, and we are always obeying their orders and accepting their verdicts. The Smiths like the new play; the Joneses go to see it, and they copy the Smith verdict. Morals, religions, politics, get their following from surrounding influences and atmospheres, almost entirely; not from study, not from thinking. A man must and will have his own approval first of all, in each and every moment and circumstance of his life—even if he must repent of a self-approved act the moment after its commission, in order to get his self-approval *again:* but, speaking in general terms, a man's self-approval in the large concerns of life has its source in the approval of the peoples about him, and not in a searching personal examination of the matter. Mohammedans are Mohammedans because they are born and reared among that sect, not because they have thought it out and can furnish sound reasons for being Mohammedans; we know why Catholics are Catholics; why Presbyterians are Presbyterians; why Baptists are Baptists; why Mormons are Mormons; why thieves are thieves; why monarchists are monarchists; why Republicans are Republicans and Democrats, Democrats. We know it is a matter of association and sympathy, not reasoning and examination; that hardly a man in the world has an opinion upon morals, politics, or religion which he got otherwise than through his associations and sympathies. Broadly speaking, there are none but corn-pone opinions. And broadly speaking, corn-pone stands for self-approval. Self-approval is acquired mainly from the approval of other people. The result is conformity. Sometimes conformity has a sordid business interest—the bread-and-butter interest—but not in most cases, I think. I think that in the majority of cases it is unconscious and not calculated; that it is born of the human being's natural yearning to stand well with his fellows and have their inspiring approval and praise—a yearning which is commonly so strong and so insistent that it cannot be effectually resisted, and must have its way.

A political emergency brings out the corn-pone opinion in fine force in its two chief varieties—the pocketbook variety, which has its origin in self-interest, and the bigger variety, the sentimental variety—the one which can't bear to be outside the pale; can't bear to be in disfavor; can't endure the averted face and the cold shoulder; wants to stand well with his friends, wants to be smiled upon, wants to be welcome, wants to hear the precious words, *"He's* on the right track!" Uttered, perhaps by an ass, but still an ass of high degree, an ass whose approval is gold and diamonds to a smaller ass, and confers glory and honor and happiness, and membership in the herd. For these gauds many a man will dump his life-long principles into the street, and his conscience along with them. We have seen it happen. In some millions of instances.

Men think they think upon great political questions, and they do; but they think with their party, not independently; they read its literature, but not that of the other side; they arrive at convictions, but they are drawn from a partial view of the matter in hand and are of no particular value. They swarm with their party, they feel with their party, they are happy in their party's approval, and where the party leads they will follow, whether for right and honor, or through blood and dirt and a mush of mutilated morals.

In our late canvass half of the nation passionately believed that in silver lay salvation, the other half as passionately believed that that way lay destruction. Do you believe that a tenth part of the people, on either side, had any rational excuse for having an opinion about the matter at all? I studied that mighty question to the bottom—came out empty. Half of our people passionately believe in high tariff, the other half believe otherwise. Does this mean study and examination, or only feeling? The latter, I think. I have deeply studied that question, too— and didn't arrive. We all do no end of feeling, and we mistake it for thinking. And out of it we get an aggregation which we consider a boon. Its name is Public Opinion. It is held in reverence. It settles everything. Some think it the Voice of God.

THE AMERICAN PLUTOCRACY I*

I was lofty in those days. I have survived it. I was unwise, then. I am up-to-date now. Day before yesterday's New York *Sun* has a paragraph or two from its London correspondent which enables me to locate myself. The correspondent mentions a few of our American events of the past twelvemonth, such as the limitless rottenness of our great insurance companies, where theft has been carried on by our most distinguished commercial men as a profession; the exposures of conscienceless graft, colossal graft, in great municipalities like Philadelphia, St. Louis, and other large cities; the recent exposure of millionfold graft in the great Pennsylvania Railway system—with minor uncoverings of commercial swindles from one end of the United

---

* *Mark Twain in Eruption.*

States to the other; and finally today's lurid exposure, by Upton Sinclair, of the most titanic and death-dealing swindle of them all, the Beef Trust, an exposure which has moved the President to demand of a reluctant Congress a law which shall protect America and Europe from falling, in a mass, into the hands of the doctor and the undertaker.

According to that correspondent, Europe is beginning to wonder if there is really an honest male human creature left in the United States. A year ago I was satisfied that there was no such person existing upon American soil except myself. That exception has since been rubbed out, and now it is my belief that there isn't a single male human being in America who is honest. I held the belt all along, until last January. Then I went down, with Rockefeller and Carnegie and a group of Goulds and Vanderbilts and other professional grafters, and swore off my taxes like the most conscienceless of the lot. I was a great loss to America, because I was irreplaceable. It is my belief that it will take fifty years to produce my successor. I believe the entire population of the United States—exclusive of the women—to be rotten, as far as the dollar is concerned. Understand, I am saying these things as a dead person. I should consider it indiscreet in any live one to make these remarks publicly.

THE AMERICAN PLUTOCRACY II*

1. *Senator Clark of Montana*

2. *Jay Gould and John McCall*

3. *Senator Guggenheim of Colorado*

4. *Young John D. Rockefeller's Bible Class*

Jones . . . telephoned and said he would like to call for me at half past seven and take me to a dinner at the Union League Club. He said he would send me home as early as I pleased, he being aware that I am

---

* *Mark Twain in Eruption.*

declining all invitations this year—and for the rest of my life—that make it necessary for me to go out at night, at least to places where speeches are made and the sessions last until past ten o'clock. But Jones is a very particular friend of mine and therefore it cost me no discomfort to transgress my rule and accept his invitation; no, I am in error—it did cost me a pang, a decided pang, for although he said that the dinner was a private one with only ten persons invited, he mentioned Senator Clark of Montana as one of the ten. I am a person of elevated tone and of morals that can bear scrutiny, and am much above associating with animals of Mr. Clark's breed.

I am sorry to be vain—at least I am sorry to expose the fact that I am vain—but I do confess it and expose it; I cannot help being vain of myself for giving such a large proof of my friendship for Jones as is involved in my accepting an invitation to break bread with such a person as Clark of Montana. It is not because he is a United States Senator—it is at least not wholly because he occupies that doubtful position—for there are many Senators whom I hold in a certain respect and would not think of declining to meet socially, if I believed it was the will of God. We have lately sent a United States Senator to the penitentiary, but I am quite well aware that of those who have escaped this promotion there are several who are in some regards guiltless of crime—not guiltless of all crimes, for that cannot be said of any United States Senator, I think, but guiltless of some kinds of crime. They all rob the Treasury by voting for iniquitous pension bills in order to keep on good terms with the Grand Army of the Republic, and with the Grand Army of the Republic Jr., and with the Grand Army of the Republic Jr., Jr., and with other great-grandchildren of the war—and these bills distinctly represent crime and violated senatorial oaths.

However, while I am willing to waive moral rank and associate with the moderately criminal among the Senators—even including Platt and Chauncey Depew—I have to draw the line at Clark of Montana. He is said to have bought legislatures and judges as other men buy food and raiment. By his example he has so excused and so sweetened corruption that in Montana it no longer has an offensive smell. His history is known to everybody; he is as rotten a human being as can be found anywhere under the flag; he is a shame to the American nation, and no one has helped to send him to the Senate who did not know that his proper place was the penitentiary, with a chain and ball on his legs. To my mind he is the most disgusting creature that the republic has produced since Tweed's time.

I went to the dinner, which was served in a small private room of the club with the usual piano and fiddlers present to make conversation difficult and comfort impossible. I found that the Montana citizen was not merely a guest but that the dinner was given in his honor. While the feeding was going on two of my elbow neighbors supplied me with information concerning the reasons for this tribute of respect to Mr. Clark. Mr. Clark had lately lent to the Union League Club, which is the most powerful political club in America and perhaps the richest, a million dollars' worth of European pictures for exhibition. It was quite plain that my informant regarded this as an act of almost superhuman generosity. One of my informants said, under his breath and with awe and admiration, that if you should put together all of Mr. Clark's several generosities to the club, including this gaudy one, the cost to Mr. Clark first and last would doubtless amount to a hundred thousand dollars. I saw that I was expected to exclaim, applaud, and adore, but I was not tempted to do it, because I had been informed five minutes earlier that Clark's income, as stated under the worshiping informant's breath, was thirty million dollars a year.

Human beings have no sense of proportion. A benefaction of a hundred thousand dollars subtracted from an income of thirty million dollars is not a matter to go into hysterics of admiration and adulation about. If I should contribute ten thousand dollars to a cause, it would be one-ninth of my past year's income, and I could feel it; as matter for admiration and wonder and astonishment and gratitude, it would far and away outrank a contribution of twenty-five million dollars from the Montana jailbird, who would still have a hundred thousand dollars a week left over from his year's income to subsist upon.

It reminded me of the only instance of benevolence exploded upon the world by the late Jay Gould that I had ever heard of. When that first and most infamous corrupter of American commercial morals was wallowing in uncountable stolen millions, he contributed five thousand dollars for the relief of the stricken population of Memphis, Tennessee, at a time when an epidemic of yellow fever was raging in that city. Mr. Gould's contribution cost him no sacrifice; it was only the income of the hour which he daily spent in prayer—for he was a most godly man—yet the storm of worshiping gratitude which welcomed it all over the United States in the newspaper, the pulpit, and in the private circle might have persuaded a stranger that for a millionaire American to give five thousand dollars to the dead and dying poor—when he could have bought a circuit judge with it—was the noblest thing in American history, and the holiest.

In time, the President of the Art Committee of the club rose and began with that aged and long-ago discredited remark that there were not to be any speeches on this occasion but only friendly and chatty conversation; then he went on, in the ancient and long-ago discredited fashion, and made a speech himself—a speech which was well calculated to make any sober hearer ashamed of the human race. If a stranger had come in at that time he might have supposed that this was a divine service and that the Divinity was present. He would have gathered that Mr. Clark was about the noblest human being the great republic had yet produced and the most magnanimous, the most self-sacrificing, the most limitlessly and squanderingly prodigal benefactor of good causes living in any land today. And it never occurred to this worshiper of money, and money's possessor, that in effect Mr. Clark had merely dropped a dime into the League's hat. Mr. Clark couldn't miss his benefaction any more than he could miss ten cents.

When this wearisome orator had finished his devotions, the President of the Union League got up and continued the service in the same vein, vomiting adulations upon that jailbird which, estimated by any right standard of values, were the coarsest sarcasms, although the speaker was not aware of that. Both of these orators had been applauded all along but the present one ultimately came out with a remark which I judged would fetch a cold silence, a very chilly chill; he revealed the fact that the expenses of the club's loan exhibition of the Senator's pictures had exceeded the income from the tickets of admission; then he paused—as speakers always do when they are going to spring a grand effect—and said that at the crucial time Senator Clark stepped forward of his own motion and put his hand in his pocket and handed out fifteen hundred dollars wherewith to pay half of the insurance on the pictures, and thus the club's pocket was saved whole. I wish I may never die if the worshipers present at this religious service did not break out in grateful applause at that astonishing statement; and I wish I may never permanently die, if the jailbird didn't smile all over his face and look as radiantly happy as he will look some day when Satan gives him a Sunday vacation in the cold storage vault.

Finally, while I was still alive, the President of the club finished his dreary and fatiguing marketing of juvenile commonplaces, and introduced Clark, and sat down. Clark rose to the tune of "The Star-Spangled Banner"—no, it was "God Save the King," frantically sawed and thumped by the fiddlers and the piano, and this was followed by "For he's a jolly good fellow," sung by the whole strength of the happy worshipers. A miracle followed. I have always maintained that no man could make a speech with nothing but a compliment for a text but I know now that a reptile can. Senator Clark twaddled and twaddled and twaddled along for a full half-hour with no text but those praises which had been lavished upon his trifling generosities; and he not only accepted at par all these silly phrases but added to them a pile—praising his own so-called generosities and magnanimities with such intensity and color that he took the pigment all out of those other men's compliments and made them look pallid and shadowy. With forty years' experience of human assfulness and vanity at banquets, I have never seen anything of the sort that could remotely approach the assfulness and complacency of this coarse and vulgar and incomparably ignorant peasant's glorification of himself.

I shall always be grateful to Jones for giving me the opportunity to be present at these sacred orgies. I had believed that in my time I had seen at banquets all the different kinds of speechmaking animals there are and also all the different kinds of people that go to make our population, but it was a mistake. This was the first time I had ever seen men get down in the gutter and frankly worship dollars and their possessors. Of course I was familiar with such things through our newspapers, but I had never before heard men worship the dollar with their mouths or seen them on their knees in the act.

Jay Gould was the mightiest disaster which has ever befallen this country. The people had *desired* money before his day, but *he* taught them to fall down and worship it. They had respected men of means before his day, but along with this respect was joined the respect due to the character and industry which had accumulated it. But Jay Gould taught the entire nation to make a god of the money and the man, no matter how the money might have been acquired. In my youth there was nothing resembling a worship of money or of its possessor, in our region. And in our region no well-to-do man was ever charged with having acquired his money by shady methods.

The gospel left behind by Jay Gould is doing giant work in our days. Its message is "Get money. Get it quickly. Get it in abundance. Get it in prodigious abundance. Get it dishonestly if you can, honestly if you must."

This gospel does seem to be almost universal. Its great apostles, today, are the McCurdies, McCalls, Hydes, Alexanders, and the rest of that robber gang who have lately been driven out of their violated positions of trust in the colossal insurance companies of New York. President McCall was reported to be dying day before yesterday. The others have been several times reported, in the past two or three months, as engaged in dying. It has been imagined that the cause of these death strokes was sorrow and shame for the robberies committed upon the two or three million policy holders and their families, and the widow and the orphan—but every now and then one is astonished to find that it is not the outraged conscience of these men that is at work; they are merely sick and sore because they have been exposed.

Yesterday—as I see by the morning paper—John A. McCall quite forgot about his obsequies and sat up and became impressive, and worked his morals for the benefit of the nation. He knew quite well that anything which a prodigiously rich man may say—whether in health or moribund—will be spread by the newspapers from one end of this continent to the other and be eagerly read by every creature who is able to read. McCall sits up and preaches to his son—ostensibly to his son—really to the nation. The man seems to be sincere, and I think he is sincere. I believe his moral sense is atrophied. I believe he really regards himself as a high and holy man. And I believe he thinks he is so regarded by the people of the United States. He has been worshiped because of his wealth, and particularly because of his shady methods of acquiring it for twenty years. And I think he has become so accustomed to this adulation, and so beguiled and deceived by it that he does really think himself a fine and great and noble being, and a proper model for the emulation of the rising generation of young men. He snivels owlishly along and is evidently as happy and as well satisfied with himself as if there wasn't a stain upon his name, nor a crime in his record. Listen—here is his little sermon:

February 16, 1906.

WORK, WORK, SAYS McCALL

Tells of His Last Cigar in a Talk with His Son.
Special to The New York Times.

LAKEWOOD, Feb. 15.—John A. McCall felt so much better today that he had a long talk with his son, John C. McCall, and told many incidents of his career.

"John," he said to his son, "I have done many things in my life for which I am sorry, but I've never done anything of which I feel ashamed.

"My counsel to young men who would succeed is that they should take the world as they find it, and then work—work!"

Mr. McCall thought the guiding force of mankind was will power, and in illustration he said:

"Some time ago, John, your mother and I were sitting together, chatting. I was smoking a cigar. I liked a cigar, and enjoyed a good, quiet smoke. She objected to it.

" 'John,' said she, 'why don't you throw that cigar away?'

"I did so.

" 'John,' she added, 'I hope you'll never smoke again.'

"The cigar I threw away was my last. I determined to quit then and there, and did so. That was exactly thirty-five years ago."

Mr. McCall told his son many stories of his business life and seemed in a happier frame of mind than usual. This condition was attributed partly to the fact that he received hundreds of telegrams today congratulating him on his statement of yesterday reiterating his friendship for Andrew Hamilton.

"Father received a basketful of dispatches from friends in the North, South, East, and West commending him for his statement about his friend Judge Hamilton," said young Mr. McCall tonight. "The telegrams came from persons who wished him good health and recovery. It has made him very happy."

Mr. McCall had a sinking spell at 3 o'clock this morning, but it was slight, and he recovered before it was deemed necessary to send for a physician.

Milk and bouillons are now his sole form of nourishment. He eats no solids and is rapidly losing weight.

Drs. Vanderpoel and Charles L. Lindley held a conference at the McCall house at 5 o'clock this evening, and later told Mrs. McCall and Mrs. Darwin P. Kingsley, his daughter, that Mr. McCall's condition was good, and that there was no immediate danger.

John C. McCall gave out this statement tonight: "Mr. McCall has had a very favorable day and is somewhat better."

Following it comes the kind of bulletin which is given out from day to day when a king or other prodigious personage has had a favorable day and is somewhat better—a fact which will interest and cheer and comfort the rest of the human race, nobody can explain why.

The sons and daughters of Jay Gould move today in what is regarded as the best society—the aristocratic society—of New York. One of his daughters married a titled Frenchman ten or twelve years ago, a noisy and silly ruffian, gambler, and gentleman, and agreed to pay his debts, which amounted to a million or so. But she only agreed to pay the existing debts, not the future ones. The future ones have become present ones now and are colossal. Today she is suing for a separation from her shabby purchase, and the world's sympathy and compassion are with her, where it belongs.

The political and commercial morals of the United States are not merely food for laughter, they are an entire banquet. The human being is a curious and interesting invention. It takes a Cromwell and some thousands of preaching and praying soldiers and parsons ten years to raise the standards of English official and commercial morals to a respect-worthy altitude, but it takes only one Charles II a couple of years to pull them down into the mud again. Our standards were fairly high a generation ago, and they had been brought to that grade by some generations of wholesome labor on the part of the nation's multitudinous teachers; but Jay Gould, all by himself, was able to undermine the structure in half a dozen years; and in thirty years his little band of successors—the Senator Clarks and their kind—have been able to sodden it with decay from roof to cellar and render it shaky beyond repair, apparently.

Before Jay Gould's time there was a fine phrase, a quite elegant phrase, that was on everybody's lips, and everybody enjoyed repeating it, day and night, and everywhere, and enjoyed the thrill of it: "The press is the palladium of our liberties." It was a serious saying and it was a true saying, but it is long ago dead and has been tucked safely away in the limbo of oblivion. No one would venture it now except as a sarcasm.

Mr. Guggenheim has lately been chosen United States Senator reputedly by a bought legislature in Colorado—which is almost the customary way, now, of electing United States Senators. Mr. Guggenheim is said to have purchased his legislature and paid for it. By his public utterances it is plain that the general political rottenness has entered into him and saturated him, and he is not aware that he has been guilty of even an indelicacy, let alone a gross crime. In many instances the palladium of our liberties has nothing but compliment for him, and justification. The Denver *Post*, which is recognized as the principal and most trustworthy reflector of the public opinion of his State, says:

It is true that Mr. Guggenheim spent a large sum of money, but he only followed the precedents set in many other States. There is nothing essentially wrong in what he has done. Mr. Guggenheim will make the best Senator Colorado has ever had. His election will result in bringing to Colorado what the State needs, capitalists and population of the desirable quality. Mr. Guggenheim will get for Colorado many improvements which Tom Patterson failed to obtain from Washington. He is just the man for the place. There is no use trying to reform the world. They have been trying that for two thousand years and haven't succeeded. Mr. Guggenheim is the choice of the people and they ought to have him, even if he spent a million dollars. The issue of the election was Tom Patterson and Simon Guggenheim, and the people chose Guggenheim. The Denver *Post* bows to the will of the people.

Mr. Guggenheim, in buying what an obsolete phrase called senatorial "honors," did not buy the entire legislature but practiced the customary economy and bought only enough of it to elect him. This has been resented by some of the unbought; they offered a motion to inquire into the methods by which his election was achieved, but the bought majority not only voted the motion down but actually *sponged it from the records.* It looks like sensitiveness but it probably isn't; it is human nature that even the most conscienceless thieves do not like to be pilloried in the Rogues' Gallery.

One of the standing delights of the American nation in these days is John D. Rockefeller, Junior's, Bible Class adventures in theology. Every Sunday young Rockefeller explains the Bible to his class. The next day the newspapers and the Associated Press distribute his explanations all over the continent and everybody laughs. The entire nation laughs, yet in its innocent dullness never suspects that it is laughing at itself. But that is what it is doing.

Young Rockefeller, who is perhaps thirty-five years old, is a plain, simple, earnest, sincere, honest, well-meaning, commonplace person, destitute of originality or any suggestion of it. And if he were traveling upon his mental merit instead of upon his father's money, his explanations of the Bible would fall silent and not be heard of by the public. But his father ranks as the richest man in the world, and this makes his son's theological gymnastics interesting and important. The world believes that the elder Rockefeller is worth a billion dollars. He pays taxes on two million and a half. He is an earnest, uneducated Christian and for years and years has been Admiral of a Sunday school in Cleveland, Ohio. For years and years he has discoursed about himself to his Sunday school and explained how he got his dollars; and during all these years his Sunday school has listened in rapture and has divided its worship between him and his Creator—unequally. His Sunday-school talks are telegraphed about the country and are as eagerly read by the nation as are his son's.

As I have said, the nation laughs at young Rockefeller's analyzations of the Scriptures. Yet the nation must know that these analyzations are exactly like those which it hears every Sunday from its pulpits, and which its forbears have been listening to for centuries without a change of an idea—in case an idea has ever occurred in one of these discourses. Young John's methods are the ordinary pulpit methods. His deductions of golden fancy from sordid fact are exactly the same which the pulpit has traded in for centuries. Every argument he uses was already worn threadbare by the theologians of all the ages before it came in its rags to him. All his reasonings are like the reasonings of all the pulpit's stale borrowings from the dull pulpits of the centuries.

Young John has never studied a doctrine for himself; he has never examined a doctrine for any purpose but to make it fit the notions which he got at secondhand from his teachers. His talks are quite as original and quite as valuable as any that proceed from any other theologian's lips, from the Pope of Rome down to himself. The nation laughs at young John's profound and clumsy examinations of Joseph's character and conduct, yet the nation has always heard Joseph's character and conduct examined in the same clumsy and stupid way by its pulpits, and the nation should reflect that when they laugh at young John they are laughing at themselves. They should reflect that young John is using no new whitewash upon Joseph. He is using the same old brush and the same old whitewash that have made Joseph grotesque in all the centuries.

I have known and liked young John for many years and I have long felt that his right place was in the pulpit. I am sure that the fox fire of his mind would make a proper glow there—but I suppose he must do as destiny has decreed and succeed his father as master of the colossal Standard Oil Corporation. One of his most delightful theological deliverances was his exposition, three years ago, of the meaning—the real meaning, the bottom meaning—of Christ's admonition to the young man who was overburdened with wealth yet wanted to save himself if a convenient way could be found: "Sell all thou hast and give to the poor." Young John reasoned it out to this effect:

"Whatever thing stands between you and salvation, remove that obstruction at any cost. If it is money, give it away, to the poor; if it is property, sell the whole of it and give the proceeds to the poor; if it is military ambition, retire from the service; if it is an absorbing infatuation for any person or thing or pursuit, fling it far from you and proceed with a single mind to achieve your salvation."

The inference was plain. Young John's father's millions and his own were a mere incident in their lives and not in any way an obstruction in their pursuit of salvation. Therefore Christ's admonition could have no application to them. One of the newspapers sent interviewers to six or seven New York clergymen to get their views upon this matter, with this result: that all of them except one agreed with young Rockefeller. I do not know what we should do without the pulpit. We could better spare the sun—the moon, anyway.

THE AMERICAN PLUTOCRACY III:

Andrew Carnegie*

Yesterday I had a message for Andrew Carnegie who has just been celebrating his seventieth birthday with the help of friends, and I went uptown to deliver it, first notifying him by telephone that I should arrive at midafternoon or thereabouts. I arrived at his palace a little after three o'clock and delivered my message; then we adjourned to a room which he called his "cozy corner" to have a general chat while I should wait for Mr. Bryce, the British ambassador, who had gone to fill an appointment but had left word that I must wait, as he would soon return. I was glad to comply, for I have known Mr. Bryce a good many years, mainly at his own hospitable table in London, and have always not only respected and esteemed him but have also revered him. I waited an hour and then had to give it up, but the hour was not ill spent, for Andrew Carnegie, long as I have known him, has never yet been an uninteresting study, and he was up to standard yesterday.

If I were going to describe him in a phrase I think I should call him the Human Being Unconcealed. He is just like the rest of the human race but with this difference, that the rest of the race try to conceal what they are and succeed, whereas Andrew tries to conceal what he is but doesn't suceed. Yesterday he was at his best; he went on exposing himself all the time, yet he seemed to be unaware of it. I cannot go so far as to say he *was* unaware of it—seemed is the safer word to use, perhaps. He never has any but one theme, himself. Not that he deals in autobiography; not that he tells you about his brave struggles for a livelihood as a friendless poor boy in a strange land; not that he tells you how he advanced his fortunes steadily and successfully against obstructions that would have defeated almost any other human being similarly placed; not that he tells you how he finally reached the

* *Mark Twain in Eruption.* (Written in 1907.)

summit of his ambition and became lord over twenty-two thousand men
and possessor of one of the three giant fortunes of his day; no, as
regards these achievements he is as modest a man as you could meet
anywhere, and seldom makes even a fleeting reference to them; yet it is
as I say, he is himself his one darling subject, the only subject he for
the moment—the social moment—seems stupendously interested in. I
think he would surely talk himself to death upon it if you would stay
and listen.

Then in what way does he make himself his subject? In this way. He
talks forever and ever and ever and untiringly of the attentions which
have been shown him. Sometimes they have been large attentions, most
frequently they are very small ones; but no matter, no attention comes
amiss to him and he likes to revel in them. His friends are coming to
observe with consternation that while he adds new attentions to his list
every now and then, he never drops an old and shopworn one out of the
catalogue to make room for one of these fresh ones. He keeps the whole
list, keeps it complete; and you must take it all, along with the new
additions, if there is time and you survive. It is the deadliest affliction I
know of. He is the Ancient Mariner over again; it is not possible to
divert him from his subject; in your weariness and despair you try to
do it whenever you think you see a chance, but it always fails; he will
use your remark for his occasion and make of it a pretext to get
straight back upon his subject again.

A year or two ago Gilder, of *The Century*, and I called at Mr.
Carnegie's upon some matter connected with Gen. Carl Schurz, who
was very ill at the time. We arranged for a visit to the Schurz family
with Mr. Carnegie, who was Schurz's nearest neighbor; then our business was over and we wanted to get away but we couldn't manage it. In
the study Mr. Carnegie flew from photograph to photograph, from
autograph to autograph, from presentation book to presentation book,
and so on, buzzing over each like a happy hummingbird, for each
represented a compliment to Mr. Carnegie. Some of these compliments
were worth having and remembering but some of them were not; some
of them were tokens of honest admiration of the man for the liberal
way in which he had devoted millions of dollars to "Carnegie Libraries," while others were merely sorrowfully transparent tokens of
reverence for his moneybags; but they were all a delight to him and he
loved to talk about them and explain them and enlarge upon them.

One was a poem written by a workingman in Scotland. It was a good piece of literary work, and sang Andrew's glories quite musically. It was in the Scotch dialect, and Andrew read it to us, and read it well— so well that no one born out of Scotland could understand it. Then he told us about King Edward's visit to him at Skibo Castle in Scotland. We had heard him read the poem before and tell about the King's visit; we were doomed to hear him read that poem many times and also tell about that visit many times, afterward. When his study seemed to be exhausted we were hoping to get away, but it was not to be. He headed us off at this and that and the other room, and made us enter each and every room under the pretext that there was something important in there for us to consider—but it was always the same old thing: a gold box containing the freedom of the city of London, or Edinburgh, or Jerusalem, or Jericho; or a great photograph with the pictures of all the iron masters whom he had reared and trained and made millionaires of—a picture which they had presented him, along with a banquet; or it was shelves which we must inspect loaded to the guards with applications from everywhere in the world for a Carnegie library; or it was this or that or the other God-knows-what in the form of some damned attention that had been conferred upon him; and one exasperating feature of it was that it never seemed to occur to him for a moment that these attentions were mainly tributes to his money and not to himself.

He has bought fame and paid cash for it; he has deliberately projected and planned out this fame for himself; he has arranged that his name shall be famous in the mouths of men for centuries to come. He has planned shrewdly, safely, securely, and will have his desire. Any town or village or hamlet on the globe can have a public library upon these following unvarying terms: when the applicant shall have raised one-half of the necessary money, Carnegie will furnish the other half, and the library building must permanently bear his name.

During the past six or eight years he has been spending six or seven million dollars a year on this scheme. He is still continuing it; there is already a multitude of Carnegie libraries scattered abroad over the planet and he is always making additions to the list. When he dies, I think it will be found that he has set apart a gigantic fund whose annual interest is to be devoted forever to the begetting of Carnegie libraries. I think that three or four centuries from now Carnegie libraries will be considerably thicker in the world than churches. It is a long-headed idea and will deceive many people into thinking Carnegie a long-headed man in other and larger ways. I am sure he is a long-headed man in many and many a wise small way—the way of the trimmer, the way of the smart calculator, the way that enables a man to correctly calculate the tides and come in with the flow and go out with the ebb, keeping a permanent place on the top of the wave of advantage while other men as intelligent as he, but more addicted to principle and less to policy, get stranded on the reefs and bars. . . .

To return to the visit of yesterday to Mr. Carnegie in his palace. One of his first remarks was characteristic—characteristic in this way: that it brought forward a new attention which he had been receiving; characteristic also in this way: that he dragged it in by the ears, without beating around the bush for a pretext to introduce it.

He said, "I have been down to Washington to see the President."

Then he added, with that sort of studied and practiced casualness which some people assume when they are proposing to state a fact which they are proud of but do not wish to seem proud of, "He sent for me."

I knew he was going to say that. If you let Carnegie tell it, he never seeks the great—the great always seek him. He went on, and told me about the interview. The President had desired his advice regarding the calamitous conditions existing today, commercially, in America and Mr. Carnegie furnished that advice. It was characteristic of Mr. Carnegie that he did not enter into the details of the advice which he furnished and didn't try to glorify himself as an adviser. It is curious. He knew, and I knew, and he knew that I knew, that he was thoroughly competent to advise the President and that the advice furnished would be of the highest value and importance; yet he had no glorification to waste upon that; he has never a word of brag about his real achievements, his great achievements; they do not seem to interest him in the least degree; he is only interested—and intensely interested—in the flatteries lavished upon him in the disguise of compliments and in other little vanities which other men would value but conceal. I must repeat he is an astonishing man in his genuine modesty as regards the large things he has done, and in his juvenile delight in trivialities that feed his vanity.

Mr. Carnegie is not any better acquainted with himself than if he had met himself for the first time day before yesterday. He thinks he is a rude, bluff, independent spirit, who writes his mind and thinks his mind with an almost extravagant Fourth of July independence; whereas he is really the counterpart of the rest of the human race in that he does not boldly speak his mind except when there isn't any danger in it. He thinks he is a scorner of kings and emperors and dukes, whereas he is like the rest of the human race: a slight attention from one of these can make him drunk for a week and keep his happy tongue wagging for seven years.

I was there an hour or thereabouts, and was about to go when Mr. Carnegie just happened to remember by pure accident, apparently, something which had escaped his mind—this something which had escaped his mind being, in fact, a something which had not been out of his mind for a moment in the hour and which he was perishing to tell me about.

He jumped up and said, "Oh, wait a moment. I knew there was something I wanted to say. I want to tell you about my meeting with the Emperor."

The German Kaiser, he meant. His remark brought a picture to my mind at once, a picture of Carnegie and the Kaiser; a picture of a battleship and a Brooklyn ferryboat, so to speak; a picture of a stately big man and a wee little forkèd child of God that Goliath's wife would have pinned a shirtwaist onto a clothesline with—could have done it if she wanted to, anyway. I could see the Kaiser's bold big face, independent big face, as I remember it, and I could see that other face turned up toward it—that foxy, white-whiskered, cunning little face, happy, blessed, lit up with a sacred fire, and squeaking, without words: "Am I in Heaven or is it only a dream?" . . .

As I have said, Mr. Carnegie mentioned two incidents of his Washington visit: one of them was . . . the four battleships; the other was the "In God We Trust." Away back yonder in the days of the Civil War, a strong effort was made to introduce the name of God into the Constitution; it failed but a compromise was arrived at which partially satisfied the friends of the Deity. God was left out of the Constitution but was furnished a front seat on the coins of the country. After that on one side of the coin we had an Injun, or a Goddess of Liberty, or something of that kind, and on the other side we engraved the legend,

"In God We Trust." Now then, after that legend had remained there forty years or so, unchallenged and doing no harm to anybody, the President suddenly "threw a fit" the other day, as the popular expression goes, and ordered that remark to be removed from our coinage.

Mr. Carnegie granted that the matter was not of consequence, that a coin had just exactly the same value without the legend as with it, and he said he had no fault to find with Mr. Roosevelt's action but only with his expressed reasons for the act. The President had ordered the suppression of that motto because a coin carried the name of God into improper places, and this was a profanation of the Holy Name. Carnegie said the name of God is used to being carried into improper places everywhere and all the time, and that he thought the President's reasoning rather weak and poor.

I thought the same, and said, "But that is just like the President. If you will notice, he is very much in the habit of furnishing a poor reason for his acts while there is an excellent reason staring him in the face, which he overlooks. There was a good reason for removing that motto; there was, indeed, an unassailably good reason—in the fact that the motto stated a lie. If this nation has ever trusted in God, that time has gone by; for nearly half a century almost its entire trust has been in the Republican party and the dollar—mainly the dollar. I recognize that I am only making an assertion and furnishing no proof; I am sorry, but this is a habit of mine; sorry also that I am not alone in it; everybody seems to have this disease.

"Take an instance: the removal of the motto fetched out a clamor from the pulpit; little groups and small conventions of clergymen gathered themselves together all over the country, and one of these little groups, consisting of twenty-two ministers, put up a prodigious assertion unbacked by any quoted statistics and passed it unanimously in the form of a resolution: the assertion, to wit, that this is a Christian country. Why, Carnegie, so is hell. Those clergymen know that, inasmuch as 'Strait is the way and narrow is the gate, and few—*few*—are they that enter in thereat' has had the natural effect of making hell the only really prominent Christian community in any of the worlds; but we don't brag of this and certainly it is not proper to brag and boast that America is a Christian country when we all know that certainly five-sixths of our population could not enter in at the narrow gate."

THE AMERICAN PLUTOCRACY IV:

The Democracy in 1877*

Noble system, truly, where a man like R. H. Dana can't be confirmed, and where a person like Jones, whose proper place is a shyster in a Tombs court, is sent to the US Senate; where it is impossible to reward the most illustrious and fittest citizens with the presidency. Look at the list: Polk, Tyler, Pierce, etc. and *almost* Tilden, with the suit pending for swindling the revenue. Half the nation voted for him. This beggarly congress of ignorance and frauds. The back-pay gang of thieves.

THE COMING AMERICAN MONARCHY I†

Thirty-five years ago in a letter to my wife ostensibly, but really to Mr. Howells, I amused myself—and endeavored to amuse him—with forecasting the monarchy and imagining what the country would be like when the monarchy should replace the republic. That letter interests me now. Not because of anything it says—for there are no serious sentences in it—but because it refreshes my memory and enables me to recall the substance of a letter which preceded it and which treated the coming monarchy seriously.

I was not expecting the monarchy to come in my own time, nor in my children's time, nor at any period which one might forecast with anything approaching definiteness. It might come soon, it might come

---

* *Mark Twain's Notebook.*

† *Mark Twain in Eruption.* (Written in 1908.) Mark Twain did not foresee totalitarianism, but he had various reflections about the coming American monarchy, and its parallels with the Roman Empire, which were not too far away from that. In his darker moments he prophesied the rise to power by a shoemaker-dictator from the Southern states—a possibility that history has been toying with. *Ed.*

late; it might come in a century, it might be delayed two centuries, even three. But it would come.

Because of a special and particular reason? Yes. Two special reasons and one condition.

1. It is the nature of man to want a definite something to love, honor, reverently look up to, and obey: God and King, for example.

2. Little republics have lasted long, protected by their poverty and insignificance, but great ones have not.

3. The Condition: vast power and wealth, which breed commercial and political corruption and incite public favorites to dangerous ambitions.

The idea was, republics are impermanent; in time they perish and in most cases stay under the sod, but the overthrown monarchy gets back into the saddle again by and by. The idea was—in other and familiar words—history repeats itself: whatever has been the rule in history may be depended upon to remain the rule. Not because, in the case under present consideration, men would deliberately desire the destruction of their republic and plan it out, but because *circumstances* which they create without suspecting what they are doing will by and by *compel* that destruction—to their grief and dismay. My notion was that in some near or some distant day circumstances would so shape themselves, unnoticed by the people, as to make it possible for some ambitious idol of the nation to upset the republic and build his throne out of its ruins; and that then history would stand ready to back him.

But all this was thirty-five years ago. It seems curious now that I should have been dreaming dreams about a *future* monarchy and never suspecting that the monarchy was already present and the republic a thing of the past. Yet that was the case. The republic in name remained but the republic in fact was gone.

For fifty years our country has been a constitutional monarchy, with the Republican party sitting on the throne. Mr. Cleveland's couple of brief interruptions do not count; they were accidents and temporary, they made no permanent inroad upon Republican supremacy. Ours is not only a monarchy but a hereditary monarchy—in the one political family. It passes from heir to heir as regularly and as surely and as unpreventably as does any throne in Europe. Our monarch is more powerful, more arbitrary, more autocratic than any in Europe, its

White House commands are not under restraint of law or custom or the Constitution, it can ride down the Congress as the Czar cannot ride down the Duma. It can concentrate and augment power at the Capital by despoiling the States of their reserved rights, and by the voice of a Secretary of State it has indicated its purpose to do this. It can pack the Supreme Court with judges friendly to its ambitions, and it has threatened—by the voice of a Secretary of State—to do this. In many and admirably conceived ways it has so formidably intrenched itself and so tightened its grip upon the throne that I think it is there for good. By a system of extraordinary tariffs it has created a number of giant corporations in the interest of a few rich men, and by most ingenious and persuasive reasoning has convinced the multitudinous and grateful unrich that the tariffs were instituted in *their* interest! Next, the monarchy proclaims itself the enemy of its child the monopoly, and lets on that it wants to destroy that child. But it is wary and judicious, and never says anything about attacking the monopolies at their life source—the tariffs. It thoughtfully puts off that assault till "after election." A thousand years after is quite plainly what it means, but the people do not know that. Our monarchy takes no backward step; it moves always forward, always toward its ultimate and now assured goal, the *real* thing.

I was not expecting to live to see it reach it, but a recent step—the newest advance step and the startlingest—has encouraged me. It is this: formerly our monarchy went through the form of electing its Shadow by the voice of the people, but now the Shadow has gone and *appointed* the succession Shadow!

I judge that that strips off about the last rag that was left upon our dissolving wax-figure republic. It was the last one in the case of the Roman Republic.

THE COMING AMERICAN MONARCHY II*

As regards the coming American monarchy. It was before the Secretary of State had been heard from that the chairman of the banquet

* *Mark Twain in Eruption.* (Written in 1906.)

said: "In this time of unrest it is of great satisfaction that such a man as you, Mr. Root, is chief adviser of the President."

Mr. Root then got up and in the most quiet and orderly manner touched off the successor to the San Francisco earthquake. As a result, the several State governments were well shaken up and considerably weakened. Mr. Root was prophesying. He was prophesying, and it seems to me that no shrewder and surer forecasting has been done in this country for a good many years.

He did not say in so many words that we are proceeding in a steady march toward eventual and unavoidable replacement of the republic by monarchy, but I suppose he was aware that that is the case. He notes the several steps, the customary steps, which in all the ages have led to the consolidation of loose and scattered governmental forces into formidable centralizations of authority but he stops there and doesn't add up the sum. He is not unaware that heretofore the sum has been ultimate monarchy, and that the same figures can fairly be depended upon to furnish the same sum whenever and wherever they can be produced, so long as human nature shall remain as it is; but it was not needful that he do the adding since anyone can do it, neither would it have been gracious in him to do it.

In observing the changed conditions which in the course of time have made certain and sure the eventual seizure by the Washington government of a number of State duties and prerogatives which have been betrayed and neglected by the several States, he does not attribute those changes and the vast results which are to flow from them to any thought-out policy of any party or of any body of dreamers or schemers, but properly and rightly attributes them to that stupendous power—Circumstance—which moves by laws of its own, regardless of parties and policies, and whose decrees are final and must be obeyed by all—and will be. The railway is a Circumstance, the steamship is a Circumstance, the telegraph is a Circumstance. They were mere happenings; and to the whole world, the wise and the foolish alike, they were entirely trivial, wholly inconsequential; indeed silly, comical, grotesque. No man, and no party, and no thought-out policy said, "Behold, we will build railways and steamships and telegraphs, and presently you will see the condition and way of life of every man and woman and child in the nation totally changed; unimaginable changes of law and custom will follow, in spite of anything that anybody can do to prevent it." . . .

Human nature being what it is, I suppose we must expect to drift into monarchy by and by. It is a saddening thought but we cannot change our nature—we are all alike, we human beings; and in our blood and bone, and ineradicably, we carry the seeds out of which monarchies and aristocracies are grown: worship of gauds, titles, distinctions, power. We have to worship these things and their possessors, we are all born so and we cannot help it. We have to be despised by somebody whom we regard as above us or we are not happy; we have to have somebody to worship and envy or we cannot be content. In America we manifest this in all the ancient and customary ways. In public we scoff at titles and hereditary privilege but privately we hanker after them, and when we get a chance we buy them for cash and a daughter. Sometimes we get a good man and worth the price but we are ready to take him anyway, whether he be ripe or rotten, whether he be clean and decent or merely a basket of noble and sacred and long-descended offal. And when we get him the whole nation publicly chaffs and scoffs—and privately envies, and also is proud of the honor which has been conferred upon us. We run over our list of titled purchases every now and then in the newspapers and discuss them and caress them, and are thankful and happy.

Like all the other nations, we worship money and the possessors of it—they being our aristocracy, and we have to have one. We like to read about rich people in the papers; the papers know it, and they do their best to keep this appetite liberally fed. They even leave out a football game or a bull fight now and then to get room for all the particulars of how—according to the display heading—"Rich Woman Fell Down Cellar—Not Hurt." The falling down the cellar is of no interest to us when the woman is not rich, but no rich woman can fall down a cellar and we not yearn to know all about it and wish it was us.

In a monarchy the people willingly and rejoicingly revere and take pride in their nobilities, and are not humiliated by the reflection that this humble and hearty homage gets no return but contempt. Contempt does not shame them, they are used to it and they recognize that it is their proper due. We are all made like that. In Europe we easily and quickly learn to take that attitude toward the sovereigns and the aristocracies; moreover, it has been observed that when we get the attitude we go on and exaggerate it, presently becoming more servile than the natives and vainer of it. The next step is to rail and scoff at republics and democracies. All of which is natural, for we have not ceased to be human beings by becoming Americans, and the human race was always intended to be governed by kingship, not by popular vote.

I suppose we must expect that unavoidable and irresistible Circumstances will gradually take away the powers of the States and concentrate them in the central government, and that the republic will then repeat the history of all time and become a monarchy; but I believe that if we obstruct these encroachments and steadily resist them the monarchy can be postponed for a good while yet.

The human race was always interesting, and we know by its past that it will always continue so. Monotonously. It is always the same; it never changes. Its circumstances change from time to time, for better or worse, but the race's *character* is permanent, and never changes. In the course of the ages it has built up several great and worshipful civilizations and has seen unlooked-for circumstances slily emerge bearing deadly gifts which looked like benefits and were welcomed, whereupon the decay and destruction of each of these stately civilizations has followed.

It is not worth while to try to keep history from repeating itself, for man's character will always make the preventing of the repetitions impossible. Whenever man makes a large stride in material prosperity and progress he is sure to think that *he* has progressed, whereas he has not advanced an inch; nothing has progressed but his circumstances. *He* stands where he stood before. He knows more than his forebears knew but his intellect is no better than theirs and never will be. He is richer than his forebears but his character is no improvement upon theirs. Riches and education are not a permanent possession; they will pass away, as in the case of Rome and Greece and Egypt and Babylon; and a moral and mental midnight will follow—with a dull long sleep and a slow reawakening. From time to time he makes what looks like a change in his character but it is not a real change; and it is only transitory anyway. He cannot even invent a religion and keep it intact; circumstances are stronger than he and all his works. Circumstances and conditions are always changing, and they always compel him to modify his religions to harmonize with the new situation.

For twenty-five or thirty years I have squandered a deal of my time—too much of it perhaps—in trying to guess what is going to be the process which will turn our republic into a monarchy and how far off that event might be. Every man is a master and also a servant, a vassal. There is always someone who looks up to him and admires and envies him; there is always someone to whom he looks up and whom he admires and envies. This is his nature; this is his character; and it is unchangeable, indestructible; therefore republics and democracies are not for such as he; they cannot satisfy the requirements of his nature. The inspirations of his character will always breed circumstances and conditions which must in time furnish him a king and an aristocracy to look up to and worship. In a democracy he will try—and honestly—to keep the crown away, but Circumstance is a powerful master and will eventually defeat him.

Republics have lived long but monarchy lives forever. By our teaching we learn that vast material prosperity always brings in its train conditions which debase the morals and enervate the manhood of a nation—then the country's liberties come into the market and are bought, sold, squandered, thrown away, and a popular idol is carried to the throne upon the shields or shoulders of the worshiping people and planted there in permanency. We are always being taught—no, formerly we were always being taught—to look at Rome and beware. The teacher pointed to Rome's stern virtue, incorruptibility, love of liberty, and all-sacrificing patriotism—this when she was young and poor; then he pointed to her later days when her sunbursts of material prosperity and spreading dominion came and were exultingly welcomed by the people, they not suspecting that these were not fortunate glories, happy benefits, but were a disease and freighted with death.

The teacher reminded us that Rome's liberties were not auctioned off in a day, but were bought slowly, gradually, furtively, little by little; first with a little corn and oil for the exceedingly poor and wretched, later with corn and oil for voters who were not quite so poor, later still with corn and oil for pretty much every man that had a vote to sell— exactly our own history over again. At first we granted deserved pensions, righteously and with a clean and honorable motive, to the disabled soldiers of the Civil War. The clean motive began and ended there. We have made many and amazing additions to the pension list but with a motive which dishonors the uniform and the Congresses which have voted the additions—the sole purpose back of the additions being the purchase of votes. It is corn and oil over again, and promises to do its full share in the eventual subversion of the republic and the substitution of monarchy in its place. The monarchy would come anyhow, without this, but this has a peculiar interest for us in that it prodigiously hastens the day. We have the two Roman conditions: stupendous wealth with its inevitable corruptions and moral blight, and the corn and oil pensions—that is to say, vote bribes, which have taken away the pride of thousands of tempted men and turned them into willing alms receivers and unashamed.

THE AMERICAN MONARCHY:

Freedom of Speech in America*

It is by the goodness of God that in our country we have those three unspeakably precious things: freedom of speech, freedom of conscience, and the prudence never to exercise either of them.

DICTATORSHIP†

. . . But it was impossible to save the Great Republic. She was rotten to the heart. Lust of conquest had long ago done its work; trampling upon the helpless abroad had taught her, by a natural process, to endure with apathy the like at home; multitudes who had applauded the crushing of other people's liberties, lived to suffer for their mistake in their own persons. The government was irrevocably in the hands of

* *Mark Twain's Notebook.*
† *Letters from the Earth.*

the prodigiously rich and their hangers-on; the suffrage was become a mere machine, which they used as they chose. There was no principle but commercialism, no patriotism but of the pocket. From showily and sumptuously entertaining neighboring titled aristocracies, and from trading their daughters to them, the plutocrats came in the course of time to hunger for titles and heredities themselves. The drift toward monarchy, in some form or other, began; it was spoken of in whispers at first, later in a bolder voice.

It was now that the portent called "the Prodigy" rose in the far south. Army after army, sovereignty after sovereignty went down under the mighty tread of the shoemaker, and still he held his conquering way—north, always north. The sleeping Republic awoke at last, but too late. It drove the money-changers from the temple, and put the government into clean hands—but all to no purpose. To keep the power in their own hands, the money-changers had long before bought up half the country with soldier-pensions and turned a measure which had originally been a righteous one into a machine for the manufacture of bond-slaves—a machine which was at the same time an irremovable instrument of tyranny—for every pensioner had a vote, and every man and woman who had ever been acquainted with a soldier was a pensioner; pensions were dated back to the Fall, and hordes of men who had never handled a weapon in their lives came forward and drew three hundred years' back pay. The country's conquests, so far from being profitable to the treasury, had been an intolerable burden from the beginning. The pensions, the conquests, and corruption together had brought bankruptcy in spite of the maddest taxation; the government's credit was gone, the arsenals were empty, the country unprepared for war. The military and naval schools, and all commissioned offices in the army and navy, were the preserve of the money-changers; and the standing army—the creation of the conquest days—was their property.

The army and navy refused to serve the new Congress and the new Administration, and said ironically, "What are you going to do about it?" A difficult question to answer. Landsmen manned such ships as were not abroad watching the conquests—and sunk them all, in honest attempts to do their duty. A civilian army, officered by civilians, rose brimming with the patriotism of an old forgotten day and rushed multitudinously to the front, armed with sporting guns and pitchforks—and the standing army swept it into space. For the money-changers had privately sold out to the shoemaker. He conferred titles of nobility upon the money-changers, and mounted the Republic's throne without firing a shot.

It was thus that Popoatahualpacatapetl became our master; whose mastership descended in a little while to the Second of that name, who still holds it by his Viceroy this day.

RULERS AND MASSES:

*Where Does the Talent Come From?**

Men write many fine and plausible arguments in support of monarchy, but the fact remains that where every man in a state has a vote, brutal laws are impossible. Arthur's people were of course poor material for a republic, because they had been debased so long by monarchy; and yet even they would have been intelligent enough to make short work of that law which the king had just been administering if it had been submitted to their full and free vote. There is a phrase which has grown so common in the world's mouth that it has come to seem to have sense and meaning—the sense and meaning implied when it is used; that is the phrase which refers to this or that or the other nation as possibly being "capable of self-government;" and the implied sense of it is, that there has been a nation somewhere, some time or other, which *wasn't* capable of it—wasn't as able to govern itself as some self-appointed specialists were or would be to govern it. The master minds of all nations, in all ages, have sprung in affluent multitude from the mass of the nation, and from the mass of the nation only—not from its privileged classes; and so, no matter what the nation's intellectual grade was, whether high or low, the bulk of its ability was in the long ranks of its nameless and its poor, and so it never saw the day that it had not the material in abundance whereby to govern itself. Which is to assert an always self-proven fact: that even

* *A Connecticut Yankee in King Arthur's Court.*

the best-governed and most free and most enlightened monarchy is still behind the best condition attainable by its people; and that the same is true of kindred governments of lower grades, all the way down to the lowest.

MAN'S MORAL SENSE*

In a moment we were in a French village. We walked through a great factory of some sort, where men and women and little children were toiling in heat and dirt and a fog of dust; and they were clothed in rags, and drooped at their work, for they were worn and half starved, and weak and drowsy. Satan said:

"It is some more Moral Sense. The proprietors are rich, and very holy; but the wage they pay to these poor brothers and sisters of theirs is only enough to keep them from dropping dead with hunger. The work-hours are fourteen per day, winter and summer—from six in the morning till eight at night—little children and all. And they walk to and from the pigsties which they inhabit—four miles each way, through mud and slush, rain, snow, sleet, and storm, daily, year in and year out. They get four hours of sleep. They kennel together, three families in a room, in unimaginable filth and stench; and disease comes, and they die off like flies. Have they committed a crime, these mangy things? No. What have they done, that they are punished so? Nothing at all, except getting themselves born into your foolish race. You have seen how they treat a misdoer there in the jail; now you see how they treat the innocent and the worthy. Is your race logical? Are these ill-smelling innocents better off than that heretic? Indeed, no; his punishment is trivial compared with theirs. They broke him on the wheel and smashed him to rags and pulp after we left, and he is dead now, and free of your precious race; but these poor slaves here—why, they have been dying for years, and some of them will not escape from life for years to come. It is the Moral Sense which teaches the factory proprietors the difference between right and wrong—you perceive the

* *The Mysterious Stranger.*

result. They think themselves better than dogs. Ah, you are such an illogical, unreasoning race! And paltry—oh, unspeakably!"

Then he dropped all seriousness and just overstrained himself making fun of us, and deriding our pride in our warlike deeds, our great heroes, our imperishable fames, our mighty kings, our ancient aristocracies, our venerable history—and laughed and laughed till it was enough to make a person sick to hear him; and finally he sobered a little and said, "But, after all, it is not all ridiculous; there is a sort of pathos about it when one remembers how few are your days, how childish your pomps, and what shadows you are!"

SATAN SPEAKS ON CONFORMITY*

"Oh, it's true. I know your race. It is made up of sheep. It is governed by minorities, seldom or never by majorities. It suppresses its feelings and its beliefs and follows the handful that makes the most noise. Sometimes the noisy handful is right, sometimes wrong; but no matter, the crowd follows it. The vast majority of the race, whether savage or civilized, are secretly kind-hearted and shrink from inflicting pain, but in the presence of the aggressive and pitiless minority they don't dare to assert themselves. Think of it! One kind-hearted creature spies upon another, and sees to it that he loyally helps in iniquities which revolt both of them. Speaking as an expert, I know that ninety-nine out of a hundred of your race were strongly against the killing of witches when that foolishness was first agitated by a handful of pious lunatics in the long ago. And I know that even to-day, after ages of transmitted prejudice and silly teaching, only one person in twenty puts any real heart into the harrying of a witch. And yet apparently everybody hates witches and wants them killed. Some day a handful will rise up on the other side and make the most noise—perhaps even a single daring man with a big voice and a determined front will do it—and in a week all the sheep will wheel and follow him, and witch-hunting will come to a sudden end.

* *The Mysterious Stranger.*

Monarchies, aristocracies, and religions are all based upon that large defect in your race—the individual's distrust of his neighbor, and his desire, for safety's or comfort's sake, to stand well in his neighbor's eye. These institutions will always remain, and always flourish, and always oppress you, affront you, and degrade you, because you will always be and remain slaves of minorities. There was never a country where the majority of the people were in their secret hearts loyal to any of these institutions."

I did not like to hear our race called sheep, and said I did not think they were.

"Still, it is true, lamb," said Satan. "Look at you in war—what mutton you are, and how ridiculous!"

"In war? How?"

"There has never been a just one, never an honorable one—on the part of the instigator of the war. I can see a million years ahead, and this rule will never change in so many as half a dozen instances. The loud little handful—as usual—will shout for the war. The pulpit will—warily and cautiously—object—at first; the great, big, dull bulk of the nation will rub its sleepy eyes and try to make out why there should be a war, and will say, earnestly and indignantly, 'It is unjust and dishonorable, and there is no necessity for it.' Then the handful will shout louder. A few fair men on the other side will argue and reason against the war with speech and pen, and at first will have a hearing and be applauded; but it will not last long; those others will outshout them, and presently the anti-war audiences will thin out and lose popularity. Before long you will see this curious thing: the speakers stoned from the platform, and free speech strangled by hordes of furious men who in their secret hearts are still at one with those stoned speakers—as earlier—but do not dare to say so. And now the whole nation—pulpit and all—will take up the war-cry, and shout itself hoarse, and mob any honest man who ventures to open his mouth; and presently such mouths will cease to open. Next the statesmen will invent cheap lies, putting the blame upon the nation that is attacked, and every man will be glad of those conscience-soothing falsities, and will diligently study them, and refuse to examine any refutations of them; and thus he will by and by convince himself that the war is just, and will thank God for the better sleep he enjoys after this process of grotesque self-deception."

THE HUMAN CONDITION AND LAUGHTER*

Satan was accustomed to say that our race lived a life of continuous and uninterrupted self-deception. It duped itself from cradle to grave with shams and delusions which it mistook for realities, and this made its entire life a sham. Of the score of fine qualities which it imagined it had and was vain of, it really possessed hardly one. It regarded itself as gold, and was only brass. One day when he was in this vein he mentioned a detail—the sense of humor. I cheered up then, and took issue. I said we possessed it.

"There spoke the race!" he said; "always ready to claim what it hasn't got, and mistake its ounce of brass filings for a ton of gold-dust. You have a mongrel perception of humor, nothing more; a multitude of you possess that. This multitude see the comic side of a thousand low-grade and trivial things—broad incongruities, mainly; grotesqueries, absurdities, evokers of the horse-laugh. The ten thousand high-grade comicalities which exist in the world are sealed from their dull vision. Will a day come when the race will detect the funniness of these juvenilities and laugh at them—and by laughing at them destroy them? For your race, in its poverty, has unquestionably one really effective weapon—laughter. Power, money, persuasion, supplication, persecution—these can lift at a colossal humbug—push it a little—weaken it a little, century by century; but only laughter can blow it to rags and atoms at a blast. Against the assault of laughter nothing can stand. You are always fussing and fighting with your other weapons. Do you ever use that one? No; you leave it lying rusting. As a race, do you ever use it at all? No; you lack sense and the courage."

* *The Mysterious Stranger.*

SATAN OUR TRUE RULER*

A person (Satan) who for untold centuries has maintained the imposing position of spiritual head of 4/5 of the human race, and political head of the whole of it, must be granted the possession of executive abilities of the highest order. In his large presence the other popes and politicians shrink to midgets for the microscope.

He hasn't a single salaried helper; the Opposition employ a million.

Much has been written about Mark Twain's final period of black despair and bitterness. Yet his last book, the Autobiography, *has been described as "one of the great daylight books of our literature" (by the editor of this volume) and his final testament—in* The Mysterious Stranger, *published posthumously, as was the* Autobiography, *where Twain was "speaking from the grave," and speaking so relevantly to us today—was about the farcical and tragical comedy of life. In a similar vein, the selections which follow here can be viewed as Twain's ironical benison; they are in their way a final blessing upon the humanity he had condemned so roundly. And in their compassion they may remind us of some almost identical statements uttered by two other American writers of comparable rank, Theodore Dreiser and Herman Melville. I am including Twain's famous description of the human race as a race of cowards in which he not only marched but carried a banner because, while it has been used often to document Twain's "weakness," it should be obvious that only a strong man could have written it, the boldest of human spirits and a ranking artist of world literature. All great writers have rehearsed this theme in one way or another; it is only small spirits who deny it. Ed.*

* Mark Twain's Notebook.

SUSY CLEMENS AND THE HUMAN CONDITION*

The summer seasons of Susy's childhood were spent at Quarry Farm on the hills east of Elmira, New York; the other seasons of the year at the home in Hartford. Like other children, she was blithe and happy, fond of play; *un*like the average of children, she was at times much given to retiring within herself and trying to search out the hidden meanings of the deep things that make the puzzle and pathos of human existence, and in all the ages have baffled the inquirer and mocked him. As a little child aged seven, she was oppressed and perplexed by the maddening repetition of the stock incidents of our race's fleeting sojourn here, just as the same thing has oppressed and perplexed maturer minds from the beginning of time. A myriad of men are born; they labor and sweat and struggle for bread; they squabble and scold and fight; they scramble for little mean advantages over each other. Age creeps upon them; infirmities follow; shames and humiliations bring down their prides and their vanities. Those they love are taken from them, and the joy of life is turned to aching grief. The burden of pain, care, misery, grows heavier year by year. At length ambition is dead; pride is dead; vanity is dead; longing for release is in their place. It comes at last—the only unpoisoned gift earth ever had for them— and they vanish from a world where they were of no consequence; where they achieved nothing; where they were a mistake and a failure and a foolishness; where they have left no sign that they have existed— a world which will lament them a day and forget them forever. Then another myriad takes their place, and copies all they did, and goes along the same profitless road, and vanishes as they vanished—to make room for another and another and a million other myriads to follow the same arid path through the same desert and accomplish what the first myriad, and all the myriads that came after it, accomplished—nothing!

* *Autobiography.*

THE HUMAN FAMILY*

There is hardly a creature which you cannot definitely and satisfactorily describe by one single trait—but you cannot describe man by one single trait. Men are not all cowards, like the rabbit; nor all brave, like the house fly; nor all sweet and innocent and gentle, like the lamb; nor all murderous, like the spider and the wasp; nor all thieves, like the fox and the blue jay; nor all vain, like the peacock; nor all beautiful, like the angel-fish; nor all frisky, like the monkey; nor all unchaste, like the goat.

The human family cannot be described by any one phrase; each individual has to be described by himself. One is brave, another is a coward; one is gentle and kindly, another is ferocious; one is proud and vain, another is modest and humble. The multifarious traits that are scattered, one or two at a time, throughout the great animal world, are all concentrated, in varying and nicely shaded degrees of force and feebleness, in the form of instincts in each and every member of the human family. In some men the vicious traits are so slight as to be imperceptible, while the nobler traits stand out conspicuously. We describe that man by those fine traits and we give him praise and accord him high merit for their possession. It seems comical. He did not invent his traits; he did not stock himself with them; he inherited them at his birth; God conferred them upon him; they are the law that God imposed upon him, and he could not escape obedience if he should try. Sometimes a man is a born murderer, or a born scoundrel—like Stanford White—and upon him the world lavishes censure and dispraise; but he is only obeying the law of his nature, the law of his temperament; he is not at all likely to try to disobey it, and if he should try he would fail. It is a curious and humorous fact that we excuse all the unpleasant things that the creatures that crawl and fly and swim and go on four legs do, for the recognizably sufficient reason that they are but obeying the law of their nature, which is the law of God, and

* Autobiography.

are therefore innocent; then we turn about and with the fact plain before us that we get all our unpleasant traits by inheritance from those creatures, we blandly assert that we did not inherit the immunities along with them, but that it is our duty to ignore, abolish and break these laws of God. It seems to me that this argument has not a leg to stand upon and that it is not merely and mildly humorous but violently grotesque.

By ancient training and inherited habit, I have been heaping blame after blame, censure after censure, upon Bret Harte, and have felt the things I have said, but when my temper is cool I have no censures for him. The law of his nature was stronger than man's statutes and he had to obey it. It is my conviction that the human race is no proper target for harsh words and bitter criticisms, and that the only justifiable feeling toward it is compassion; it did not invent itself, and it had nothing to do with the planning of its weak and foolish character.

THE HUMAN RACE*

Every man is in his own person the whole human race, with not a detail lacking. I am the whole human race without a detail lacking; I have studied the human race with diligence and strong interest all these years in my own person; in myself I find in big or little proportion every quality and every defect that is findable in the mass of the race. I knew I should not find in any philosophy a single thought which had not passed through my own head, nor a single thought which had not passed through the heads of millions and millions of men before I was born; I knew I should not find a single original thought in any philosophy, and I knew I could not furnish one to the world myself, if I had five centuries to invent it in. Nietzsche published his book, and was at once pronounced crazy by the world—by a world which included tens of thousands of bright, sane men who believed exactly as Nietzsche believed but concealed the fact and scoffed at Nietzsche. What a coward every man is! and how surely he will find it out if he will just

* *Mark Twain in Eruption.* (Written in 1907.)

let other people alone and sit down and examine himself. The human race is a race of cowards; and I am not only marching in that procession but carrying a banner.

ON LIFE AND DEATH

To Adam we owe the two things which are most precious—Life and Death. Life, which the young, the hopeful, the undefeated hold above all wealth and all honors; and Death, the refuge, the solace, the best and kindliest and most prized friend and benefactor of the erring, the forsaken, the old, and weary, and broken of heart, whose burdens be heavy upon them, and who would lie down and rest.*

The dignity of death—the only earthly dignity that is not artificial—the only safe one. The others are traps that can beguile to humiliation. Death—the only immortal who treats us all alike, whose pity and whose peace and whose refuge are for all—the soiled and the pure—the rich and the poor—the loved and the unloved.†

* *Mark Twain's Speeches.* (Written 1880–1885.)
† *Mark Twain: A Biography.*

INDEX